Twin Peaks Unwrapped

Photo by Scott Ryan

Twin Peaks Unwrapped

BY BEN DURANT
& BRYON KOZACZKA

Twin Peaks Unwrapped

© 2020 Scott Ryan Productions
ScottRyanProductions.com
Bluerosemag.com

Book designed by Scott Ryan
Front & back cover design: Josh Howard
Senior Editor: Tracey Durant
Co-Editors: Jill Watson, Rebecca Saunders
Managing Editor: Scott Ryan

Published in the USA by Scott Ryan Productions
Columbus, Ohio

Contact Information
Email: twinpeaksunwrapped@gmail.com
Twitter: @TwinPeaksUnwrap
Podcast: twinpeaksunwrapped.com

ISBN: 978-1-949024-14-2
eBook ISBN: 978-1-949024-15-9

Dedicated to our listeners.

CONTENTS

Foreword by John Thorne...*01*

1. Introduction *03*

Season 1

2. Season 1: The Pilot...*06*

3. Season 1: Episode 1...*17*

4. Season 1: Episode 2...*24*

5. Season 1: Episode 3...*31*

6. Season 1: Episode 4...*39*

7. Season 1: Episode 5...*44*

8. Season 1: Episode 6...*49*

9. Season 1: Episode 7...*55*

Season 2

10. Season 2: Episode 8...*59*

11. Season 2: Episode 9...*64*

12. Season 2: Episode 10...*69*

13. Season 2: Episode 11...*74*

14. Season 2: Episode 12...*78*

15. Season 2: Episode 13...*82*

16. Season 2: Episode 14...*85*

17. Season 2: Episode 15...*89*

18. Season 2: Episode 16...*93*

19. Season 2: Episode 17...*97*

20. Season 2: Episode 18...102

21. Season 2: Episode 19...105

22. Season 2: Episode 20...109

23. Season 2: Episode 21...113

24. Season 2: Episode 22...117

25. Season 2: Episode 23...122

26. Season 2: Episode 24...126

27. Season 2: Episode 25...130

28. Season 2: Episode 26...134

29. Season 2: Episode 27...138

30. Season 2: Episode 28...143

31. Season 2: Episode 29...147

Fire Walk With Me

32. *Fire Walk With Me*...154

Season 3

33. Getting Back To *Twin Peaks*...166

34. Season 3: Part 1...176

35. Season 3: Part 2...183

36. Season 3: Part 3...188

37. Season 3: Part 4...194

38. Season 3: Part 5...203

39. Season 3: Part 6...210

40. Season 3: Part 7..216

41. Season 3: Part 8..222

42. Season 3: Part 9..230

43. Season 3: Part 10..237

44. Season 3: Part 11..244

45. Season 3: Part 12..250

46. Season 3: Part 13..258

47. Season 3: Part 14..263

48. Season 3: Part 15..269

49. Season 3: Part 16..276

50. Season 3: Part 17..283

51. Season 3: Part 18..291

52. The Curtain Call...300

Acknowledgments

Ben & Bryon Thanks...302

More *Twin Peaks* Products..310

Foreword

Let's start with the words of David Lynch: "Don't do the work for the fruit of the action. Do it for the doing. Do it for the happiness you get."

I can't think of two happier people than Ben Durant and Bryon Kozaczka. These guys love to talk about *Twin Peaks*! Just listen to any one of their over 200 *Twin Peaks Unwrapped* podcasts and you'll hear what I mean: No matter if they're dissecting an episode of the original series, theorizing about a scene from *The Return*, or interviewing an actor from the series, Ben and Bryon are unabashedly joyful when talking about their favorite show.

Here's a fact you probably already know: Fans of *Twin Peaks* need to talk about *Twin Peaks*. Whenever we can, we discuss it and debate it and decrypt it. We share our silliest thoughts and our craziest theories. We reveal what delights us and confess what scares us. And we seek out those kindred spirits who understand just how important *Twin Peaks* is. That's why we listen to podcasts like *Twin Peaks Unwrapped*; it's a place to celebrate *Twin Peaks* with our equally enthusiastic friends.

Buoyed by the enigmatic, enthralling art created by David Lynch and Mark Frost, Ben and Bryon have managed to produce a new *Twin Peaks Unwrapped* podcast every week for over four years. That's quite an accomplishment. It's not easy to create new content week in and week out; you have to have passion and commitment for your subject. That's especially true when you're not making money (take it from me, talking (or writing) about *Twin Peaks* is *not* a lucrative business). No, Ben and Bryon are not doing it for profit (the "fruit of the action"); they're doing it because they fell under the spell we've all felt. They were compelled to share their love of *Twin Peaks* with anyone who would listen.

Now they're sharing it with us on the printed page. Welcome to *Twin Peaks Unwrapped: The Book!* What you hold in your hands is a labor of love distilled from a labor of love.

Over the years Ben and Bryon have delved deep into the many wonders of *Twin Peaks*: They've analyzed plot and characters and themes; they've interviewed actors, writers, musicians, and dozens of other artists; and they've kept in touch with dedicated fans whose own creative endeavors help keep *Twin Peaks* alive. Much of the great material Ben and Bryon have recorded over the years is documented in this book. (And there's a lot more, too. You're in for plenty of surprises in these pages!) That's perfect. We can peruse this indispensable information at our leisure. The fascinating revelations we remember from the *Twin Peaks Unwrapped* podcast are now at our fingertips.

And rest assured—the happiness is still here, too. Can't you sense it already? That same spell is working its magic; Ben and Bryon are about to take you back to *Twin Peaks* with the all the infectious enthusiasm they've always had. There's dedication here. There's sincerity, too. And though what follows may be words on a page, read closely and you'll hear it: The delight in Ben's voice, the cheer in Bryon's. Two great fans: happy, still, to be doing it for the doing.

— **John Thorne, December 9, 2019**

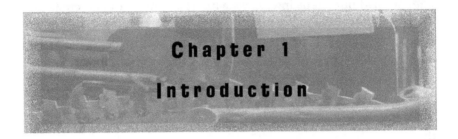

Chapter 1
Introduction

Ben: Welcome to *Twin Peaks Unwrapped*, the book. I'm your co-host, I mean co-author Ben Durant and beside me is ...

Bryon: Bryon Kozaczka, co-author. We say co-authors because we have written this book based on our five-year *Twin Peaks* podcast. Ben, do you want to share how this whole journey began?

Ben: For those who don't know the story, it was my 40th birthday party in March 2015 and Bryon, I knew you had gotten the *Twin Peaks* Blu-ray set for Christmas.

Bryon: I had waited so long to finally watch this series. I knew little to nothing about it, but I knew you were a big fan.

Ben: Talking to you at the party, I was surprised you still hadn't watched it three months after getting it. Right then and there I had an idea to do a *Twin Peaks* podcast with you. You had been doing a podcast for years, which I really enjoyed listening to, and I figured with your podcast experience, we could put a show together.

Bryon: I remember you pitching me the idea that day.

Ben: You, the *Twin Peaks* noob, and I, the veteran, would watch *Twin Peaks* through your fresh eyes and along the way, I would share my long-time experience.

Bryon: I was in. Over 200 shows later, we are still going strong. We covered Seasons 1 and 2, *Fire Walk with Me*, and Season 3 (called *The Return* by Showtime).

Ben: We had numerous interviews with *Twin Peaks* cast and crew.

Bryon: And a lot of help from the community, giving a platform to everyone who shares the same passion we do for the world of *Twin Peaks*, David Lynch, and Mark Frost.

Ben: The *Twin Peaks* community is by far the best fan community out there.

Bryon: With 2020 being the 30th anniversary of *Twin Peaks* and us ending our show at the end of 2020, it seemed like a good time to put out a book based on our podcast and to include new interviews and contributions from the *Twin Peaks* cast and crew as well as the community.

Ben: This companion book should be read after watching Seasons 1 and 2, *Fire Walk with Me*, and Season 3 for best enjoyment and to avoid spoilers.

Bryon: We should explain how most chapters will be structured. This is Chapter 1, the introduction, and Chapter 2 is on the pilot. Therefore, Chapter 3 focuses on Season 1, Episode 1.

Ben: Right, so we don't count the pilot episode in numbering the episodes and we continue numbering in order right through Season 2. So, the first episode of Season 2 is Episode 8 instead of Season 2, Episode 1. Many long time fans have numbered the show this way. I do remember that the *Twin Peaks* Seasons 1 and 2 VHS box set was numbered this way.

Bryon: And what about the German titles?

Ben: I don't like them and Lynch/Frost originally did not give Seasons 1 and 2 episode titles. These titles are based on the titles Germany assigned when it aired in that country. Streaming services like Netflix and Hulu have since adopted the German titles, so we provide them as an easy aid to sort out the episodes.

Bryon: Most chapters are broken down into four parts: "The Log Line", "Behind the Curtain", "Bringing Back Some Memories", and "Community Commentary".

Ben: "The Log Line" gives a brief summary. For example, Episode 1: Agent Cooper meets Audrey Horne for the first time.

Bryon: "Behind the Curtain" is cast and crew sharing stories and thoughts about *Twin Peaks*.

Ben: Then, in "Bringing Back Some Memories", we share our favorite moments and quotes from the show.

Bryon: The chapter ends with "Community Commentary", where *Twin Peaks* fans share their experiences.

Ben: So sit back, relax, pour yourself a damn fine cup of coffee, and enjoy *Twin Peaks Unwrapped*, the book.

Ben Durant & Bryon Kozaczka in Snoqualmie,
Washington at Twede's Cafe (Double R diner) in 2017.

Chapter 2

Season 1: The Pilot
Aired: Sunday, April 8, 1990
Written by Mark Frost & David Lynch
Directed by David Lynch

The Log-line

FBI Agent Dale Cooper begins his investigation in the town of Twin Peaks after the adored teenager Laura Palmer is found dead, "wrapped in plastic."

Behind the Curtain

Months before the pilot aired on ABC, *Twin Peaks* was previewed to the press. Co-creators David Lynch and Mark Frost took questions about the serial drama. Lynch expressed, "Everybody loves a mystery, and we're all detectives of sorts and we want to know what's going to happen. And I think we'll like getting to know these characters and spending time with them" ("Bizarre 'Twin Peaks' Coming to ABC." *Waterloo Courier*, January 16, 1990). *Twin Peaks* gave the TV viewer the opportunity to be a detective, actively participating in solving the mystery of who killed Laura Palmer. This would not be a passive show where people could tune in and out. This would be a show which required viewers to be invested and pay strict attention. For fans, this would include community discussions, flow charts of all the characters and their relationships between each other, and multiple rewatches to discover new details. But it all began with the dead body of a young girl that washed up on a shore.

Mark Frost (Co-Creator) on the origins of Laura Palmer: Hazel Drew [a young New York girl in 1908] was murdered, I'd say, less than two miles from the lake where I grew up and where I spent every summer growing up. My grandmother knew that story intimately and the pond that her body was found beside was allegedly haunted. She and her sister, my great aunt, had a great story about going down there one night and thought they heard a ghost moaning and wailing. And it turned out the next day, they discovered that a cow had gotten stuck in the fence. It was sort of lowing for help. The calf, I'm happy to report, survived the ordeal.

Then when I was about 13, a friend of the family—his father worked with my dad—their oldest daughter was murdered. She was about Laura's age. She was at a private school in central California. So we lived through that tragedy and her younger brother was one of my closest friends at the time. That was an indelible experience that also, I think, figured into the *Twin Peaks* history as well.

Tony Krantz (past Agent to David Lynch and Mark Frost): David and I would go to Nibblers, this restaurant on Wilshire Boulevard in Beverly Hills, all the time. We'd go to Du-pars and Nibblers, places that he liked. And I wanted to get David into television because that was the world that I worked in principally. And I said to him, "You know, this world of Nibblers is sort of the world you should write about. The world of regular people."

I honestly don't remember how I first met Mark Frost, but Mark was also a client. He had come out of [the TV show] *Hill Street Blues*. So this idea of David and Mark together, that sort of yin and yang of the two of them was a perfect idea. And I screened for the guys *Peyton Place*, the movie. I said, "This is sort of further than the Nibblers thing. This is what you guys should do."

It was off of that the guys created an idea called *Northwest Passage*. I took them in to Chad Hoffman who was the drama executive at ABC. I was covering ABC at the time and Chad basically bought it in the room. David unfurled the map to Twin Peaks, which he then subsequently gave me one year for my birthday, described what the world would be like and this and that, and Chad ordered it as a script. It was the first time a movie person like David had worked in television.

Robert Bauer (Johnny Horne): David, I think, was the first real heralded film director to come to television to bring his filmic directorial brand and star power to television. Once they heard the pitch, they're like, "Done, whatever you want." And gave him carte blanche to do what he did. And I think that first season paid the dividends of ABC's belief in David. It was a big moment in the television landscape for ABC, that they had David Lynch on television, having created this show, and it was groundbreaking on every level.

Map Courtesy of Tony Krantz.

Scott Frost (Writer): The first I knew of *Twin Peaks* was when Mark gave me an early draft of the pilot script to read, which was, at that point, called *Northwest Passage*. It was kind of interesting, but it didn't seem to be anything incredibly unique at that point. Then the ball started rolling and it turned into one of the greatest pilots ever made.

Mary Jo Deschanel (Eileen Hayward): The idea of this small town and all the things that people know about each other: I love that. All the dark underbelly, the layers, and layers of secrets.

Duwayne Dunham (Editor and Director of Ep. 1, 18, and 25): I first came in contact with David through *Blue Velvet*. I didn't know David. I knew of his work. I was living up in the Bay Area, just finished with George Lucas, and David wanted to edit in Berkeley, and there's a pretty small pool out there. So he called and said, "I want you to cut *Blue Velvet* for me." And so we met and talked about it.

We did *Blue Velvet,* had a really good time, and got on pretty good. Then I edited a couple of commercials for him and he sent me the script for *Twin Peaks.* He said, "I'm sending you this script. ABC will never air it, but they're gonna give us four or five million dollars so let's just go have some fun and make the movie." And that's kind of what we did.

Isabella Rossellini (was offered to play Giovanna Pasqalini Packard, which became Josie Packard): *Twin Peaks* was a real revolution in the world of television. I was sorry I couldn't be part of it because a series shoots during many long months. I was then having a great modeling career that required much traveling and couldn't commit. I was, and still am, very sorry not to be part of it. It also signed the end of my love story with David Lynch … that was even sadder.

Charlotte Stewart (Betty Briggs): I had done *Eraserhead* with David. He knew me and my roommate at the time. I was sharing a house with Jack Nance [Pete Martel]. So David came to dinner one night and told us about the show, which then was called *Northwest Passage.* And because there had been another show called *Northwest Passage,* they decided to change it to *Twin Peaks* so there was no confusion.

Sherilyn Fenn (Audrey Horne): I was 24 and had done a few things. I think at that point I'd done [the movie] *Two Moon Junction* already and I wasn't very happy. I went to a prominent manager's Christmas party. And she spoke to me a day or two later and said that she had been observing me. She said, "Don't try to be likable or who you think people want you to be. If you're kind of sarcastic, if you're a smart ass, if you're shy, whatever you are, try to stay in that center of yourself and the good directors will want to work with you."

David (Lynch) just looks at 8X10s and decides who he wants to bring in. There was no specific role that I was told I was up for. He had a photograph of me where I had a short, platinum blonde pixie. So I went in. I was quiet. He did most of the talking. He asked me, "What do you think of the script?" I answered, honestly, "Well, everyone's sleeping with everyone." What did I know? I was just a kid. And he's like, "Yeah, they are, you know, it's kind of a soap opera." I left and the casting person called my manager and said that I should have been more positive, et cetera, et cetera.

Johanna Ray (Casting Director): I think [David Lynch saw in Sherilyn] what everybody else in Hollywood saw in her. Of all the young actors around, she was *the* beauty. She has this certain sensuality about her and was stunningly beautiful.

Sherilyn Fenn (Audrey Horne): A week later they called and said that (David Lynch) was writing a role for me. Audrey Horne was not in *Northwest Passage* until I got to meet him. And then he wrote her in. So it was an incredible verification of being one's true self. I got this role written for me that pretty much changed my career and my life.

Johanna Ray: If he clicks with and likes the actor, he'll hire them for a role that is not the way it's described in the script.

Kimmy Robertson (Lucy Moran): I was a guest in the pilot and then in the first season. For some reason, the only thing they could do for me was make me have a recurring [guest] role status. Now, I don't understand the politics of Hollywood at all. I've never been good at playing that, "Oh, I can't do that part because there's not enough lines" kind of thing. But that actually exists. But all the weirdness that has to do with your image and what producers think of you is more important than just being the person they want for the part. That sorta had something to do with that back then because I was an absolute nobody.

Eric Da Re (Leo Johnson): I was working in production at Propaganda Films and then I was assisting my mom [Johanna Ray] in the casting of it. It was pilot season, which a lot of the actors come in after like 10:00 PM 'cause they were shooting pilots for other networks.

Johanna Ray: We were working at a table together, usually the assistant is in a different room from me, but we were sitting next to each other at a table. We didn't have any choice. It was right when we first started making deals with the stars and ABC had insisted on seeing David's choices audition. So David had all the actors that we'd cast in the room. David hated doing that. Personally, I think it was insulting to him.

So on that particular day, I was negotiating deals and David said, "Can you come in and fill in and read for the roles that we haven't cast?" And I couldn't. So I sent Eric in.

Eric Da Re: And they asked me if I'd stay because I was there late anyway and read with them, which I really didn't want to do. I was kind of quite embarrassed to do that. So I reluctantly did it one night and I did it the second night. I think I did it like two or three times.

[Actresses] were reading for Shelly Johnson at that time and I was reading the part of Leo. But the thing about script read through—because I've seen them and operated them before in production—is just reading the lines just to see how they hear. You're not actually acting it out, really. You can, but it's generally just reading them and then the writers can hear the dialogue and decide what can be removed and what doesn't sound natural and so forth. I was just literally reading the words off of the page at that point. I didn't want them to think I wanted to be an actor and that I was trying to. But after doing it a few more times, it just became natural to do it a little bit more other than just reading the words off the page.

David went to New York to look for actors there and in fact, if I remember correctly, at the time Brad Pitt read for my role and Richard Tyson.

Johanna Ray: After [auditions] finished, David came up to me and he kind of was very secretive. He said, "Johanna, Eric is amazing. Can I have your permission to cast him?"

Eric Da Re: David called me from New York at the production office that night and offered me the part. I think I said to him, "You're full of shit!" even though I wasn't in a relationship with him well enough to talk to him like that, but I really thought he was pulling my leg. He wasn't laughing and he told me not to laugh. He had said originally if I'm not mistaken, I reminded him a lot of [an early] Dennis Hopper. And he goes, "I mean it. Will you consider it?" And I said, "Sure." The next thing I knew, that was it.

I got up to Washington from LA, they had a production party the night before shooting the pilot. I was with everybody having a great time and having such a good time that we wanted to continue, even though the party was over. So somebody told me they left keys in the production van. So Michael Horse, Sheryl Lee, and I got one of the vans, took it into town. I don't want to get into details, but Michael Horse had to bail me out of jail in Seattle at five o'clock in the morning and drive me directly to the set. Keep in mind, this is my very first acting job. Very first time. My scene was the first scene to be shot of the pilot. Totally out of order. So I got right out of jail, right to the set, action. Literally, that scene where I'm sitting across from [Mädchen Amick] with Crème de Menthe looking at the ashtray. Thank God for Michael Horse.

Sherilyn Fenn: [I wore my own clothes] all the time. I would have been in really big sweaters, big huge sweaters like the girls in the [pilot]. I'm like, "Nuh-uh." I ran and grabbed my baby pink cashmere antique sweater, which David ruined, by the way, because when they put me against the wall with the Norwegian, he kept saying tighter, tighter, tighter. He pinned it and wrapped it into a ball behind my back and totally stretched it out, but it was worth it.

Audrey was barely in the pilot. So they're like, "Oh, we don't care if she wears a pink sweater." It just didn't matter and then all of a sudden, it really mattered.

Mary Jo Deschanel (Eileen Hayward): Someone came up and said, "We don't have time" [to film everything] and I was standing there and David just took the script and he ripped out a few pages and he goes okay there you go. He really stuck to it. It wasn't like he went back. It wasn't just a display. I thought, "Oh, that is fantastic."

Kyle MacLachlan (Agent Dale Cooper): Diane was a great device to be able to explain and talk about what was happening in Twin Peaks. I think the wonderful thing was the reveal of the character in that opening episode when Cooper drives up to the mountain and just what he does, how he comments. He's giving up information, but you're really learning about the quality of this guy through his observations, what's important to him, how he speaks, his cadence, everything that goes on. So, it was a great character reveal just in that one shot, that one drive up the mountain.

Lesli Linka Glatter (Director of Ep. 5, 10, 13 and 23): I was around a lot because I wanted to learn from [David Lynch]. I wanted to soak in the environment. So, there was a scene in which Kyle Maclachlan and Michael Ontkean go look [at Laura Palmer's] safe deposit box and on the table is a moose head. The scene's incredible. So as I got to know David, I asked him how he got the idea to put the moose head on the table. He looked at me like I was kinda crazy. He said, "It was there." I was like, "Well, what do you mean it was there?" He said, well, the Set Decorator was going to hang up the moose head on the wall, but he walked into the set and saw the moose head lying there and said, "Leave the moose head." And something cracked open for me. Have your plan, know what you want, but be sure you're open to the moose head on the table. Be sure you're open to life happening all around you. For me, that's David Lynch right there.

Duwayne Dunham: We were up in Washington shooting, and David was out in very adverse weather conditions, which just made for a beautiful look because it was the deep blues, greens, and blacks of the forest. The actors were freezing, so their cheeks are red and noses are running. He was shooting with coral filters to warm it all up. It was just a really great feel.

One day he said something like, ABC had just informed him that they cannot and will not air a pilot episode if they don't pick this up. They said, "We need a closed ending." Well, there was no closed ending. In other words, you have to answer the 'who-done-it.'

A couple days later, it's like our last or next to last day up there and about midnight, this delivery guy brought up a cartload of film into the room. And I said, "You gotta be mistaken. We're done. We leave in the morning. That can't be for us." "*Twin Peaks*, right?" I said, "Yeah." And he said, "Well, it's for you." I grabbed the roll of film, and I put it on the flatbed, and I started looking at it. It was Bob down in the basement being crazy. It was the one-armed man and him talking about "Living above it and I mean it like its sounds," and all this weird stuff. David hadn't mentioned a word of it. So that became the so-called closed ending. In David's mind, that was closed enough.

Todd Holland (Director of Ep. 11 and 20): I thought the pilot was extraordinary and I really credit Mark Frost with always being this leveling force in David's weirdness. That synergy between the two of them was just beautiful because this has such an accessible ground as humanity, and yet there was this deep dark spin that was utterly unique. I thought they really were beautiful collaborators. (*Courtesy of* The Red Room Podcast, *Ep125*)

Mary Jo Deschanel: When we were doing the pilot, it was just a goof, kind of. I don't mean that [David] didn't take it seriously. I mean goof in the sense that we're doing this thing, but it's never going to go on television. It was so unusual and groundbreaking. That was the feeling during the pilot.

Ray Wise (Leland Palmer): We had no idea really how it was going to be perceived by an audience. As we were doing the pilot, we knew that it was good writing, great characters. We were doing good work. But how it would be taken, we had no idea. And I remember we went to see a screening of the pilot and we thought, "You know, pretty good. Ah, different. But I don't know, it's on ABC."

It's amazing it got on the air, but it did because of the strength of force of its own being. It had to come out. They were forced to put it on the air because everybody liked that pilot so much. Once it was, everybody responded to it and it had to go on. (*Courtesy of* FWWM *event at Studio 35 Cinema & Drafthouse, July, 2019*)

Tony Krantz (previous Agent to David Lynch and Mark Frost): Brandon Tartikoff [then President of NBC] famously said about the pilot after he saw it, "The tried and true is dead and buried."

Duwayne Dunham: I'm very proud of that pilot episode of *Twin Peaks*. It's a great movie.

Brings Back Some Memories

Ben: Reflecting back on the pilot, I remember you were surprised how much it was like a soap opera.

Bryon: The acting, the presentation, the music almost felt soap-opera-like and dreamlike. And when you watch a soap opera, it always has that fuzziness around it. I'm like, what am I getting myself into here?

Ben: Why did I suggest you watch this? I believe you thought the killer was Jacoby in the pilot?

Bryon: I do remember thinking Jacoby did it only because of his odd behavior when they first met him.

Ben: Cooper and Harry get off the elevator and Jacoby asks if they're going to see Laura's dead body and if he can come along.

Bryon: He was almost like sexualizing the situation and being very creepy. And I thought that was very odd, especially when it is one of your patients in town. In this day and age, that would be the first person I would think would be the killer.

Ben: Yes, I could definitely see that. I watched it originally in 1990 when I was 15 and what I loved about the show was that it was so odd. Teenagers would dance in the hallways, boys barked like dogs in jail cells, and an FBI agent talked to his tape recorder about chocolate bunnies. It was like nothing else on television at the time and you really never knew what was going to happen next.

Bryon: When I first watched the pilot in 2015, I had to detach myself from the current television that I was watching, like *True Detective, American Horror Story* and a lot of good current television. I had to get myself into a headspace of early '90s television because it's a different way you told stories back then.

This was my first gateway into Lynch, so he tells things a lot differently than I'm used to. A slower pace. It felt like a very odd soap opera. Very different. Very '90s. I think *Twin Peaks* was a trailblazer at the time of its airing and now you can definitely see how *Twin Peaks* inspired shows like *True Detective.*

Favorite Quotes and Scenes

Ben: My quote is from good old Pete Martell, "She's dead, wrapped in plastic." It's a classic line and it gets to the essence of the mystery of a young girl who was killed in a peculiar way. I also can't imagine anyone delivering that line better than Jack Nance!

Bryon: My favorite quote is from Dale Cooper. He's with Sheriff Harry Truman in the sheriff cruiser staking out the Roadhouse.

Dale Cooper: You know why I'm whittling?
Sheriff Harry S. Truman: Okay, I'll bite again. Why are you whittling?
Dale Cooper: Because that's what you do in a town where a yellow light still means slow down, not speed up.

I enjoy this scene because it shows you how Cooper is taking to this town very quickly and he likes the slow pace of the town and it makes him feel like a kid in a candy store. He loves everything about the town and you don't want him to leave it and you don't want him to leave your television. That's one of my favorite scenes from the pilot.

Ben: In David Lynch style, more emphasis was put on everyday objects like a phone, including cord and receiver, a fan, and a traffic light than what most audiences were used to in 1990. The emphasis on the atmosphere in and around the town played a big part in the show and there was no one better to point out the details than Special Agent Dale Cooper. From his first appearance dictating, "Diane, 11:30 a.m. February 24th, entering the town of Twin Peaks," he made the mundane facts he observed, like "What kind of trees are these?" delightful. It's my favorite scene in the pilot.

Bryon: The Twin Peaks town hall meeting is a very clever way to meet the townspeople and to learn about them as well through the eyes of Dale Cooper. We see Harry and Cooper sitting in the front facing the entrance while Cooper asks Harry about all the different people walking into the hall, like, "Who's the glad-handing dandy?" We also get our first glimpse at the Log Lady. In an episode filled with great moments, this is one of my favorites.

Community Commentary

Charles de Lauzirika (DVD and Blu-ray Producer and Filmmaker): I was at Glendale Community College in California and I was on the newspaper staff. Having been a fan of David I heard that he had this new TV show that was in the works and I actually got tickets to an early screening of the pilot. I can't remember how far in advance it was before it was actually on television. I got to brag about it for a while. With my friends, I was like, "Oh my God! You're not going to believe this thing! I saw it." And so instantly from day one, I was a *Twin Peaks* maniac.

Chapter 3

Season 1: Episode 1
"Traces to Nowhere" (German title)
Aired: Thursday, April 12, 1990
Written by Mark Frost & David Lynch
Directed by Duwayne Dunham

The Log-line

Agent Cooper meets Audrey Horne for the first time, as well as other townspeople that may be connected to the death of Laura Palmer.

Behind the Curtain

After the pilot was completed, ABC gave the green-light to Lynch/Frost to create a seven episode season. David Lynch expressed, "When we talked about television, the main pull for me was being able to do a continuing story, one where you can really get to know the people." (Buck, Jerry. "Contrast Is 'Twin Peaks' Lynchpin." *Daily News*. April 6, 1990). With the opportunity to continue the story, sets were built on a soundstage to replicate places from the pilot, and writers and directors were hired to assist in developing the episodic murder mystery drama.

Tony Krantz (previous Agent to David Lynch and Mark Frost): [ABC] ordered *Twin Peaks* only for mid-season for seven additional episodes. The show benefited from that because it was being screened everywhere, and the word of mouth just started building and building. And when the [pilot] show went on the air initially, the last half hour of it, I think, had something like a 39 share. That was in a different world than the world we exist in now. But what that means is that 39% of all televisions that were in use in America in the last half hour of the pilot of *Twin Peaks* were watching that show. It was a massive audience. That's what fueled it and it became a phenomenon.

Duwayne Dunham (Editor and Director of ep. 1, 18, and 25): I really love working with David. When we were finishing *Twin Peaks* [the pilot], I asked him one day if he was going to do anything and he said no, he was going to take some time off. And I said, "Okay, well I just want to know because I'm going to go get another editing job and I just want to make sure if you're going to do something, I'd rather work with you." And he said, "Nope I'm not doing anything.

Then like a week later, he walked back in with Monty Montgomery. Monty had this project, *Wild at Heart*, [and he] had been saying that he himself was going to direct it and David walked in and he said, "Hey, I'm gonna direct *Wild at Heart* and I want you to cut it." And I kinda looked at the two of them and said, "I thought that was Monty's project?" David says, "Nope it's mine now." I said, "Well, do you have a script?" And he said, "No, but it won't be hard to get one." And I said, "Well, when do you plan on shooting?" And he said, "Maybe six weeks away or something." And I said, "Wow, that's ambitious, but the problem is we had talked and you said this wasn't going to happen so I got another job and I start as soon as this one's finished in a few days." And he said, "No, no, you have to cut *Wild at Heart*." I said, "I can't do that, David. I can't trade one editing job for another. I just can't do that." And he said, "Well, okay, what would it take for you to cut *Wild at Heart*?" And I said, "I'm in this business for one reason. I want to direct and make my own movies. If that situation came upon me, then everybody would understand that's an important move and it's not trading an apple for an apple." He thought for a moment and he said, "Okay, I'll tell you what. ABC just picked us up for seven episodes. You can direct the first episode and a few others. Now will you cut *Wild at Heart* for me?" And that is how it happened.

Scott Frost (Writer): My wife and I were living in Minnesota at the time. I was a museum guard at that point and a screenwriter. So I was writing scripts and I had already gotten an agent and I'd had a couple things optioned and then Mark, who's as surprised as anybody else, called up and said, "They picked it up. Why don't you come out?"

Richard Hoover (Production Designer): While we did not know the secrets, the potential discoveries excited us. Each setting, each surface, and each object we found wanted to play into this potential. David allowed us such joy in this discovery.

Duwayne Dunham: I didn't have directorial experience, but outside of David and probably even Mark, I knew the movie as well as anybody. I knew the characters and I was still actively working on them. So the one advantage was I was very comfortable in being confident that I would be able to get the actors right where they were from the pilot. So it was just a matter of reminding them of who that character was because we had shot that over a year earlier. And then it was a kind of a crazy time because I finished the pilot of *Twin Peaks* and then David started shooting *Wild at Heart* and I started cutting *Wild at Heart* and then I took a break to go direct.

Kyle MacLachlan (Dale Cooper): So much of [the character of Cooper] was written in the script and I just kind of took that and expanded it and made it my own. We sort of found it together, David [Lynch] and I. He had certain mannerisms and I'm speaking now of course of the first incarnation I adopted as Dale Cooper. Some of the hand clasping in front of the body, some of the intonation and delivery, and we both are fairly enthusiastic people. So that wasn't too difficult. He was quirky. Yes. But there was a serious side to him as well, which it was important to bring out from time to time, just to remind people that this wasn't all about sort of the crazy, wonderful world of the town of Twin Peaks.

Duwayne Dunham: Gosh, [Cooper] is a handsome guy? [Audrey] is a very attractive young woman and the character she played was so outrageous. The whole idea of somebody who leaves the house wearing these clothes to school and puts on red high heels. That tells you a lot about that character.

Sherilyn Fenn: There was no plan. Dale Cooper ended up at the hotel, so put him with Audrey. We weren't supposed to be together, but after we worked together, something was on film that really worked. And instead of having his character go towards Joan Chen (Josie Packard), which was their original plan, they had him start to come towards me.

Duwayne Dunham: When you're doing episodic work, you can ask questions and say, "David or Mark, where is this going? Is this going to lead to anything?" And you can ask questions like that and sometimes certain things are revealed that help you. It was just a human attraction. It didn't have anything to do with the real people. It was just those characters in that environment, in that situation. [Audrey] came prancing into the room and caught [Cooper's] attention and kinda had him. I think I played it where he was a little bit dumbfounded. Wasn't quite sharp as he would be otherwise because she kind of got under his skin and that then makes him a little more human.

Twin Peaks update—
• Laura Palmer found murdered
• The FBI arrives
• James Hurley arrested.

▲ TWIN ▲
PEAKS
Like every town you've ever seen.
And no place you've ever known.
New Series Premiere
9:00PM abc 9 13 20 50

Photo courtesy of TV Guide

Charlotte Stewart: I knew I was playing Betty Briggs. I didn't know what that meant. I was totally surprised when I met Don Davis who plays my husband, Major Briggs. Somehow I thought he would be this big tall, handsome guy and here's this kind of slightly rounded, redhead, middle-aged guy. I misjudged him completely. Don Davis is, was, God rest his soul, he was one of the more interesting men I have ever met. He was a painter. He was a teacher. He became a very good friend. And I miss him.

Duwayne Dunham: David doesn't move the camera a lot. Lucas doesn't move the camera a lot. I suppose that style probably came out of my having worked closely with material from both those guys. But it's also knowing as an editor that my strength is in editing and so I would shoot sorta say around the movie.

I just knew I needed these pieces. Somebody like Spielberg, he'll go and just shoot the movie. He knows exactly what he wants and how to get it and what it is. I shoot around it. I go out and I just make sure I got all the pieces so when I go back to the cutting room, I can empty that sack of pieces and somehow put it together. David's a bit that way, in a strange way, the characters are still developing and certain ways that the story is going together continues to evolve and it comes out of yet another editorial style.

I also am aware that you don't have much time to edit those things. So if I could get it in one [shot], a oner, and actually everybody challenged one another. You've got to have one scene and in these first seven episodes, that's a oner. You got to do a one. I think mine was Audrey's dance. Started on her saddle shoes and pulled back and her dad comes in.

The first episode of *Twin Peaks* we shot in seven days and I finished the same day David finished shooting the feature *Wild at Heart*. So we met back at the cutting room and now we had the first episode of *Twin Peaks* and we had the feature *Wild at Heart* and then David started directing the second episode of *Twin Peaks*. So, we had those seven episodes going on at the same time the feature, *Wild at Heart*, was going on and it kind of sounds crazy, but it wasn't.

Brings Back Some Memories

Bryon: Cooper is an amazing detective, but it was his discovery of James's motorcycle in Laura's eye that really proved to me how unbelievable he was.

Ben: Right! It is only because Cooper pauses on Laura's eye in Laura and Donna's picnic videotape that he's able to confirm it's James Hurley's bike.

Bryon: Who would see that? It's unbelievable. But it was kind of clever and cool.

Ben: I also think it's Lynch/Frost telling the audience to pay attention! There are clues throughout the show in images, sounds, names of people, and places for the fans to discover; Easter eggs. When you first watched, you thought that Laura and Donna were a couple because on the videotape they were dancing.

Bryon: Because in this show everybody's having affairs! Nobody's just with somebody. They also have someone on the side. You see them dancing and I'm wondering, "What if Laura and Donna had a fling?"

Ben: And you thought Leo was the killer.

Bryon: Leo had construction going on in his house with the plastic on the walls. Plastic, of course, makes me think of when Laura was found dead wrapped in plastic. He also had blood on his shirt and wanted Shelly to wash it.

Ben: We got to witness the living Laura Palmer in this episode. She comes alive through the dancing picnic video, a flashback of her giving the half heart necklace to James and she delivers an audio message from the dead to Dr. Jacoby (and the audience) by means of a cassette tape. She was important to everyone in town and in this episode we begin to understand why.

Favorite Quotes and Scenes

Ben: My favorite scene in Episode 1 is at the Great Northern with Agent Cooper having breakfast with "a damn fine cup of coffee" and he meets Audrey Horne. Kyle MacLachlan and Sherilyn Fenn had great chemistry and their characters were similar in that they both could have a serious conversation about something one second and then the next second be asking a random question about Douglas fir trees or "Do your palms ever itch?" They were charming, peculiar, and beautiful together. The 15-year-old me who originally saw the show had such a crush on Audrey.

Bryon: As someone with fresh eyes, I thought their relationship was inappropriate right away, whereas old-time fans liked the idea of Cooper and Audrey together. Their flirting was cute, but I didn't want it to go beyond that.

You mentioned the damn fine coffee, my favorite quote from the episode is from Pete Martell:

Pete Martell: Mr. Cooper, how do you take it?
Dale Cooper: Black as midnight on a moonless night.
Pete Martell: Pretty black.

This quote is classic for explaining how to have coffee, but just as Agent Cooper is having his first sip of rich, black coffee Pete comes in and says ...

Ben: "There was a fish in the percolator." That's my favorite quote! Just the oddness of a fish getting into a percolator. The coffee that Cooper and the townspeople love is ruined by the fish.

Bryon: And it was probably Josie. She's not as innocent as she seems and maybe she was throwing them off by putting fish in their coffee.

My favorite scene is at the Double R with Dale Cooper and Sheriff Truman having some coffee and cherry pie while working on the case together. We see that the Log Lady is also at the counter area of the diner and Dale Cooper wants to ask her about her log. "Many have," Truman says to him. At the end of the scene, the Log Lady approaches Dale Cooper and Sheriff Truman, telling them that her log saw something (the night Laura died). Dale says back, "What did it see?", and she, knowing full well he is not ready for what she will clap back to him, replies, "Ask it." Dale Cooper has nothing. He's not sure if he knows how to take this whole thing. Was this a joke? Was she serious? But deep down, I think he wasn't ready to ask and the Log Lady knew it. Seeing Dale and Truman bonding over coffee and pie, two iconic hallmarks of *Twin Peaks*, while we get some new information about the townsfolk and the promise of a possible answer from a log down the road makes this one of the most interesting scenes in this episode. It sets up the juxtaposition of the folksy, small town with the bizarre and nightmarish quality that is at the heart of *Twin Peaks*.

Community Commentary

Scott Ryan (*The Blue Rose* magazine, Managing Editor): *Twin Peaks* hit me like a sandbag on the head at a Miss Twin Peaks Contest. I remember sitting on the couch at my college girlfriend's house watching the pilot episode on regular network television. You see, back then we had to watch TV when it was on. I remember when the girl runs across the high school campus screaming and crying at the news that Laura Palmer had died, that my girlfriend's father stood up, shook his hands at the screen and said, "This is crap." He left the room. 30 years later, I am still sitting on a couch riveted by the town of Twin Peaks, by the music of *Twin Peaks,* and by the community of *Twin Peaks* fans.

Chapter 4

Season 1: Episode 2
"Zen, or the Skill to Catch a Killer"
Aired: Thursday, April 19, 1990
Written by Mark Frost & David Lynch
Directed by David Lynch

The Log-line

Cooper dreams of being with Laura Palmer in a red room with a little man who speaks backwards and may hold the answers to who killed the homecoming queen.

Behind the Curtain

The pilot and first episode had strange moments and strange characters, but in Episode 2, David Lynch took the audience to a whole new strange place with a dream sequence of backward walking and talking characters. "I like places that make you dream and give you new feelings." David Lynch expressed right before Episode 2 aired (Shales, Tom. "Creator of 'Twin Peaks' wants to make dreams." *Washington Post*. April 18, 1990). Cooper's dream was a television game changer and after this point, the show would never be the same again.

Kyle MacLachlan: Before *Twin Peaks* my film experiences were pretty wide at that point in time. I started off from *Dune*, which is its own kind of beast, to kind of a long lull before *Blue Velvet*, which was the second, both with David. So that was the common thing. *Blue Velvet* was much smaller. I think everybody was much more comfortable and kind of understood this story. There were a lot of moving parts in *Dune*. And shortly after that, I did the movie called *The Hidden*, which was a kind of a departure, but also had some kind of early Dougie (Jones) stages in some ways. A little bit of the object discovery with this character which was fun to explore. Didn't quite know how to react to this human environment.

Then the *Twin Peaks* thing was really something that I was very excited about. I was primarily excited because of the character. I liked the character. It's not that I was having a hard time, but I was struggling a little bit in Los Angeles with film and things are coming and stuff, but it's not really consistent yet. And I said, "This is a great character. And I get to work with my friend David" and I said, "Okay, this could be fun."

Scott Frost: For the first season, I worked on the production side on set as a Production Assistant. I just sort of absorbed the whole part of production, which came in to be very useful later in my career when I was on shows as a producer. 'Cause you learn it from the ground up. I was able to spend a lot of time watching directors work. You also learned that what a lot of writers never learn in Hollywood is how frickin' hard it is to work in production and the insane hours you work.

Robert Bauer: I got a call from my agent that David [Lynch] wanted to see me for the role of Johnny Horne. I didn't know anything about *Twin Peaks*. There was no script; there was nothing. It wasn't floating around, at least in my solar system. Evidently, he saw my headshot and was like, "Have him come in." I'm sure along with many, many others. But that's how I got the audition, literally off the picture.

I remember the dinner scene with the mashed potatoes. David Lynch just wanted me and the actors to explore and be in the moment. I would fling the mashed potatoes more than I would serve it to myself. There were things that were very specific and needed to be specific, but he seemed very journey oriented. The goal will reveal itself in the process. It's like, what color do you want to paint with? This color? Oh, let's try that. Oh, that's a neat color. What if we add this and what if we add that? It was a hand-in-hand collaborative thing. What do you think about the scene? I'm thinking this, what do you think? That seems kind of good. Let's try that. It was a very responsive and embracing and back-and-forth thing.

Connie Woods (The New Girl): Well, obviously I had no idea what enduring cinematic gravitas I had stumbled into standing there that day in the huddle of hopefuls on location. We didn't know why we were called outside and asked to form a line but suddenly there he was. David Lynch slowly strolled through our lineup and peered into our souls. His trademark angst and sticky, twisted cynicism permeated the set even when cameras weren't rolling. My eye twitched, knees melted just as he quietly said: "It's her ... that's her."

Eric Da Re: It was like four o'clock in the morning. We're in Malibu Canyon and very unusual for California, it was below freezing when we shot [the woods scene with Leo, Bobby and Mike]. David Lynch said action. I think Dana did his dialogue to me and I just had no recollection of what my lines were or anything, but I just kept staring at him. David off of camera said, "Don't cut, don't cut," and I just sat there and he just let me just stand there.

Finally after looking at Dana for about 45 seconds and clearly I forgot [my lines], I just looked straight down at the ground, veering like I was looking directly at my shoes and that's when David said, "Leo needs a new pair of shoes.", and that must be what he wants for me to say and I said it. That's how that came about. I still to this day don't remember what [the line] was because it became that and it was a one-take thing.

Michael Horse on Hawk wearing oven mitts during the Copper rock-throwing scene: It's actually kind of funny cause they said, "Here put these oven mitts on." and I'm going, "What is this?" And they said, "Oh, we just wanted to see you with oven mitts on." I went to pick up the pot with them on and I went, "Oh, it's like *Kung Fu*."

Sherilyn Fenn: The second episode where I had to dance, well that very day David said, "Okay, Sherilyn Fenn and Lara, we're rewriting this scene, get a cappuccino." He rewrites the scene. I'm panicked, "Oh my God! I already worked with Roy [acting coach]. David is rewriting this scene. What am I going to do?" I called Roy. Roy says, "Sherilyn, it's David. Don't worry about it. Just do what he says." I'm like, "Oh, okay."

I was frightened. What do you mean I have to dance? I don't want to dance. [Speaking as David Lynch] "We wrote you music and you're just gonna put it on and you just groove." And I was like, "Oh my God." If you look closely enough my hands are shaking. I felt silly [laughs]. I mean, I did. Look at me dancing.

Ray Wise (Leland Palmer): I remember when I'm holding a picture [of Laura Palmer] and doing a little dance and Grace comes in and I smashed that picture and I actually cut my thumb for real and I bled all over that picture.

And it was one of those real *Apocalypse Now* moments. (*Courtesy of* FWWM *event*)

How the Red Room originated during the editing of the pilot.

Duwayne Dunham: David had this sort of a maroon, deep purple Mercedes, a real beautiful car, old car. And we had been in the cutting room and we walked out into the parking lot over at CFI, the film processing plant [in LA].

Brian Berdan (Assistant Editor): All I remember was, they'd just repaved the parking lot, dark black asphalt…and it indeed was really hot. We'd just come out of the totally dark cutting room—"black as midnight on a moonless night…that's pretty black"—and it had to be dark so we could see the footage that the DP, Fred Elmes, had shot—so very dark. So dark, that we called it the Fred Elmes disease.

Duwayne Dunham: We were talking about something and [David Lynch] just leaned onto the car and all of a sudden he just sprung back and my recollection is he said, "I can't talk. I gotta go." And he jumped in his car and he sped away. And I just kinda stood there like, "Okay, that's David."

David Lynch (Director): My hands were on the roof and the metal was very hot. The Red Room scene leapt into my mind. 'Little Mike' was there and he was speaking backwards. I told Duwayne that I had an idea that I thought he would like very much, but that I couldn't talk about it. For the rest of the night I thought only about The Red Room. (*Lynch on Lynch*, Chris Rodley, p165)

Duwayne Dunham: We were already deep in post when David got that idea. Then he set it up there at the stage. We shot it there. We recorded dialogue and re-recorded it played backwards so that the actors could learn their lines backwards and they said it backwards. When we got it back in the cutting room, we reversed it again. So now backwards was forwards. It's a really wonderful technique that David came up with and it worked really great.

Kyle MacLachlan: The Red Room sequence was definitely odd. It's David, so you know you're going to be in some interesting environments. I thought it was pretty cool and it felt very otherworldly at the time.

The pilot, the first movie, I say movie because it was actually built to be close-ended and they called it at that time a backdoor pilot. Which means, if it did not get picked up, then at least ABC could air it as a movie of the week. They put an ending on it. I don't think that was David's intention to ever close it up, but he sort of had to do it. So we filmed that end sequence. That whole sequence made its way into Episode 2.

The whole Red Room stuff, you kind of do it and it's very strange because Mike Anderson is there, Little Mike, and he's walking backwards. He was actually very proficient at talking backwards and was pretty good at being able to make this sound believable as words. Fortunately, I didn't have to

Ben and Bryon in The Red Room in 2017 at Mary Hutter's house.

speak backwards, but everyone else did. And I was like, what's this going to be like? I had no idea. It seemed very strange. And then you saw it and you were like, whoa, that is pretty brilliant. So you don't really appreciate it until, of course, you see it and it's played backwards and then you go, wow, pretty awesome.

Brings Back Some Memories

Ben: This was the episode where you either got the show or you didn't. Back in the day, there were some people who thought the Cooper dream sequence was too much for them. They thought it was too weird and they stopped watching the show. But for others, like you and me, this was the episode that cemented the love of the show.

I remember when we talked about Laura in the Red Room and how she said, "Sometimes my arms bend back." We connected it to how Nadine's arms bent back when she used the rowing exercise machine. You thought I had spoiled the killer and it was Nadine!

Bryon: I think I was half-joking. Although some part of me was like Nadine is an odd character and her arms did bend backwards!

Favorite Quotes and Scenes

Bryon: My favorite quote in this episode is from Agent Cooper when he is sitting in the Double R and says, "This must be where pies go when they die." Cooper is so overwhelmed with great tasting coffee and amazing pie and it's just fun watching him enjoy the little things in this small town.

Ben: He's in Heaven.

Bryon: This episode has it all: the long dinner scene with the Horne family and Ben and Jerry stuffing their faces with baguettes, Big Ed spilling oil on Nadine's drape runners, Norma and Big Ed flirting at the Double R, Dale Cooper's Tibetan rock throwing, the classic Audrey Horne dance in the Double R, getting to finally meet the sharp-tongued Albert Rosenfield, and the meltdown of Leland Palmer spinning in circles with a picture of Laura Palmer while the peppy sounds of Glenn Miller's "Pennsylvania 6-5000" play in the background. All this happens in one episode of *Twin Peaks*, but what scene will light your socks on fire?

Ben: Cooper's Red Room dream!

Bryon: The moment Dale Cooper puts his head down on that pillow, all hell breaks loose. Flashing lights of the Palmer house, the fan, BOB behind the bed and an echoing sound of "Laura," from Sarah Palmer calling out from the void. We see a one-armed man speaking directly to us, "Through the

Darkness of future past…," he seems to be reciting a poem.

Ben: That's my favorite quote for this episode. "Through the darkness of future past, the magician longs to see. One chants out between two worlds, Fire … walk with me." A lot of cryptic information, which leaves a lot to the imagination. All these years later and we are still trying to make sense of it, which is what I love.

Bryon: Over the next five episodes, Mark Frost and other writers will translate the dream to the reality of the Laura Palmer murder case. You can not think of *Twin Peaks* without the Red Room and it's impossible not to have this one scene be the best part of Episode 2 and quite possibly the most important part of the whole series.

Community Commentary

David Bushman (Author of *Conversations with Mark Frost, The Women of David Lynch*): I came upon *Twin Peaks* in a somewhat unusual fashion. I was a TV editor at *Variety* and we were running stories almost weekly in anticipation of the great David Lynch's transition to television. So I originally appreciated it in the context of what was unfolding within the industry at that time. The imperative for broadcast television to reinvent itself as it was under siege from alternative forms of entertainment: home video, original cable programming, gaming, etc. So, for me that was *interesting*. But once it began airing, interest became *passion*. I fell in love with it as a viewer. Even now it's this peculiar alloy of cerebral and emotional engagement—mind and heart, Lynch and Frost—that obsesses me about it. That and of course Donna Hayward. And let's be clear here, by that I mean *the* Donna Hayward, as portrayed by Lara Flynn Boyle, especially in Season 1.

Scott Ryan (*The Blue Rose* magazine, *The Women of David Lynch*) Bushman says, "Especially in Season 1," because he knows that *FWWM* Donna, Moira Kelly, is the *ultimate* Donna.

Chapter 5

Season 1: Episode 3
"Rest in Pain"
Aired: Thursday, April 26, 1990
Written by Harley Peyton
Directed by Tina Rathborne

The Log-line

Twin Peaks residents attend the funeral of Laura Palmer.

Behind the Curtain

At the end of Episode 2, Agent Cooper calls Sheriff Truman and tells him, "I know who killed Laura Palmer." Many eagerly awaited for Episode 3 to reveal who the killer was. Mark Frost, co-creator, responded to the mounting anticipation, "This is not a show about instant gratification. It's a journey, not a destination. And people should just relax and enjoy the ride." (Moore, Colleen. "Viewers Enter Whodunit Spirit." *Florida Today*, April 26, 1990). Lynch/Frost were interested in gradually exploring the town, its people, the darkness in the old woods, which included who killed Laura Palmer and why. Answers would emerge slowly starting with decoding Cooper's dream.

Tina Rathborne (Director of ep. 3 and 17): When I was casting *Zelly and Me* [1988 film], Isabella [Rossellini] didn't like the people that I was thinking of casting and she said, "Please try David [Lynch]." And I said, "No. Isabella, he's a great director." I'm very stubborn and sometimes just so stupidly so. And she said, "But I don't feel anything towards the people." And I knew that I hadn't found the right person. And she just said, "Please just try David." And within the first, I don't know, three minutes, it was clear that David was the right person.

Duwayne Dunham: When I got the script for the first episode, I don't know the exact page count, but it was in the low seventies and I was saying the script is too long. An hour program, it's like 43 minutes of show. And I said, "This is gonna be way long and we're gonna wind up getting rid of stuff." And so by about the third or fourth episode, because my episode came in way long, David's [episode], Tina's [episode], then they finally got down in the ideal length I think was 34 pages full for 43 minutes of program.

So that influenced the editorial style because sometimes you're pushing something, sometimes you're holding back, sometimes you're letting a moment play, sometimes you're celebrating a moment or creating a pause or whatever. But the rhythm of the piece is really, in my opinion, it's the rhythm of the dialogue and the manner in which those characters deliver that dialogue. So when you start with the pilot and then go Episode 1 and 2, that's me and David upfront, it starts to lock in and then everybody starts falling into that pattern.

Tina Rathborne: I always have written and directed my stuff. So this was a totally new experience for me when David said, "Well Teen, would you like to do [a *Twin Peaks* episode]?" I said, "Oh, sure, I've never done it. This could be really fun." And it turned out that I actually loved directing material that wasn't my own.

I can't tell you that I actually talked with David during shooting in the first season, but I had spent so much time with him and I had so immersed myself in what he was doing. I must have watched his pilot fifteen times. When I say fifteen, all I'm saying is that I watched it and watched it and rewatched. It was my template and then I took it and infused the script with it. Harley's script was wonderful. I so immersed myself in David's pilot and then in Harley's script that I was able to make it my own.

Harley Peyton (Writer): One day, Mark Frost called me and said, "I did this TV pilot with David Lynch, of all people. You should come see it. We're doing a screening at the Directors Guild." So I went to it, saw that two-hour pilot, and like everybody else there, just had my mind blown. I went up to Mark in the lobby afterwards to congratulate him and said, "I've never written television before, but if you need anyone to write an episode just call me cause I'm ready to go." Luckily for me, he then said, "Great! Come write the third [episode]."

It was Laura Palmer's funeral. I was lucky I got to walk into that story.

In my experience, the best episodes of television that you write are ones that have a sort of thesis and have a kind of idea behind it. You don't always have the opportunity to do that, but because this was Laura's funeral, it was an episode about death. That's what I was always thinking about: how these various characters are going to respond to that. And that's very rich material and the actors were all so wonderful. That was just a lucky break. When Mark said to me, "Here's what's happening in three," I just thought, "Oh man!" I knew that I was in very good shape from the start.

I went in all sorts of crazy directions with it. I had a great time writing it. And really the process was very much like it would be throughout the entire show, which was you'd sit down with Mark. He would go through an outline with you that he and David had worked on or a story, and then you were given a lot of freedom within those scenes to kind of navigate as you could. But I had no idea how he'd react.

The phone rang. It was like close to midnight. [Mark] had just finished reading the script and he was thrilled. I came to know later why he was thrilled because when you're running a television show, just to know that you have a writer who can write something that you feel you're not going to have to rewrite substantially, that you can count on, it's a rare thing. It's something that when you read it, you know it.

Tina Rathborne on Agent Cooper picking up Laura's hand and putting it back on her chest in the morgue: It's one of my favorite shots. The emotion in it was very deep to me, but I was laughing at myself as I was watching it and I went, "Tina, she would have had rigor mortis. He wouldn't have been able to do that."

Harley Peyton: Mark, he's the one who finishes [all the scripts]. You knew if you've really written a good script because then Mark wouldn't have to change much of it. There are always production things that he needed to fix. And there are other things, too. I remember the first episode I wrote where Truman and Josie are talking about death and she has a speech. The speech I wrote was so ridiculously long. Because who knew? I just figured I'll let her go. [Josie recites from *Tao Te Ching* on the subject of death.] Mark knew a little bit more about how that was going to work than I did. So it was always great to know that he was going to come in and make you look even better than you looked already. So no matter how good a job you did, you knew it was going to be even better by the time it was shot.

Charlotte Stewart (Betty Briggs): I never told them about when I wore the happy face button to Laura Palmer's funeral. Nobody on the show noticed at all. Everybody was too involved. The funeral scene was the whole cast plus a whole bunch of extras. People were paying attention to other things and I wore this big yellow happy face on my suit, but the fans picked it up. I started getting happy face everything. So when I go [to fests] I always bring a big bag of happy face buttons. You know you're never fully dressed unless you're wearing a smile.

Ben and Charlotte Stewart at The Great Southern Twin Peaks Fest 2016.

Robert Bauer (Johnny Horne): I knew that [Johnny] had mental issues. Maybe he was on the spectrum. Back then, they weren't even referring to people as autistic or otherwise as being on the spectrum. It was just he had emotional problems and came from a complex family and had some anger issues. Basically, a child in the body of a young man. The preparation I did was to watch a lot of cartoons. I remember very distinctly that the first scene we shot was the graveyard scene. That was the full cast burying Laura. That was the first day I worked and these guys had all worked together before.

I went to a bookstore to look for books that I felt might be meaningful to Johnny. I found a first edition of *Peter Pan* that kind of opened up a world that I felt I could inhabit as this character. Not growing up, forever a child and comfort in that. Not a struggle, but a real comfort in that. I had this book and that was sort of my talisman I used and carried into the scene with me.

Dana Ashbrook (Bobby Briggs): We starting to shoot the series and there was a little get-together at the production office. [Robert Bauer] was there and had his *Peter Pan* book he was carrying around. I remember not knowing him at that point and then when I met him I was finally like, "Dude, I was just laughing at you for having that book." I was a stupid asshole kid then.

Robert Bauer: He dug that I had this book and once made fun of me for it. We were just actors fucking around and we just clicked right out of the gate.

Dana Ashbrook: We became really good friends. We became best friends.

Robert Bauer: It's rare, but there's times where you meet people you feel like an immediate comfort and immediate connectivity to that person. It's a part cosmic thing, to be sort of weird about it. And it's part alchemy, it just is.

I think [being] given that immediate level of comfort helped drive Dana. I'm not speaking for him. We've never really talked about it. I remember him grabbing me very specifically [during the funeral scene] and moving me to the side. But the way he grabbed me wasn't with anger but with purpose and care. He didn't throw me aside to make his entrance.

Tina Rathborne: Toni [Morgan], the editor, she and I became very close and in this particular show, she said, "Tina, I have something to tell you. I've never edited a film before in my life." She was brilliant. There was no bump there. You know how much the editor has to do with how smooth or sinuous a scene is. And I give Toni a lot of credit for that. She paired the drama down to Bobby ultimately saying it was all our fault. Bobby, he really nailed it.

We didn't have enough footage, so that's why we did it in slow motion [for Bobby and James going after each other]. I remember it actually made it much better.

Ray Wise: Originally when I met with David, I thought I was going in for the part of the sheriff, Sheriff Truman. And then a couple of days later when I got the call that said David wants you to play Leland, I thought, wait a minute, I gotta look back at the script and see Leland. He finds out that his daughter is dead and he cries and then he goes to the morgue and identifies his daughter's body and cries. All this guy does is cry. Ah, but therein lies the challenge. I thought I have to show different levels of crying and different types of grief. And then as I started to show them what I could do, they started writing more and more of the outrageous things that Leland did, throwing himself on a casket and dancing with himself. (*Courtesy of* FWWM *event*)

Tina Rathborne (Director of ep. 3 and 17): I basically storyboard my films in huge detail and what it allows me to do is to be completely flexible when I get to the set. In other words, since I know I have a plan to fall back on, I'm not anxious so I can use anything that anyone brings to me.

The thing about the funeral scene is Gregg Fienberg, the producer, had said to me some time at the beginning of making the show that he was $200,000 in the hole. Then it came time to do the funeral scene and most of the cast was in it. We had tracks running through the gravestones. The way I had designed it is that the characters were walking to the funeral, or many of them, through the gravestones. Now being Southern California, it was hard to avoid the palm trees. [So long shots were scrapped for just medium and close-up shots]. Greg had given me one day and at the end of the day, he said to me, "You just saved me $200,000. That was supposed to be three days, that shoot. You did it in one, and thanks very much."

I loved rehearsing and on *Zelly and Me*, David and Isabella wanted to rehearse all the time. So we were peas in a pod. So I get *Twin Peaks* and I think, "Oh, we need to rehearse." Not we need to, it's just that's what one does to make something better. I called Michael [Ontkean] and I said, "Michael, would you like to rehearse?" and he said, "I've never heard of you? Why should I rehearse?" And I said, "Oh, that's fine. I totally understand."

I remember in the diner where Shelly is mimicking the coffin going up and down and then it goes over the heads into the booth. Well nobody knew their lines. Not one of the people [Everett McGill, Michael Ontkean, and Michael Horse] in the booth knew their lines. What I did, and 'cause it's my responsibility to make the day, when I realized they didn't know their lines, I said, "Action." They learned them pretty quickly.

Now the last day of shooting, three sets were going at the same time 'cause we had to fill holes. We didn't have the time or Toni said you need a close up of this. I guess I was working on the Leland falling on the coffin [scene] and then I felt a presence on my left shoulder and I turned around and I said, "Oh, hi Michael, how are you?" And he said, "I'm fine," or whatever. And then he said, "Tina, I won't do my close up without you." [The actors] came to trust me. And that is incredibly, deeply rewarding.

Brings Back Some Memories

Ben: This is the episode where Leland Palmer is watching the soap opera, *Invitation to Love*, and his niece Maddy Ferguson, who looks exactly like Laura Palmer but is a brunette instead of a blonde, stops by the Palmer house to go to Laura's funeral with him. When you first watched the show, you brought up that Laura could still be alive.

Bryon: I really honestly thought Laura was in disguise as Maddy.

Ben: There were clues in Laura and Maddy's names that you were right.

In the 1944 film *Laura*, a detective investigates the murder of Laura Hunt only to discover she is not dead. The victim who everyone thought was Laura was actually a woman named Diane Redfern and she was killed by Waldo Lydecker. In Twin Peaks, there is a mynah bird named Waldo and a veterinarian named Bob Lydecker.

In Alfred Hitchcock's *Vertigo*, Detective Ferguson investigates a redhead named Judy, who looks like a blond woman named Madeleine, who had committed suicide. It turns out that Judy and Madeleine are one and the same person.

It has been widely speculated that Lynch/Frost were inspired by these movies and were sort of giving a little wink to them by naming *Twin Peaks* characters after characters from those films

Bryon: I knew there had been movies where one actress played two different people, maybe twins, and one dies and the other takes the other person's identity. I thought *Twin Peaks* was going in that direction. Laura was still alive.

Ben: Regarding the killer, Mike Nelson (one of the bad boys of Twin Peaks High School) didn't seem like a very important character to you and you joked that maybe he was the murderer.

Bryon: Sometimes it's the one person you least expect who is the killer.

Favorite Quotes and Scenes

Ben: My favorite quote from this episode is from Cooper who says, "Break the Code. Solve the Crime." To solve the case, Cooper needs to understand the Red Room dream in waking life. For instance, Cooper connects Laura saying in his dream, "Sometimes my arms bend back" to Agent Albert Rosenfield telling Cooper and Truman that Laura was tied up twice the night of her death. If Cooper can figure out the codes in his dream, maybe he'll figure out the killer whose name Laura whispered in his ear. As the show continues, the focus will be on connecting Cooper's dream (Lynch's vision) to Cooper's investigation (Frost's storytelling).

Bryon: My favorite quote is from Major Briggs who says, "Any time a man dies in war, he dies too soon." Major Briggs is a serious character who has a complicated backstory. These very few words establish his character and give some weight to a rather quirky town.

The funeral scene is definitely my favorite moment in this episode. The fact that we get to see the town mourn Laura is heartfelt but at the same time, it gives us a small glimpse into what each main character is feeling. We get to see the raw emotion come from Bobby as he lashes out on the town and goes after James. We witness Leland break down and jump on the coffin. Looking back now, I feel this was the real Leland that had no idea what BOB had done.

Ben: I agree the funeral scene is the best scene in the episode, but I disagree about Leland. Agent Cooper watches everyone at the funeral and I think he is wondering if the killer is among them. Leland/BOB is practically begging to be caught with his reckless actions of throwing himself on Laura's casket. Not knowing Leland is the killer, it is heartbreaking to witness a father have to bury his young daughter. Knowing that he is the killer and that he sexually assaulted his daughter, it is disturbing to watch him on top of the casket as it lowers and raises.

Community Commentary

James Roday (*Psych*): *Twin Peaks* not only shaped my love of storytelling — it lit a fire in me that it didn't have to be what everyone thought it had to be. That was prime time network television and our jaws were hitting the floor every week. Thirty episodes changed the game.

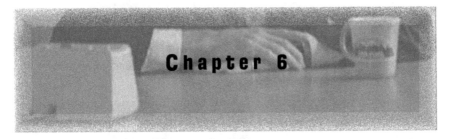

Chapter 6

Season 1: Episode 4
"The One-Armed Man"
Aired: Thursday, May 3, 1990
Written by Robert Engels
Directed by Tim Hunter

The Log-line

Cooper meets Phillip Gerard, a one-armed shoe salesman, who leads him face to face with a llama in Bob Lydecker's veterinary clinic.

Behind the Curtain

After completing the pilot and during the first season production of *Twin Peaks*, David Lynch worked on the film *Wild at Heart* and relied on others to keep the show going. Richard Beymer (Ben Horne) remarked, "The series really depends on David's quirky, off-center take on life. So he's picked people he's had relationships with or whose work he likes to direct [episodes]" ("Maintaining the Momentum." *Santa Maria Times*, February 23, 1990). Tim Hunter, a classmate of David Lynch's at American Film Institute (AFI) and director of *River's Edge*, directed Episode 4.

Tim Hunter (Director of ep. 4, 16, and 28): I had been at the AFI with David Lynch in the first class when the program started in 1970. So I knew David and when the show was starting up, I got a call, actually, from Mark Frost. I met Mark for lunch and they asked me if I wanted to work on it. And of course, I was delighted to say yes.

In television, you have as many days of prep as you have to shoot. So you have seven or eight days of prep, seven or eight days of shooting. And it's very unusual if you get the script before you show up for work on the first day of prep. At that point, there's usually some casting to do, probably less on *Twin Peaks* than on other shows because it was a large ensemble cast that had already been set. And a certain amount of locations of scouting to do. And I remember doing some of that on *Twin Peaks* for the exteriors.

We would go out to look for exteriors largely in the woods. I remember there was a park at the top of Beverly Drive, off Mulholland Drive that was a nature preserve. We went to Westlake Village, which had a certain amount of a woods and an outdoors feeling to it.

So you do whatever testing you need to do. You find whatever locations you need to find. You have a certain number of production meetings with the department heads and the producers and then organize whatever it is you need to organize for the show. And then you just plunge in and shoot the thing. TV, even on *Twin Peaks*, is often for a director like being dealt a hand of poker and you just have to sort of take the cards you're dealt and play it the best way you can. Fortunately at the beginning, *Twin Peaks* was wonderful material and everybody knew that we were working on something really special.

Bob Engels (Writer): Warren Frost was my professor at the University of Minnesota when I was there, and I've known Mark since he was 12. I could walk you through episodes of *Twin Peaks* and you can see all sorts of Minnesotans we hired. We hired Chris Mulkey [Hank Jennings], who is one of my best friends. I wrote Hank for Chris. The parole board [members] are all Minnesota. The cast is full of friends, which is how you should do it.

Tim Hunter: You shoot whatever you're given. And on any given day they can often just throw a set of colored rewrite pages at you in the middle of production. Television is run by producers/writers for the most part. So it's rare that they want the directors to encourage the actors to deviate from the script. Sometimes you're told that a certain actor, they like the way he reworks the dialogue to suit his own cadences. It's okay to let them go. Sometimes they say if an actor wants to do another line or you have an idea for another line, just run it by us first. Sometimes they say if you feel that the dialogue is being changed and it's expedient for you to shoot it, shoot it, but make sure you have the scripted dialogue in the can so it can be restored or worked anyway the producers want to in the cutting room. I don't think anybody was ad-libbing very much on *Twin Peaks*. It was very specifically written with certain cadences and in a very stylized manner. So the actors were all into it and it was a lot of fun because there was always an element of the mysterious about it.

I do remember Russ Tamblyn doing this sleight of hand stuff and of course, it was a lot of fun. Whether or not I let him do it on my authority or whether it was sanctioned from above, I don't remember. But obviously, everybody enjoyed it.

Sherilyn Fenn: Me and my brothers were the kids that were left behind in pursuit of whatever [my parents] were in pursuit of. And so then my grandparents were sort of raising us. For me, acting became a way of expressing things and exploring things that I didn't understand or needed to learn more about.

I believe until we take our last breath, we grow here. It was an amazing gift that I met Roy [London, acting coach]. I met him after I'd done the pilot. He taught me how to uncover truths for myself and what the gift is of acting and made me fall in love with it again.

What Roy showed me was, where are you? You are a young woman who is discovering her power, who has a certain amount of innocence, who is incredibly romantic and wants to fall in love and has daddy issues. You just use your truth. The truth is far more interesting than a lie or demonstrating something that's not real. A, you have the courage to really see yourself where you are and then B, have the courage to illuminate that sort of human struggle and be filmed while you're doing it.

Jed Mills (Wilson Mooney): Everything about the experience was Class A! Top notch! Just the best! So, what can I say? Or did I already say it? I could go on ad infinitum, just a pleasure to work on.

Thank you *Twin Peaks* for that wonderful gig. And by the way, I fell in love with my scene partner actor, Peggy Lipton (Norma Jennings). Then again, who, after meeting her, wouldn't fall in love.

Tim Hunter on the llama at the Vet's office: I suggested the llama [in Lydecker's vet clinic] and I imagine it was because driving around places like Topanga Canyon, where in fact we were actually going to shoot that sequence in the vet's episode, there were llamas all over the place. There's a lovely moment there where Kyle MacLachlan and the llama actually make eye contact for a second. And that's the thing I remember most about that episode.

Brings Back Some Memories

Ben: A scene from the script that I wish had made it into the show was Leland dancing with his secretary, who would have been played by Director Lesli Linka Glatter. Leland says about Laura, "She loved dancing. She loved to dance ... she'd stand on my shoes ... I taught her ... come and dance with me ... She was a good little dancer ..." The scene would have explained why Leland liked to dance so much after Laura's death because dancing was something special Dad and daughter used to do together.

Lesli Linka Glatter (Director of ep. 5, 10, 13, and 23): I never shot the scene. I was all dressed and ready to go and waiting in the trailer and waiting in the trailer and something happened on the set and the scene was never shot. It was a great scene and I love the idea of being Leland Palmer's dancing secretary.

Ben: In looking at episode 4, we were very much into the idea of visions vs dreams. Merriam-Webster defines a vision as "something seen in a dream, trance, or ecstasy." Sarah Palmer's vision could be considered a dream.

Bryon: When Cooper's having a dream he could be on a different plane of existence. I don't see a vision necessarily being a dream. A vision happens when someone is staring off into space and seeing things that are not there.

Ben: Does Lynch/Frost look at visions as being part of the astral dream plane? This idea of an out of body experience where the universal consciousness resides.

Bryon: In Season 2, was Cooper having a dream of The Giant because he was lying on the ground on death's doorstep or was The Giant physically in that room like a vision to Cooper? They kept it very ambiguous.

Ben: Cooper asked the Giant where he comes from. He says, "The question is, where have you gone?" The Giant is saying Cooper is in another place, which could be a spiritual plane of existence. Maybe the White Lodge? But we are getting ahead of ourselves.

Favorite Quotes and Scenes

Ben: My favorite quote is when Cooper says he is a strong sender. We learn that Sarah and Cooper both saw BOB in a vision and a dream. I love that

Cooper is concerned about influencing Sarah during the questioning of her. He follows Bureau protocol, but he also follows his own spiritual protocol.

Bryon: My favorite quotes comes from FBI Regional Bureau Chief Gordon Cole. The conversation between Cole and Cooper shows that Cooper will always stick up for what is right. His boy scout mentality is on full display.

Ben: The name Gordon Cole comes from a character in the film Sunset Boulevard, which happens to be one of Lynch's favorite films.

My favorite scene is the questioning of the one-armed man. Cooper, Harry, and Andy are at the motel to question him. There is this whole intrigue of who this man could be. When they finally meet him they see he is just this harmless shoe salesman. His name comes from the show *The Fugitive*, where Police Lieutenant Philip Gerard is on the hunt for Dr. Richard Kimble, who has been wrongfully convicted of killing his wife.

Bryon with Al Strobel in 2017.

Community Commentary

Mya McBriar (Author of the blog *Twin Peaks* Fanatic; Contributing Writer in *The Women of David Lynch* book, *Blue Rose Magazine* & 25 Years Later): In 1990, *Twin Peaks* was, for me, the sound of the lonesome foghorn blowing. It was the wind in the trees. It was a girl wrapped in plastic and the sadness surrounding her death. *Twin Peaks* grabbed hold of my heart and captured my imagination. It was haunting, atmospheric, and had levels of depth that I felt intuitively. *Twin Peaks* was beautifully flawed, masterfully surreal, complex in its simplicity, and pure in its own reality.

Chapter 7

Season 1: Episode 5
"Cooper's Dreams"
Aired: Thursday, May 10, 1990
Written by Mark Frost
Directed by Lesli Linka Glatter

The Log-line

Agent Cooper, Sheriff Truman, Deputy Hawk, and Doc Hayward take a walk in the woods and run into the Log Lady's cabin where she informs them they are two days late.

Behind the Curtain

"The thing about all these characters is they all have a story. You will find out things that make them seem less weird, that will humanize them. They're not just there as jokes." -Mark Frost ("Hype over 'Twin Peaks' fails to acknowledge co-creator's contribution." *Detroit Free Press*, May 2, 1990). Margaret Lanterman, aka the Log Lady, was known for switching on and off lights at town meetings, carrying a log everywhere she went and telling Agent Cooper that her log saw something the night of Laura Palmer's death, but she was more than an odd townsperson. She had been married to a logging man who died the day after their wedding from a fire. She was connected to the woods, understood about the owls and the darkness in the woods. She was able to deliver the message to Agent Cooper that two men and two girls had been in the woods and a third man soon followed the night Laura was killed. Margaret was a complicated woman who seemed bizarre to many people, but she was a wise woman who lived in the woods and understood many of the town's supernatural secrets.

Scott Frost: I live in this little community where Mark and I spent our summers as kids. It goes back to our grandparents. Part of it was sort of the genesis of the original *Twin Peaks*. And this idea of a small town where you had all these quirky characters. And particularly when we were kids, there were some very quirky characters who lived up here. And there still are. You get back in the woods and there's some of those people out there. And there was a murder, which I guess has gotten a lot of play lately. A woman [Hazel Drew] who was found in a pond down the mountain from us. It's been overblown as the inspiration for *Twin Peaks*, but I think this place was more of an inspiration for Mark in terms of the kind of bizarre people we would see as kids around here. And there were some real characters.

While shooting Eraserhead, *Lynch mentioned to Catherine Coulson about a TV show idea called, "I'll Test My Log with Every Branch of Knowledge," and Catherine would play the Log Girl.*

Catherine Coulson (Log Lady): [The Log Girl] was going to be the person going to the experts to find out [things] with a little boy. Ask, like, a dentist to put on one of those little blue things with the clips around the log and probe the rings. We would learn about wood, ponderosa pine log, the only log. We would also learn about dentistry and the importance of keeping your teeth clean. And there was an idea we talked about and joked about for a long time, but then we didn't actually ever do [it] because it manifested [in *Twin Peaks*].

Lesli Linka Glatter: I was a very new director. A thousand years ago, I was a modern dancer and a choreographer. Back in the dark ages when the American government sponsored the arts, I had spent about five years in Paris and London dancing and choreographing modern dance. And then I got a grant to teach, choreograph, and perform throughout the Far East. When I was living in Tokyo, I was told a series of stories that I knew I had to pass on and I knew it wasn't dance. So that is the only reason I ever made a film.

The thing about David and Mark is they really encouraged directors to make it their film. I think everyone did that. And that whole sequence in the woods, I wanted to do this shot, people call it the Mount Rushmore shot, where all our main male actors, their heads go into the shot one by one. And they're all in focus and the amount of light it took to be able to do that shot, it was kind of amazing. I think when I thought of it in my mind, I actually didn't understand at that point what a technological challenge that was. It's one thing if the first person is sharp or even the first two, but [to have four people sharp in the scene]. It was a huge technological challenge. And it was at night. [But] we ended up being able to do it.

Catherine (Coulson) was a Camera Assistant so that was her first [acting] scene. She had not acted before. I mean she had wandered around carrying the log, but [this scene] was like an eight-page scene. It was a long scene and it was all about the looks in between people.

Catherine Coulson on the spirit of the Log Lady's husband being in the Log: I think we hold fast to totems that remind us of the people we love. I wouldn't say the spirit of him is in the log. I would say that she holds fast to the memory of her dead husband, but really the log is just a log and we never answer who morphizes the log. Not a she or he. It's just a good log though.

I have [the Log] in trust, in a secure undisclosed location. I have what I call the travel log. It's in my suitcase. Otherwise, the airlines won't let me carry it because they said it could be used as a bludgeon. Once I called United Airlines and said, I have this log and I want to carry it on. And they said, "*The Log.*" It was very funny.

Harley Peyton (Writer): [Catherine Coulson] was just amazing and she was such a dear friend of David's and so integral to the spirit of the place. We had wonderful actors in all of those parts. It's hard for me to think of a single one [that wasn't wonderful]. And that's lucky. I think that is a part of David's genius too. He doesn't even read actors. He just meets them. There's a kind of way he vibed it out. When you look at David and Mark's contribution to the show, I give [David] a ton of credit in the casting. It's almost like Catherine was already in *Twin Peaks*. She was so natural and so perfect. And that's such an original character. Also, just as everyone who has ever met her knows, she was just a lovely, lovely person and sort of interesting and sweet and gentle and strange and exemplified the best of that show.

Lesli Linka Glatter: I did a shot of the needle going into the groove of a record [in Jacques's cabin]. [David Lynch] was such a great collaborator and I remember him saying, "Les, I loved that shot. Can't we look at that for a long time?" And that shot was on for, like, a long time. That was in the editing because we would sit and look at the cuts together.

Scott Frost: I made an appearance on camera. I played, in the first season, one of the Icelanders at a party. We were short of extras and I looked fairly

Scandinavian even though, well, I'm sure the Vikings must have rampaged their way through Northern England and Scotland. That was my Hitchcock moment.

Scott Frost on screen in Episode 5. Courtesy of CBS.

Lesli Linka Glatter: Then, of course, there were all the Icelanders dancing at the end, which was insane and wonderful, and coming up with a dance that Leland could be doing, that Piper Laurie (Catherine Martell) could pick up on that would look like she was trying to cover. It was great.

Brings Back Some Memories

Ben: This episode is all about the Log Lady for the most part.

Bryon: It did a great job of intertwining each storyline and a great balancing act of each character and bringing them together.

Ben: When we started the podcast you really thought that the Log was talking to her and you saw that the wood has history in this town. That the trees knew everything because they surrounded the town. I kinda liked that.

Bryon: We learned that the Log Lady's husband died in the woods. He was a lumberjack. A woodsman?

Ben: So you had this theory back when we recorded this that the three men that passed the Log Lady's cabin that night were Jacques, Mike Nelson, and the third person being Bobby or Hank. That third person was to be the killer so I'm guessing you thought it was Bobby or Hank.

Bryon: I was close. [laughing]

Favorite Quotes and Scenes

Bryon: My favorite scene is when Cooper, Hawk, Sheriff Truman, and Doc Hayward find the Log Lady in her cabin. To me, this scene is as mysterious as the Red Room scene. She speaks in riddles, sort of like Yoda. Her log channels what had happened the night of Laura's death that gives the guys more clues to go on. I enjoyed seeing these four guys investigating Laura's death and wish we had gotten more scenes like this later on. Nothing will ever beat that shot of Cooper finding the cabin and we see Cooper step into frame, then Truman, Hawk and then Doc.

Ben: The whole Log Lady's log cabin scene is my favorite scene, too. In a previous episode, the Log Lady tells Cooper to ask her log about the night Laura died and he doesn't.

Bryon: My favorite quote is when the Log Lady is communicating for the Log. This dialogue between Cooper & the Log Lady pretty much lays out the ending of *FWWM*. It really shows the power of the Log Lady's words.

Ben: My favorite quote comes from the Log Lady where she says, "Shut your eyes and you'll burst into flames." I remember you asking me, "What does that mean?"

Community Commentary

Morgan Higby Night (Director of Regrettes' music video "Unknown Species," featuring intro by Catherine Coulson): "I was so starstruck meeting Catherine. The Log Lady is literally my favorite TV character of all time. She put me right at ease and continued to follow up to see how the video was coming along. Every time I'd get a text from Catherine, it made me so happy. Simply the best person." (*See Photo below.*)

Chapter 8

Season 1: Episode 6
"Realization Time"
Aired: Thursday, May 17, 1990
Written by Harley Peyton
Directed by Caleb Deschanel

The Log-line
Agent Cooper and Audrey Horne go undercover at One Eyed Jacks and Waldo, the Myna bird, is silenced.

Behind the Curtain
Twin Peaks was David Lynch's first venture into television. In April 1990, he expressed issues with commercials interrupting the show, "Just thinking about breaking the show in seven different places ... That's this form, and once you get the hang of it, it's kind of interesting. But if you think about it another way, it's totally absurd. It would be so absurd to have a big symphony going, and after every little movement, four different people come in and play their own little jingle and sell something, and then you go back to the symphony. It's a very weird thing that we've cooked up for television. Of course, it's what makes the whole thing work, but it's pretty weird." (Pond, Steve. "'Peaks' bears Lynch's wonderfully weird earmark" *The Orlando Sentinel.* April 8, 1990)

Mary Jo Deschanel (Eileen Hayward): Caleb [Deschanel], my husband, went to the AFI (American Film Institute) with David. So I met him the first year. There were 15 Fellows with Caleb, David, Terrence Malick, Tom Rachman, and Gill Dennis.

There were no classes [laughs]. Directors would come and give lectures. It was at the old Greystone Mansion and it was very casual at that moment. And then everybody was working on films.

We had dinners all back and forth at people's houses because it was really hard to get a credit card. People didn't go out to eat that much. So we had these dinners with all these [people].

Then when he was doing *Twin Peaks*, well, I just got a call from my agent and it was just a meeting. There was no casting per se. I guess he knew my work and I think also the way I looked was probably quite right for the part. One of the main things that I had done to that point was *The Right Stuff*. I played Annie Glenn; I had a bad stutter. I seemed to do well playing someone with some kind of disability. I don't know why he chose me. I just went and talked to him and then I got the part. One of the things that I really admire about David is that he can just have a meeting with someone and cast them.

After the pilot [Caleb and I] went to see the screening and we saw David. Caleb said, "David it's great!" David said, "Oh, you want to direct one of them?" And Caleb said, "Yeah."

Caleb Deschanel (Director of ep. 6, 15, and 19): I'd never directed any television. I directed tons of television commercials. I really loved the [*Twin Peaks*] pilot and for me, it was really exciting to get to do that.

The big advantage and the reason why you're able to shoot things really quickly is because all the actors developing their characters are already set. There's a lot of shorthand involved with that. In the case of David and Mark, they allowed us to have some input.

[*Donna, Maddie, and James listen to one of Laura's tapes.*] You hear the sound because they're playing the tape recorder and you start over the piano and then you sort of push in and you see Maddie first, and then Donna, and then you don't even see James there until he sort of steps in and you aren't sure who it is at first 'cause you don't see his face and then it's revealed that it's James. It's cinematography in the sense that you show an image and then you're keeping the audience in the dark a little bit until you reveal what's going on. The whole show was very much like that. There were a lot of secrets as secrets are dangerous.

I realize there's so many different stories going on. Some are better than others for sure. Any show in television now you have at least three or four stories going at the same time and in *Twin Peaks* you'd have like five or six in the same show. Really complex, but it keeps people interested. There are so many references to [other shows and movies]. For instance, when the insurance man comes in, his name is Mr. Neff [based on the character from *Double Indemnity* film].

There's a scene where [Waldo the bird] gets shot and there was always such an obsession with all the donuts, I thought really a great way of showing that the bird got shot was just to have the cage swigging and have the blood slurping down on the donuts. You bring these ideas up to Dave and he goes, "Oh yeah, that's really cool!" There wasn't much resistance when you would come up with a good idea. So it sort of made it fun.

Harley Peyton: Mark was so happy with [Episode 3] he said, "Oh boy! Come back and write number six." They say it's who you know, in a weird way it's one of those circumstances where it's just based on our friendship. But that's really how it kind of started for me. And it was obviously a pretty substantial break.

Caleb Deschanel on Leland Palmer looking disturbed in the dark of the Palmer living room: It's sort of a telling scene because the scene that I did in the second year where you find out that he's the killer, it's kind of a nice sort of a premonition of that. But of course, at the time we didn't know that. So many things in the show set up so many people as the potential murder or potential evil-doer. There's so many affairs going on and so much conniving. It's a very complex series of stories in each one of the episodes and each one is suggesting that maybe you need to follow on with that path. And maybe that person is a killer and maybe it's not Jacques Renault. Maybe it's Leland Palmer.

Tim Hunter: TV is staggered. So while one director is prepping, the other director is shooting. And then once that director starts shooting, a new director starts prepping and it's just checkerboarded that way without anybody losing a day.

Caleb Deschanel: Some of the episodes at One Eyed Jacks, it was sort of like tag-team directing because we only had the location for a period of time and all the extras and everything. David would direct and then I'd come in and then I'd direct my scenes from my show and then Mark would be there.

Scott Frost: When my mom was a little girl, there was a house just up the road from where she grew up. [The area had] a little lake that is a mile long and there's maybe 50, 60 houses around it at most and there was a house just up beyond where she grew up that was owned by a Madam in Troy. And this was where her working girls would come up to get away from the summer heat and occasionally some of the gentlemen callers would visit. My mom would tell stories of seeing these fancy cars driving up and going, "Now who are all these visitors going up there?" I think there is some inspiration in a connection to One-Eyed Jacks that way.

Caleb Deschanel: The show was really subversive because what would happen is that they would submit the scripts to ABC, then they would come back and they would erase things that were not approved to be done on television, only to eliminate the most obvious stuff and allowing the most subversive things to get through. Like when Audrey Horne ties the cherry stem in a knot is much more subversive than some of the language that was excised by the lawyers at ABC.

Harley Peyton: We were watching television with my 11-year-old daughter and someone did the cherry stem trick and my wife turned to my 11-year-old and said, "You know, your dad invented that." I, of course, had to explain that I popularized it. I was at a Mexican restaurant called the Border Grill with these friends of mine. Sarah Stanton said, "Watch me I'm going to tie a cherry stem in my mouth." She does it at this restaurant and the next day I pitched it and then the next day after that I put it in the script and two weeks later we were shooting it and two months later they're writing about it in New York magazine. That's the immediacy of television. Also just your ability as a writer to kind of take advantage of things that are just happening when you walk out the door.

Brings Back Some Memories

Bryon: I would say this is the *Casino Royale* episode of *Twin Peaks*.

Ben: Cooper shows off his gambling skills at blackjack at One-Eyed Jacks.

Favorite Quotes and Scenes

Ben and **Bryon:** Our favorite scene is the Cooper and Audrey scene in Cooper's hotel room.

Ben: At 15 years old in 1990, I thought Cooper and Audrey had great chemistry. I wanted more scenes between the two of them, but I did not expect to see Audrey naked in Cooper's bed at the end of Episode 5. There was so much tension in the room. What would Cooper do when a vulnerable Audrey Horne pleaded not to make her leave?

Caleb Deschanel: It's sort of this wonderful moment where [Audrey is] in [Cooper's] bed and he's being like the perfect Boy Scout. It's one of those scenes that has so much sort of hidden meaning because at the same time people are watching it saying, "Hey, come on, Cooper." No, he's goody two shoes.

Sherilyn Fenn with Ben in 2017.

Bryon: Wonderful tension, but Cooper gives Audrey the fatherly talk.

Ben: Fatherly talk? He's still attracted to her but knows friendship is best for their relationship.

Bryon: Cooper says, "What I want and what I need are two different things, Audrey." This scene is closing that whole romantic chapter that's been going back and forth between the two of them all season. Cooper is basically saying, "Hey, I'm an FBI agent and you're a high school student and this can't work." This scene speaks volumes of who Dale Cooper is and how he lives not by the code of the FBI but a moral code that he holds himself up to as well. If this scene had gone the other way as some (or many) at the time wanted, I do not think we would be talking about Cooper with such high regard as we do today.

Ben: I agree it was good that Cooper didn't sleep with Audrey, but he wasn't the perfect Boy Scout. We learn in Season 2 that he fell in love with and slept with a married woman that happened to be his partner's wife.

Ben and **Bryon:** Our favorite quote is one of the best in television history from Dale Cooper who says, "Harry, I'm going to let you in on a little secret. Every day, once a day, give yourself a present. Don't plan it. Don't wait for it. Just let it happen. It could be a new shirt in a men's store, a catnap in your office chair, or two cups of good, hot, black coffee."

Harley Peyton: My line. God, I loved writing for Cooper. The men's store was in the Crescent Department store in Spokane. I like cat naps and I love a good cup of coffee.

Ben: These are words to live by. We all have rules in life we try to live by. There is the golden rule in which you treat others as you'd want to be treated, but I think the number two rule in life should be to treat yourself right. That's what this quote is saying. Remember to take care of yourself each and every day by doing something for yourself.

Bryon: Also don't plan it, don't wait for it, just let it happen. I think of this quote almost on a daily basis. This quote should be part of those inspirational posters you see in offices.

Community Commentary

Clare Nina Norelli (Author of *Angelo Badalamenti's Soundtrack from Twin Peaks*): I discovered *Twin Peaks* as a teenager during the latter half of the 1990s. I'd seen *Eraserhead* prior to watching the show and had fallen in love with David Lynch's unique aesthetic. The world he conjured in the film was like nothing my young mind had ever encountered, and it completely challenged my ideas as to what cinema could be. I wasn't sure of what I had seen—it was all so strange—but I did know that I wanted more of the same. My friends and I began to rent the large VHS sets from our local video stores and episodes were watched out of order owing to the fact we would simply rent whatever happened to be available at the time. This lack of adherence to the show's narrative did not concern me too much as I was so taken with the town of Twin Peaks and its offbeat citizens that I was happy to watch them even without context.

I was particularly fascinated with the tragic Laura Palmer's mysterious double life, as well as impressed by Audrey Horne's confidence and savvy. As a young musician, I also became enamored with Angelo Badalamenti's evocative music for the show, which provided both a wonderful soundtrack for my adolescence and a source of inspiration for my own musical compositions. I'm still finding new things to appreciate about *Twin Peaks* with every re-watch. Even all these years and viewings later, when I press "play" and take in the iconic opening credits, it still leaves me as breathless and excited as it did the first time.

Chapter 9

Season 1: Episode 7
"The Last Evening"
Aired: Wednesday, May 23, 1990
Written & Directed by Mark Frost

The Log-line

An arrest is made in the case of Laura Palmer and a fire is started at the Sawmill.

Behind the Curtain

On May 21, 1990, just two days before the first season finale, some of the cast of *Twin Peaks* and Mark Frost went on *Donahue*, a TV talk show, to promote *Twin Peaks*. Frost announced that the show had been picked up for the fall. *Twin Peaks* would get a second season. The same day, ABC announced its Fall TV schedule and *Twin Peaks* would be moving to Saturdays at 10 p.m. Presumably if ABC had canceled *Twin Peaks* in May of 1990, the Fox network was going to pick it up.

Eight days later, Fox announced their Fall lineup and *American Chronicles*, a half-hour documentary-style program produced by Mark Frost through Lynch/Frost Productions was scheduled to air on Fox on Saturday at 9:30 p.m., preceding *Twin Peaks* on ABC. "Fox, fortunately for us, goes off the air at 10," Frost joked. "I haven't yet persuaded them to put a little subliminal message about switching to your local ABC affiliate. But I'm working on it" (The Lynch/Frost View of America, *The Los Angeles Times*, July 29, 1990).

Harley Peyton (Writer): I remember in Season 1, the last episode, one of the things I loved about it, Mark [Frost] directed it and wrote it, is that it had all these great cliffhangers and also great resolution as well. And for me, that's what you want for a season finale. You want cliffhangers that'll take you into the next year and resolution of things that you've been following.

Kyle MacLachlan: Mark is a super talented director and has a great sense of humor and knows how to tell a story. We had a great time and had a good laugh and he was terrific. And that was true, really, of all the directors. We had a really interesting mix of people directing those first seven. You've got to remember, we weren't shooting them and then airing them. We shot everything and then banked it. We had no idea of knowing what the reception was going to be. We filmed the seven episodes and then we were going to see what happened. And then they came out and of course, everything exploded.

Harley Peyton: In the first season, it's not that [David Lynch] wasn't there, but really Mark was the kind of everyday guy who was really sort of making sure that everything was working. I didn't meet David until the second season because there were no offices like there were in the second season. We were not producers. So as a freelance writer, Mark said to come to the set when they shoot your episodes and so that's when you would go there, but you wouldn't see David there that much. David was directing what he was directing, but he was also doing *Wild at Heart*. He was a fairly busy fellow in that first season.

Erika Anderson (Jade/Emerald from *Invitation to Love*): It is a rare thing for an actress to be a part of something that changes the landscape of a medium, and in television, *Twin Peaks* changed everything. It truly was revolutionary and its influence is seen in so many shows that we see today.

I am so grateful to Mark Frost and David Lynch for allowing me to play the dual role of Jade/Emerald and letting me be part of a show that I thought was the best thing on television at that time. We had so much fun shooting *Invitation to Love* and watching the show take off as a cultural phenomenon. To watch the show each week was thrilling and filled us all with anticipation as to what would happen next. The idea of the dark and hidden side of American small towns really resonates with me and I feel honored to have been a little part of that history.

Lesli Linka Glatter on being the humpback seamstress: David and Mark kind of put everybody in [the show] at some point. This was kind of a joke. I mean, thank God no one recognized me on the set. I would have been horrified because I had this huge hump on my back. They put pink lipstick so far over and under my lips. I had like a huge wart with a hair coming out of it and a hairnet on. I walked onto the set and here I'd been around all the time; I had just directed. No one recognized me.

Sabrina Sutherland (Production Coordinator): I was working on another TV show when the first season aired and I was captivated by the pilot. We'd record it and we played VHS tapes at night while we were shooting and we'd be watching *Twin Peaks*. We didn't have time otherwise and we just loved it.

Sabrina Sutherland with Ben in 2017.

As soon as my show was done, I called the production office of *Twin Peaks* and they were just going to be starting the next season. So it was a very lucky call. They needed somebody and asked me to come down the next day, which I did and I got hired.

Ken Scherer (Chief Operating Officer for Lynch/Frost Productions): Mark had created a show for Fox that I love to this day. It was called *American Chronicles* and it was really an incredible show. The way the show got picked up by Fox was that Barry Diller, who was running Fox at that time, said, "*Twin Peaks* should have been on my network." He may have been right. I think if we were on a more upstart network like Fox they might've been more patient with the show than ABC.

Scott Frost: The fun part of it for everybody, particularly that first season, was just the surprise that it became what it did, 'cause no one was expecting it.

Brings Back Some Memories

Bryon: This episode gave us some answers, but also gave us a lot of cliffhangers.

Ben: Many people were expecting to find out who killed Laura Palmer, but were instead left wondering if Agent Cooper survived being shot.

Favorite Quotes and Scenes

Ben: My favorite quote is "Bite the bullet, baby," which is so disturbing coming from a close up of Jacques Renault's mouth. He tells Cooper about the sexual encounters Leo Johnson, Laura Palmer, Ronette Pulaski, and he had with Waldo, the Myna bird, pecking at Laura's neck and Leo feeding Laura a poker chip. Laura was put in a horrible situation with men who laughed at her pain. The quote is haunting and a reminder of the brutality she faced.

Bryon: My favorite scene is when Andy and the guys are in the police station talking about the big bust they had and how Andy took the shot that brought down Jacques Renault. Lucy sees his heroic story and they meet in the supply closet. This scene plays out with such amazing comic timing between Andy and Lucy. This scene is one of my favorite scenes of Season 1. I love the way it was shot and just seeing these two play off each other is pure magic.

Ben: My favorite scene is Leland suffocating Jacques with a pillow. After Jacques' hands are tied up and he is suffocated, it is revealed that Leland is the one who killed him. The look of pain and agony as he completes the act, and then the fire alarm going off and seems to shake him out of whatever it was going on in his head. The scene started with me thinking a malicious person was murdering Jacques. The scene ends with me feeling bad for Leland, who believes Jacques killed his daughter. But his intentions will get more complicated in Season 2.

Bryon: My favorite quote is from Cooper while talking to his tape recorder, "As you can hear from the ambient sound around me, and I notice with some relief, that the Icelandic group staying on my floor has either checked or passed out." This episode didn't give us the killer, but it did give us closure on the Icelandic group, clearly something we all wanted closure on.

Community Commentary

Steven Miller (TwinPeaksBlog.com): "There is always music in the air." My journey to a place both wonderful and strange began with the music of Angelo Badalamenti and Julee Cruise. After hearing the *Wild at Heart* soundtrack (my first David Lynch film), I wanted to hear more music by Angelo. I borrowed the *Twin Peaks* soundtrack on vinyl from my local library and the rest is history. This was late September 1993. Years later, I have discovered the best part about *Twin Peaks*—my fellow Bookhouse Boys and Blue Rose Task Force Members. We share a passion for unanswered questions and find beauty in the obscure. It's the best fan community because we understand that life has meaning, every life, even those that are full of mysteries.

Chapter 10

Season 2: Episode 8
"May the Giant Be with You"
Aired: September 30, 1990
Story by Mark Frost & David Lynch
Teleplay by Mark Frost
Directed by David Lynch

The Log-line

Agent Cooper is visited by a Giant who wants to help.

Behind the Curtain

The summer of 1990 was a busy time for the creators of *Twin Peaks*. David Lynch's *Wild at Heart* released in theaters after winning the Palme d'Or at the Cannes Film Festival and Mark Frost was overseeing two fall TV shows, *American Chronicles* and *Twin Peaks*, while also working on pre-production for his upcoming film, *Storyville*. While *Twin Peaks'* first season reran over the summer, merchandise started to be released. Many heard *Twin Peaks* music in the air with the soundtrack album as they read the dark secret life of a troubled young girl in *The Secret Diary of Laura Palmer*. Both products were well received.

Kyle MacLachlan appeared on the season premiere of *Saturday Night Live* and during his opening monologue, he was asked by an audience member (*SNL* writer Jim Downey), "Are we gonna find out this year who killed Laura Palmer?" Kyle immediately responded, "Yeah. It's Shelly the waitress. And they're gonna reveal that in the last episode." The gag continued with Kyle going into the *SNL* control room and receiving an angry phone call from a fake David Lynch. Besides the monologue, Kyle also performed a hilarious *Twin Peaks* skit as Agent Cooper.

There was a lot of excitement and positive momentum heading into the new season, but some viewers, after starting to watch the season premiere, were taken aback and stopped watching. Some thought Cooper laying on the floor for 10 minutes as a confused old waiter and a Giant interacted with him was self-indulgent. Yet, David Lynch is known for not caring about how slow the pace is. "Slow is not boring, necessarily, and fast is not interesting, necessarily. Mystery and a mood require a certain pace and feel or it just doesn't happen," expressed David Lynch (Shales, Tom. "Creator of 'Twin Peaks' wants to make dreams." *Washington Post*. April 18, 1990). Like the Red Room scene in the first season, some people just didn't get it and would rather watch a more traditional TV show than something as unique as *Twin Peaks*.

Ken Scherer (Chief Operating Officer for Lynch/Frost Productions): Propaganda Films had produced the original pilot and the first abbreviated season. [They] were really a hot young shop in those days and they were doing music videos and some other things. David had a lot of regard for them and it was being run by two guys who had also been at AFI [American Film Institute]. So I think David had some knowledge of that, as fellows at AFI. David and Mark realized how much money they were paying them. [They] decided, well, if we're going to do this, let's create our own company.

I was working at the AFI. David knew me a little bit. I met Mark at a party and told him my ambitions and I wanted to get into producing and so he said, "Well, you know, we've got this thing going and if we can make it work and get picked up for the second season, we're going to start our own company. Would you be interested?" And of course, the answer was immediately, "Yes!" And luckily for me, ABC picked it up.

I met [Mark Frost and David Lynch] at Musso and Frank's in Hollywood. They were in a small booth when I joined them. We sat there for a while and my ass fell asleep. I was only sitting on one cheek, which wasn't big enough for me to slide in. And so I said, "Hey, do you mind if we get a bigger booth? I'll go facilitate this." So I went up to the Maitre d' and I said, "Look, it's David Lynch for Christ's sake. He needs a bigger table." And we got it. And David said, "That's very impressive." So I think that's how I got the job. But, it was really through my friendship with Mark. David made it very clear he never wanted to see a lawyer, never wanted to see an agent. I was to run interference for them. And that's the role that I tried to play.

Harley Peyton: One of the biggest changes was that there were these two huge warehouses out in the valley in Los Angeles, and they were like *Twin*

Peaks land. We had these offices on the second floor. You'd walk down into the warehouse and there was every set. So it was all in this one place, which is sort of magical in and of itself and every set, every interior, every house obviously.

As a producer, I got my first office as a writer. I'm using a Mac computer for the first time. They made a deal with Mac and so we all had Macs and were all working there that way as well. I worked on a typewriter prior to that. My job started out as writing my scripts and doing whatever I could do to pitch in.

Mark and I sat down with [Steven] Spielberg in his living room, prior to the second season starting, to see if he wanted to direct the first episode. Kate Capshaw was my then wife's best friend. So I knew Steven pretty well and I knew him through my wife and through Kate and I knew that he was a huge fan of the show. And I said to Mark, "Look. This is crazy, but I'm pretty sure that Steven would direct an episode. So we went and sat down with him and he couldn't have been more enthusiastic and he said, "Just make it as weird as possible. I love this show so much. It would be so much fun to do." So that was what we were thinking about doing and then David said, for all the right reasons, "I think I'll direct the first episode, but Steven could come in and direct episode," or whatever he said. Then it didn't happen after that. That's one of those alternate history moves, but that is something that nearly happened.

David was making it clear that, unlike the first season when he was doing *Wild at Heart*, he was going to be focused on this and in a pretty substantial way. And so, he was going to direct the first episode and subsequent episodes.

Scott Frost on Ray Wise dyeing his hair white: Ray was pretty freaked out about having white hair to begin with. It was either Mark or somebody who told him that that's what they wanted to do and he wasn't thrilled with that idea, but I think then he realized, "Oh, this is going to help me play this." Most actors, when they see an edge to getting a hold of a character, they take it for all it's worth.

Mak Takano (Jonathan): As a huge fan of David Lynch films, it was an honor for me to be cast in *Twin Peaks*. A good friend of mine who is a well-known writer/director recommended me to Harley Peyton, and so I was able to get a meeting with Mark Frost and was cast for the role of Jonathan "Asian Man."

I was so excited to be on the set on the first day of the second season which David Lynch was directing and to meet him for the first time. David had just gotten back from winning the Palme d'Or award at Cannes for *Wild at Heart* and he was away when I was cast. As I was on the set ready to work, Producer Bob Engels came up to me and told me that David saw my headshot and he was not happy with the casting. I just thought if anything I will have a story to tell being fired by David Lynch on my first day. When David came out on set, I introduced myself to him as he just took a good look at me and said I looked different from my headshot. Then, we proceeded to shoot Season 2, Episode 1 and I ended up being in 5 episodes.

Brings Back Some Memories

Ben: I started watching *Twin Peaks* in the summer of 1990. I discovered the show after it had started and decided to wait until summer reruns to watch it. What was wonderful about watching during the summer was that I didn't have to wait too long to find out what happened to Agent Cooper after he had been shot. Two weeks after Season 1 reruns ended, Season 2 started. While I waited, I enjoyed listening to the soundtrack and quickly read through the disturbing accounts of *The Secret Diary of Laura Palmer*. I also got the audio cassette *Diane: The Twin Peaks Tapes of Agent Cooper* performed by Kyle MacLachlan! I got to hear Cooper tell Diane, about the giant before the episode even aired.

Bryon: I thought the old waiter and the Giant were one and the same. It was the bowties that made me think they were the same person. Also, I thought Cooper was having a fever dream as he was laying on the ground.

Ben: Back in the day, I thought the same thing as well. You don't see many people with bowties. In Episode 29 the Giant says, "One and the same," which I took to mean the waiter, who just gave Cooper coffee, and he were the same person or that the Giant was a spirit and the waiter was the host.

Bryon: Back then, I also thought that BOB was the third person and is the killer, but still unsure why or how. Was BOB real or was he someone else from another town? Was BOB hired by Hank to kill Laura Palmer?

Favorite Quotes and Scenes

Ben: Some might not like the slow pace, but my favorite scene is with Cooper on the floor and the interaction with the waiter. The hard-of-hearing Great Northern Hotel employee is charming with his winks, thumbs up, and telling Cooper, "I heard about you."

I love David Lynch's pacing for this scene. I think *Twin Peaks* lost a lot of viewers because of the waiter taking forever. I'm sure a lot of people thought they were never going to solve the mystery and it seemed they had nowhere to go. But to me, this was just classic David Lynch.

Bryon: My favorite scene is when Cooper and Big Ed are talking in the hallway in the hospital about Nadine. We learn how she lost her eye in a hunting accident on their honeymoon. You have this really deep and emotional conversation about this tragic story and its intercut with Albert trying not to laugh and mock Big Ed. Everett McGill really carries this scene with his anguished face and body language and Miguel Ferrer's Albert counters the with cruel comedy.

My favorite quote is from The Giant who says, "The owls are not what they seem." Out of the three clues given, this one seems to be the most interesting. In some Native American tribes, owls are a symbol of death. In *Twin Peaks*, I have always seen the owls as watching and maybe a warning of evil. I really love what Mark Frost did with this part of the mythology.

Ben: I believe the owls are another form that the spirits, like BOB and Mike, take. In the next episode, Cooper will dream of BOB with an owl over his face, which to me means BOB is an owl.

My favorite quote comes from Major Briggs. The words performed by the outstanding Don Davis is a breakthrough moment for father and son. Bobby asked his father about his work, which Major Briggs says is classified, but the military man lets down his guard so he can make a connection with his son. He not only tells Bobby that he thinks about him, but that he has visions of him having a positive future where the two of them will have a close loving relationship.

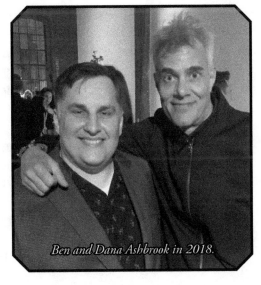

Ben and Dana Ashbrook in 2018.

Dana Ashbrook: Don Davis was such a giving actor. As a young actor myself, it was really nice to see someone that was so professional and such a great talent. He was amazing in that scene.

Community Commentary

Mark Givens (Co-author of *Blonde, Beautiful, and Dead*): I was annoyed at *Twin Peaks* when it was first broadcast. I was 15 and not in the mood to try this trendy new soap opera that everyone was raving about (and I knew absolutely nothing about). Eventually, the seemingly nonstop press bombardment about cherry pies and ladies with logs aroused my curiosity and I decided to take a peek during the summer repeats. My parents conspired to keep me out of this strange new world by planning a summer vacation to Alaska and trying to force me out to dinner with them exactly when the pilot would be airing. I held my ground and by the time they had returned hours later, it seemed like my world had been turned upside down and inside out—nothing seemed more important than following this moody murder mystery to its end. Even after all these years and the unexpected gift of the third season, we are still left wondering how or if the story will end. For a show that has always had secrets and mysteries burning at its core, that feels eternally appropriate.

Chapter 11

**Season 2: Episode 9
"Coma"
Aired: Saturday, October 6, 1990
Written by Harley Peyton
Directed by David Lynch**

The Log-line

Margaret Lanterman, aka the Log Lady, tells Major Briggs, "Deliver the message," which he does: COOPER/COOPER/COOPER.

Behind the Curtain

Ken Scherer: The thing about that period of time, it was intense and very short. There's so much happening. I'd be in Balboa Boulevard studios [where

Twin Peaks was shot in studio warehouse] by eight in the morning and be driving home at eight at night. I have great empathy for people who have this sudden burst of success and you just become overwhelmed. I said to [a *New York Times*] interviewer, because it had been announced that I was now the C.O.O. of Lynch/Frost production, "Two weeks ago I was making all of $48,000 working for the American Film Institute and now you want to know my opinion on the Fall [TV] season. America is a great place."

Don Amendolia (Emory Battis): It was truly an exciting and creative project. I'm glad to have worked on it.

Harley Peyton: There was no writers' room, but the closest we got would have been in the second season. Bob (Engels) had his office, I had my office, but that was really it for any writers on the show. Anyone else who came in and wrote, Barry Pullman or Scott Frost or actually my then-wife, Tricia Brock, they all came in as freelance writers, which never happens now. So there really wasn't a room in particular because Mark and David or just Mark were really working out the outlines. You'd kind of sit down and go through it with them and that's how the process worked. It would be act one, first scene we're going to be at the diner, we're going to accomplish this. Second scene, this is where we're going. So you would have a very, very detailed roadmap to work with before you started writing a script. If you figured out something along the way that you thought might be interesting, you could do that, but the stories, particularly when you're telling a serial story like that, you've got to hit certain marks along the way so that is what we would do. So it really never was a kind of writers' room where people were pitching ideas.

Tony Krantz: I was very involved with the guys. I was both their agent. I don't know if I would say that I was sort of the business guy behind the show, but in many ways I was. I was the person who would be dealing with them every single day and representing Lynch/Frost and all of it. I also started representing David in the movie business and I think that the rise of *Twin Peaks* in the sort of canonizing of David as America's newest genius, *Time* magazine cover, all those things, created a fracture in the relationship between Mark and David. It was seen as David Lynch's *Twin Peaks* and Mark was doing a lot of the work with the scripts and all that stuff. I think he was feeling a bit marginalized. After the first season, the show got, I dunno, 15 Emmy nominations or some incredible number like that. The guys were barely talking to each other.

Brings Back Some Memories

Bryon: I was really confused about what was going on at this point and I tried to rationalize everything. One of the theories I had was that BOB was haunting the Palmer house. Did he die there? What if Leland had killed BOB in that house when he was younger and now he doesn't remember it (suppressing his memories of it). I had come to that conclusion because Leland seemed to kill Jacques Renault so easily without any remorse. He seemed to have that killer instinct in him.

I also had some wild theories about Cooper's tape recorder just being named Diane and nobody was really at the receiving end of those tapes. Also one of my craziest theories was that Dale Cooper and his partner escaped the mental ward together and Cooper is pretending to be an FBI agent this whole time and he was the killer. I know those last two were not true and were on the crazier side of things.

Ben: When Dana Ashbrook appeared on *Late Night with David Letterman* (May 4, 1990), they joked about who the killer was. Letterman said, "It's the FBI guy. Who else would have done it? If the thing is nuts to begin with, doesn't he make the logical choice? He is as goofy as they come."

I remember the Sunday morning after Episode 9 in 1990, the Twin Peaks Sheriff's Hotline phone services launched. Viewers could call a 1-900 number where Lucy and Andy would update the caller on what's been happening on *Twin Peaks* and then a mystery man would interrupt and take over the phone call to provide more information. I thought the service at the time was a little expensive. It cost $2 for the first minute, $1 each additional minute with a maximum of $3 a call. When I called, I got a kick out of the banter between Lucy (Kimmy Robertson) and Andy (Harry Goaz):

Lucy: Hello, Twin Peaks Sheriff's station, this is Lucy speaking. Boy, has stuff been happening or what?! I heard through the Meals-on-Wheels people, I used to help them on my days off, that Donna went to see this old lady whose little kid took her creamed corn and held it in his hands like it was just a bunch of corn! Which, I guess it was, except it was creamed, and that is just about the worst food in the history of the world. Speaking of creamed corn, do you believe that story about Deputy Brennan?

Andy: I like creamed corn.

Lucy: So now you're listening in on my calls!

Andy: I was not. I was just walking by the phone and it blinked. What are you talking about…?

Ben: The service ran for the eight weeks *Twin Peaks* was on the air, ending after episode 16. No one, including the mystery man, ever really gave any big answers to the mysteries of the show, but I probably would have called every week to hear the characters of Lucy, Andy, and once Doc Hayward if I didn't fear getting in trouble with my mom over a costly phone bill!

I find it interesting that the same week the Sheriff Hotline launched, Episode 9 had a stranger call the station who wanted to talk to the sheriff but refused to give Lucy his/her name, which forced her to hang up on the caller. This exchange does not appear in any scripts I've seen. With that scene, were they actually promoting the Sheriff Hotline on the TV show?

Ken Scherer: I don't remember specifically, but we were looking for ways to engage the audience and just to see what kind of traffic we'd even get on it.

Favorite Quotes and Scenes

Ben and **Bryon:** Our favorite scene is when Donna Hayward delivers meals-on-wheels to Mrs. Tremond, who does not like creamed corn. Her grandson, played by Austin Lynch, David Lynch's son, performs a magic trick by making the creamed corn disappear from Mrs. Tremond's plate and reappear in his own hands. Mrs. Tremond says her grandson has been practicing magic.

Bryon: This creamed corn (we find out later on it means pain and sorrow) had really no meaning at this point in the show or in the mythology of *Twin Peaks* but would come into play later on in *Fire Walk with Me*. It's Lynch's amazing ability to make the normal things like creamed corn become extraordinary and out of this world.

Ben: When Mrs. Tremond said she didn't know Laura Palmer very well, she looks away, which seems to be a tell that she is lying.

Bryon: I always thought she was talking to someone else. I took it as someone else was in that room with her. Was Laura Palmer in that room with them?

Ben: My favorite quote comes from Agent Albert Rosenfield, "I performed the autopsy on Jacques Renault. The stomach contents revealed, let's see, beer cans, a Maryland license plate, half a bicycle tire, a goat, and a small wooden puppet, goes by the name of Pinocchio." He's listing off all these things and when he gets to the name Pinocchio we realize he is calling Jacques a whale, which is mean, but hilarious.

Bryon: My favorite quote is from the Log Lady to Major Briggs: "My log has something to tell you. Do you know it?" This quote has stood the test of time. If you hear this line in public you automatically go to *Twin Peaks*. This scene also shows how Major Briggs takes what The Log Lady says to heart as delivering a message. This scene tells the audience that the Log Lady is not a joke but someone to be taken seriously.

Community Commentary

Ben Rojas: I was 13 years old when *Twin Peaks* originally aired and it felt like it had arrived at the perfect time in my life. While the other kids in school were trying to decide which *90210* characters they wanted to be, I was contemplating the mystery in the woods. *Twin Peaks* changed television forever and it also changed the way I thought about the world around me. It showed me that life can be beautiful and tragic at the same time, hilarious and frightening, wonderful and strange. It taught me that things are not always what they seem and that I won't always have the answers. In many ways, *Twin Peaks* shaped who I am as an adult today and it continues to be my longest running obsession.

Photo courtesy of Ben Rojas

Chapter 12

Season 2: Episode 10
"The Man Behind the Glass"
Aired: October 13, 1990
Written by Robert Engels
Directed by Lesli Linka Glatter

The Log-line

Leland says he knows the man in the sketch and Donna Hayward discovers Laura Palmer's secret diary.

Behind the Curtain

Lesli Linka Glatter: The beginning of the second season felt very similar to me as the first, except that all of a sudden people's attention was on *Twin Peaks*.

Ian Buchanan (Dick Tremayne): Johanna Ray, who cast most of David's stuff, I had met before. She cast me in the Obsession [commercial] that David was directing. The day he shot it was the day that I met him and he asked if I could go meet him on Tuesday with Johanna. Then he said I would make a perfect Dick. There was a buzz about *Twin Peaks*, which was airing already. I don't think I was supposed to tell anybody and I really didn't, but I went to a party on that Friday night and had a cocktail and told everybody.

Lesli Linka Glatter on conventions at the Great Northern: Yes it was my idea. I just thought how funny that every time you go in there, whether anyone ever notices or not, I had a cheerleader and marching band convention, I think I had like a Tri Delta sorority convention, the American Indian Movement. It ended up being this great little detail.

Ken Scherer: Because of the incredible cult nature of [*Twin Peaks*], there were opportunities for ancillary kinds of income. The first one was a publishing deal that David and Mark's agents have brought to us. *The Secret Diary of Laura Palmer* was a huge bestseller across the world. That was one of the things that I oversaw.

David and Mark talked a lot about these kinds of things, but [the Diary] was Mark's vision. Mark is the storyteller. It was Mark who thought, "How do I get inside David's head so that the book has an authenticity to what I know he and I've been talking about all these years?"

Jen Lynch (author of *The Secret Diary of Laura Palmer*): When I was 12, I'd fantasized about finding another girl's diary.... I remember telling my father in the car, "I want to find somebody else's diary, another little girl's diary, tuck it under my jacket and run home and see if she's fantasizing about the same things, if she's afraid of the same things, if she thinks the same things about herself are right or wrong and all of this." Then years later my dad said, "Hey, do you remember that thing you said to me about a diary?" I said, "I do. I'm glad you remember it." And he says, "Will you write Laura's diary?" (Courtesy of *Nerd/Noir podcast, David Laribee and Alex West*)

Ken Scherer: Jennifer ... was an exceptional person and is, because she was really smart and she has the mindset of her father and brought that diary home. She knew the material. She knew the character. She knew the arcs that her father was going [for].

Jen Lynch: I had fallen in love with the whole epistolary approach in high school when one of the assignments was to write letters to a dead person. And the gift in that was, you can say anything you want. They're not gonna read it. And if they do, they're dead. So that's kind of miraculous in and of itself. And anybody else who reads it can't really judge because they're reading somebody else's mail. So I got to play and invent Laura. And really I was given total control. I was told, this is who killed her, these are the things you need to mention, and go.

When I was writing *The Secret Diary of Laura Palmer*, I lost it. I wrote it straight in nine days. It was when computers had just sort of come out. I flew to New York with it and everything was lost. The disks were empty and there I was at Simon and Schuster and like, fucked. Devastated.

I called my high school writing teacher who had truly changed my life. He said, "Well, it wasn't any good to begin with if you can't rewrite it." And I was like, "You fucking asshole!" Terrible fucking thing to say. And we talked about it later. He said, "I knew how dangerous and awful a thing that was to say to you, but I also knew that you would be angry enough to prove me wrong. And that it would only probably get better." I ended up writing it again in a hotel in New York in three days because of what my teacher had said.

I insisted on a typewriter after that whole computer debacle. So what had echoed in me about what I thought was good in the first one, I wanted to try and say again. I had grown so attached to Laura as a character and as a girl, I thought, she deserves for these moments to be good and I want to give her those moments. Like I can't tell that part of her story poorly. (*Courtesy of* Nerd/ Noir *podcast*)

Ken Scherer: Jennifer got deep, she got dark.

Harley Peyton: *The Diary* was amazing and of course I read it and it was a wonderful way to sort of get into the head of the character. But it didn't feed in a direct way [into the show].

Ken Scherer: I remember flying with Jennifer the day she was on *Good Morning America* to talk about the book when it was about to be released.

Jen Lynch on *Good Morning America*, September 17, 1990: I will say that some of the clues in the Diary become more evident once the series begins again, some of them stick out like sore thumbs, but the careful reader, I think, will find those clues that are more like gum wrappers under the table. Things most might not notice. So *Peaks* fans, in my opinion, should know who the killer is.

Brings Back Some Memories

Ben: *The Secret Diary of Laura Palmer* expanded the world of *Twin Peaks*. Readers got to learn more about Laura Palmer and many of the characters of *Twin Peaks*. Was Josie Packard jealous and attracted to Laura Palmer? Was she bisexual? We already knew from the show that the characters were filled with secrets, but the book dove deeper into their personal dark lives.

Bryon: Even though originally the book came out before the TV show revealed who murdered Laura Palmer, you had me wait to read the book.

Ben: I didn't figure out who killed Laura Palmer from the book, but I had heard many had and I didn't want to take the chance of ruining the TV experience for you.

Bryon: Honestly, reading it after I know who the killer was I don't think I could have figured it out from the book. Maybe those who have are just very good at reading between the lines.

Ben: It was written by Jennifer Lynch at age 22, and was on *The New York Times* Best Seller list, reaching number four. It is crazy to think that some bookstores wouldn't allow this to be in their store because they thought it was pornographic. Yes, there are sexual situations in the book, but it's an extremely disturbing story of abuse of a girl, which is still very relevant today. I think this book could be a tool used to educate young people about sexual abuse. I would also recommend people check out the audiobook version of *The Secret Diary of Laura Palmer* performed by the incredible actress who played Laura Palmer, Sheryl Lee. She also plays a creepy BOB in the audiobook.

Bryon: In the show, I thought Harold could have been the killer. He kept the secret diary of Laura Palmer as a souvenir. His front is that he's a shut-in.

Favorite Quotes and Scenes

Ben and **Bryon:** Our favorite scene is when Leland tells Truman, Hawk, and Cooper that he knows the man in the sketch. His grandfather had a summer home and a man named Robertson would flick matches at Leland. "You want to play with fire little boy?!" It was a great scene because it seemed like everything was coming together. The killer had left letters under his victims' fingernails (R. T. B.), which turned out that he was spelling his name.

Ben: It's crazy to think that we had this sketch all along and all of a sudden now Leland is identifying who this might be. Leland was in the room when Andy was drawing the sketch with Sarah Palmer back in Season 1, but he was too busy mocking Sarah to even notice. If he had paid attention to the sketch back then, would he have known right away it was Robertson?

Bryon: This scene plays even better knowing now who the killer is. We have the killer(s) right under the noses of Harry, Hawk, and Cooper and he tells them about Pearl Lakes and that Robertson (Bob is short for Robert) could have lived in a white house near his family's lake home. Was Leland (BOB) trying to divert the guys from getting any closer to solving the case? Or was this a real story on how BOB found Leland? This scene plays so differently after knowing who the killer is. Genius.

Ben: What I love about *Twin Peaks* is that there are often different ways to interpret a scene. Does Leland not know he is the killer? Is he suppressing what he did? Is he confessing without realizing he's confessing?

Bryon and **Ben:** Our favorite quote comes from Agent Albert Rosenfield, "While I will admit to a certain cynicism, the fact is that I am a naysayer and hatchet-man in the fight against violence."

Ben: Albert Rosenfield isn't as bad a guy as everyone thinks! He may say bad sarcastic things to everyone, but deep down he cares and shows that through being the best at forensics.

Bryon: Albert has become a beloved character over the years and this turning point really helped with that.

Community Commentary

Charles de Lauzirika (DVD and Blu-ray Producer and Filmmaker): In between Seasons 1 and 2, there was a charity benefit for this organization called Tree People. And it was held at Union Station in downtown Los Angeles, which is the famous train station where they shot *Blade Runner*. So they had this party there and a huge amount of the cast was there. Mark Frost was there. I don't think David was there, but everyone else was there. There was this glow of love for the show because it was between those two seasons.

It was very exciting to go and completely unauthorized, I went in with my little tape recorder and I just started walking up to various people and interviewed them for my college newspaper. I interviewed Kyle MacLachlan, Ray Wise, Jack Nance, Dana Ashbrook, James Marshall, Richard Beymer and Sheryl Lee. I felt like I shouldn't have been doing what I was doing, but I did. And then it was in my college paper and I became sort of like the de facto *Twin Peaks* expert at my college, basically.

That night, they had a contest to guess who the killer was. Now, keep in mind this is between Seasons 1 and 2, but it was after Laura's diary came out, which I had read. I felt like I had a pretty good handle on who the killer was. The contest was basically to write your name down and your contact info and who you thought the killer was. So I did and I put down Leland Palmer. And again, it was mostly out of the Diary that I came up with that.

When I interviewed Ray Wise that night, this was like the first time the public had seen him with the white hair, I asked him, "I read the Diary and I think you're the killer." And then he just kind of laughed. I'm not even sure he knew exactly, but he was like, "Yeah, sure, sure." So years later when I shot his interview for the *Secrets from Another Place* documentary, I told him the story that a month later they called me up and I had won, but I didn't know what the prize was. They said, "Hey, you're the winner of the romantic dinner with your dream killer contest!" And I said, "What?" They said, "Yeah, you get a romantic dinner with Ray Wise!" I told Ray that story and he goes, "Man, I'm glad you didn't collect that prize. That would have been very awkward."

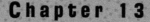

Chapter 13

Season 2: Episode 11
"Laura's Secret Diary"
Aired: October 20, 1990
Written by Jerry Stahl, Mark Frost,
Harley Peyton & Robert Engels
Directed by Todd Holland

The Log-line

Leland Palmer is interrogated about the murder of Jacques Renault and Judge Clinton Sternwood comes to town.

Behind the Curtain

Todd Holland (Director of ep. 11 and 20): My episode opened in that interrogation room. Leland Palmer sits before Sheriff Truman. I went and sat in that tiny box of a set. I said, "Okay. How does this scene start?" Cause it wasn't indicated in the script, it just said, "Interrogation room. Boom, dialogue." I looked straight ahead and saw that acoustic tile and I thought, "What if we start inside Leland's head and we think we're in this terrible cave and we're pulling out and spiraling and hearing sound and it's nightmarish and then we pull out and reveal we were ultimately in this most mundane of places." I went and pitched it to them and Mark totally got on board.

In 1990, it was a very complicated and expensive shot to pull off. We had to build that tunnel in like five times scale and shoot it with a fiber-optic camera that required all this special lighting. You had to light it to like T30 or something like that. Melt the scenery, stop to shoot that thing, but they got on board.

They loved the director with a vision. If you were speaking their language, they would just jump on board and support the creative. Top to bottom it was a show designed around supporting David and therefore it chose to become, very organically, a show that supported the director's vision, for every single director who came through. So living up to David is hard, but you kind of do your thing and hope that it fits into his world.

I was completely involved. You were given those episodes as your little films. You are expected to come into every color correction, every sound spot, every music spot and scoring. I designed all that sound [coming out of that acoustic tile]. ... Sheryl (Lee) came in and we got all those ADR [Automated Dialog Replacement] and crafted into that whole acoustic soundscape.

I presented it to Mark Frost and there was only one line he made me take out. Laura Palmer saying, "Daddy, no!" He made me take out the "No." He said, "You can't say that." I thought, "Oh, I got a little close to something." I didn't know Leland Palmer was the killer. I felt it was intriguing but I didn't really know what it meant. I began to suspect when he made me take it out.

[Ray Wise's performance] was masterful. It's breathtaking to watch it again. I remember being in awe of him. He had to do that scene three or four times for different takes and was just heartbreaking, authentic, so grounded and real. It set the whole tone for the episode. It was amazing. (*from* The Red Room Podcast *Ep125*)

Harley Peyton: Jerry Stahl was someone none of us knew. This guy worked on *Alf,* for crying out loud. He was a fascinating character. He seemed like just the kind of guy you wanted to write *Twin Peaks.* As everyone learned later because it is in his own autobiography [*Permanent Midnight*], he is clearly having some problems at the time. So the script that came in, part of it was handwritten and it was not finished. He was [also] not available suddenly.

Every time you have a freelance writer, you're going to do a certain amount of rewriting. You never take credit for that. You don't. That's just the way the game is played. By the way, when you take credit for something you're also taking money out of the writer's pocket. So that was something that we would never do. On certain episodes, there was a lot of rewriting that was done, but in this case, because we really had to just pitch in and do the entire script basically, that was the one time where we did take credit with a freelancer.

Todd Holland: I went to them and I said, "You know, it hasn't rained in Twin Peaks since the pilot. I would love to construct an arc of this approaching storm in four acts. Starling sky, the storm approaches, the storm breaks, the storm passes." Again, they loved it.

Bellina Logan (Desk Clerk Louie Budway, Female Doctor in Season 3): I was so thrilled to get the call to work on *Twin Peaks* Season 2. David didn't direct my episode, but I remember speaking with him before my big day on the set, telling him I was excited to play the desk clerk in Mr. Horne's hotel. He then replied in that very specific Lynchian dialect, "Oh—she's not just a desk clerk, Bellina. She's Louie 'Birdsong' Budway! Don't you ever forget it." And I didn't. Props didn't either because they had a nice, shiny, gold name tag with 'Louie' ready for me when I got to the set the next day. It made a difference in how I played her knowing her name. Even though she's still just listed as 'Desk Clerk' in the credits, it warms my heart to this day to know that at least me, David, and the props guy know she had a name.

Todd Holland: Four people knew who [Mr. Tojamura] was and I was one of them. They brought me into the office and said, "Here's what we're doing. No one knows. No one is to know." I met Piper [Laurie] the first time in that makeup, and I went to the makeup trailer in some secret location and saw her makeup test. We came on a set and I introduced [Fumio Yamaguchi] and Richard Beymer has a cigar in his hand and he says hello and Fumio just nodded and he pulls his head and goes, "Okay, what's the story?" I said, "I've never met him before." He [asked] me, "Who is playing the part?" He did not recognize Piper while we shot that scene. He didn't know what was happening, but he knew there was something happening. We didn't reveal it that whole shoot. It wasn't like at the end of the day it was revealed. Fumio left the set and went home. I don't know what episode it was revealed to the cast, but it was not revealed at first at all.

Somewhere in my archive of little answering machine cassette tapes, I have David calling me, "Todd, it's your buddy David Lynch. I just watched your episode." He sounds like Howdy Doody and he has this affable Midwestern loose song lilt to his voice. He was very complimentary and he had a couple notes and we made his changes, but I just always remember him calling personally, which is the way *Twin Peaks* worked. *(from* The Red Room Podcast *Ep125)*

Favorite Quotes and Scenes

Bryon and **Ben:** Our favorite scene has to be the interrogation of Leland Palmer.

Ben: That opening shot with the camera coming out of the ceiling tile with the voice of Laura Palmer saying, "Daddy," and the sound of a heart monitor beeping was brilliant.

Bryon: This scene plays out beautifully. Ray Wise goes from cold and calculating to crying hysterically seamlessly. We witness some of the best acting this show can offer.

Ben: My favorite quote is from the conversation between Judge Sternwood and Cooper. Judge Sternwood is an incredible character and I kinda see him as an older version of Dale Cooper. He is a by the book good man who tries to do the right thing. When Sternwood asks Cooper what he thinks of this place with everything that is happening, Cooper still sees the best in Twin Peaks and I think that is wonderful. It's so easy to become cynical of the world, but there is still beauty, good things and good people all around us.

Bryon: I totally agree. My quote is from Judge Sternwood as well, "The law provides us structure to guide us through paralyzing and trying times." This quote from Judge Clinton Sternwood is an interesting one because it seems to mix Law & Order with a religious undertone, some William Shakespeare sprinkled in and ends with Norse mythology. Now Valhalla is a hall (or place) where heroes slain in battle are received for honor, glory, or happiness. Valhalla could be an academic's heaven as well. This is how I understand it in the context being said here. I love the way this was written; it gives the viewer a look into Sternwood as a person, as a judge and how he sees the world.

Community Commentary

Counter Esperanto: *Counter Esperanto Podcast* grew up in *Twin Peaks*. We (Karl Eckler and Jubel Brosseau) discovered another kind of town, a funhouse mirror version of the place we had just left. There were one too many pairs of saddle shoes, sinister jazz took the place of grunge on the radio, and the population was off by an order of magnitude, but in many unlikely ways we were unnerved by the similarities: there were modern crimes done in ancient, foreboding pine forests which lured in DEA and FBI agents. There were UFOs, the Air Force, and kooky locals. There was even a feud between two "lodges" of ceremonial magicians; one light, one dark. Every time we make our own return, we see deeper into the fractal brilliance of this TV gem. The visions therein lead us through the curtains of perception into a strange, distant land. A land where only COUNTER ESPERANTO is spoken.

Chapter 14

Season 2: Episode 12
"The Orchid's Curse"
Aired: October 27, 1990
Written by Barry Pullman
Directed by Graeme Clifford

The Log-line

Agent Cooper pursues a rescue mission to free Audrey Horne from One-Eyed Jack's.

Ken Scherer: We put some merchandise into the field, T-shirts, cups, all kinds of good stuff. That was part of what I was trying to do to find some other revenue. I just wish social media had existed then. I brought a coffee deal into ABC and it was a natural coffee and it was turned down because I was told at the time by practice and standards at ABC, there would never ever be product placement in a TV show.

A few years later came *Seinfeld* and that was the end of it. We were a little bit ahead of our time. Some of the things we were trying to put in place didn't work because of all these restrictions, but we made some nice headway at marketing. We knew people were watching *Twin Peaks* collectively. When you measure by Nielsen, in those days, it didn't track that. And so we were trying to prove to the network that a lot of people were watching the show. We thought if we could do a big merchandising effort, it would drive revenue, but more importantly, it would be another way to engage with our fans. That was really primarily where I went every day in my head and then just tried to help people who were producing the show make it possible and negotiate with the networks and the promotional pieces of that.

We had this company representing the show and they had exclusive [merchandise] rights. They would take me into meetings and we would pitch and then we would bring the deals back to David and Mark. Mostly David had final approval on everything, especially from the creative perspective, because I don't care how creative you are, you can't replicate David's vision.

Galyn Gorg (Nancy O'Reilly) on her fight scene with Kyle MacLachlan: We definitely had to block that out 'cause when you do any kind of fight or any kind of a scene like that, we have to do some blocking—even though it's television [and] we're kind of moving fast. Since my background is as a dancer, I had to kind of contract my body [when] he hits me against the wall. The thing that is funny is somebody sent me these images from the episode [and] so I posted a picture on Twitter of Kyle when he had his arm back and I'm back behind the wall right before he punches me and oh my gosh, people went crazy over it.

Harley Peyton: Before the second season started, Mark actually called me up and he called up Bob [Engels] as well and said, "If you have any ideas for any stories you want to do for the second season let me know." I came to him and pitched the story that became the Harold Smith story. There actually is a real character named [Arthur Crew Inman], who wrote these diaries who lived in Boston, who never left his house and wrote diaries about the world he wasn't participating in. The real-life guy was a fairly perverse character, the scion of a very rich family and he had all these crazy notions and he would write these very long diaries. He would pay people [Talkers] to come in and talk to him and he'd write these stories down. I picked up those books and so that was one of the things that in the second season that I brought to [Mark] and said, "Let's try this." And he'd said, "Great! We're doing that," and we did.

[Harold Smith's] connection was really to Donna and to Laura, and it was really about this guy who was tangential to the main story then gradually became a larger and larger part of it, but it was really meant to be about the relationship that Donna had with him.

Lenny Von Dohlen (Harold Smith): Very happy and proud to be a part of the mosaic. *Twin Peaks* and *Fire Walk with Me* were the most extraordinary experience from beginning to end. Sweet, wildly talented people both behind and before the cameras, all inspired by Mr. Lynch to do [their] best, bravest work. And *Twin Peaks* fans, the most brilliant by far.

Brings Back Some Memories

Ben: As you were getting close to finding out who killed Laura Palmer, I remember you didn't want to see my reaction when you said who you thought it was and you whispered on the podcast, "Ben Horne is the killer," at the very end of the show. The writers led you exactly where they wanted you to go!

Bryon: This show led me down many paths of who the killer could be but everything seemed to be pointing at Ben Horne. He wasn't a very trustworthy person and he could easily cover it up and pin it on someone else because of his status in the town. I felt he had killed Laura Palmer not out of passion but rather because she knew something he didn't want to get out. A cover-up of sorts. He knew about that cabin in the woods and saw an opportunity to silence Laura knowing full well that that the other two dirtbags could easily take the fall for her murder.

Favorite Quotes and Scenes

Bryon: My favorite quote comes from Harold Smith, "There's things you can't get anywhere. But we dream they can be found in other people." This quote from Harold Smith really has some layers to it. Reminds me of Cooper's dream and how he meets Laura and gets clues to find the killer that he would otherwise not find anywhere else. I see parallels between him and Cooper and it almost makes me feel that Harold has had some experience in the lodges or knows about them because of the stories he was told over the years or maybe has experienced them himself at some point in time. This does make his character a little bit more interesting and mysterious.

Ben: Maybe the true mysteries of life are discovered through the connections we make with other people. I think we both feel this way, that, having discussed *Twin Peaks* for all these years, we actually enjoy just being in the company of our friends more than whatever subject we're talking about. My favorite quote is from Andy Brennan, "I'm a whole damn town."

Bryon: My favorite scene is with Judge Clinton Sternwood, Harry Truman, and Agent Cooper sitting at the bar after the trial. The judge orders three Black Yukon Sucker Punches and wants to get the temperature of the town. He gives some advice, "Keep your eye on the woods. The woods are wondrous here."

Ben: Could Judge Sternwood be a Bookhouse Boy?! The Bookhouse Boys seem to know something about the dark woods and now we hear the judge bring them up. My favorite scene is when Cooper and Harry rescue Audrey. Hawk says, "You guys are terrible at keeping secrets."

Community Commentary

Aaron Cohen: As someone who discovered *Twin Peaks* briefly at the age of 7 during its original airing (by "borrowing," without my parents' knowledge, VHS tapes of episodes they recorded), I never dreamed of the positive impact it would ultimately have on my life. The announcement of the third season was a shock in the best possible way and I quickly then discovered the incredibly passionate and dedicated fan community through the *Twin Peaks* UK Festival, as I was living just outside of London at that point in my life.

What I've been most thankful for though are the friendships of those I've met in the fan community—truly some of the most wonderful, creative, passionate, talented, interesting, and loving people that I could have possibly ever met. To anyone reading this that I might have met and spent time with during my travels, please know that I truly value your friendship, anything you've shared with me, and the joy you have brought to my life. I only hope I've been able to bring something to yours as well.

Chapter 15

Season 2: Episode 13
"Demons"
Aired: November 3, 1990
Written by Harley Peyton & Robert Engels
Directed by Lesli Linka Glatter

The Log-line

Regional Bureau Chief Gordon Cole pays a visit to Twin Peaks and without chemicals the one-armed man provides answers.

Behind the Curtain

Piper Laurie (Catherine Martell): Being on *Twin Peaks* was more creative fun—and just plain fun—than I've ever had. Never thought being an actress would allow that.

Bob Engels: [My wife was] the waitress in the Great Northern. She's Trudy. When I do a script, I would always write a scene at the Great Northern, kind of an inside joke. She's a wonderful actress, but she does musical comedy.

Lesli Linka Glatter: I directed David Lynch the first time David was in *Twin Peaks*, which was almost impossible for the crew to keep a straight face. He goes in to talk to [Cooper] and, of course, it's a private meeting, but, of course, everyone in the whole office can hear because he's screaming and literally behind the camera we were on the floor laughing so hard. Well, I was crying. I knew at that point [Leland] was the killer. But there were various scripts around, as I recall. I think there were several bogey scripts out there. For a while, I think I wasn't sure who was who. A bogey script would have Ben Horne listed for Leland's dialogue.

Favorite Quotes and Scenes

Bryon: My favorite quote comes from Mike The One-Armed Man: "He is BOB, eager for fun. He wears a smile, everybody run." Another amazing performance by Al Strobel, delivering these lines in such a chilling and frightening way. Also, a very cryptic line of dialogue that Cooper seems to hang on every line.

Ben: That's my favorite scene. Not only do we get a great performance from Al Strobel, but we get a lot of information about BOB and Mike and their relationship.

Bryon: My favorite scene was when Gordon Cole is waiting for Dale Cooper at the police station. The greeting between the two is classic. The rapport these two have is golden. Also, we get more information about Cooper's last case that got him wounded. Gordon sees that he is 100% invested in this town to the point of letting it consume him. He notices that lack of sleep, but Cooper reassures him that his "mind, body and spirit are up to the task." We also get another hint about his ex-partner, Windom Earle.

Ben: My favorite quote comes from Gordon Cole, "Cooper, you remind me today of a small Mexican chihuahua." But what does it mean?!

Bryon: After watching this episode again, I think I figured out what this quote means. It's not just a funny thing that Gordon Cole says. Because later on Dale Cooper asks Gordon about this chihuahua, and Gordon reminds Cooper about Philadelphia and the investigation where he was shot. It was because of his lack of sleep and not taking care of himself he was off his game. This is where the "You remind me today of a small Mexican chihuahua" comes in. Gordon sees that Cooper is under a great deal of stress with the

Lesli Linka Glatter and David Lynch. Courtesy of Lesli Linka Glatter.

investigation and he is reminding him not to go down that path again. So hence the Mexican chihuahua comparison.

Ben: He also knows that his old partner Windom Earl has escaped, so not only is he trying to figure out the Laura Palmer case, he has to deal with the fact his ex-partner could show up at any time. So he has a lot going on with the townspeople and on a personal level. So I think that's what the meaning is and not just a funny phrase or some cryptic Gordon Cole talk. I think you nailed it.

Bryon: If David Lynch and Mark Frost had their way, I think Season 2 could've gone in that direction. But with ABC saying that the ratings are on the decline and people are getting fed up, you need to give us the killer, they had no choice.

Community Commentary

Andreas Halskov (author of *The Art of Paradox: The Films of David Lynch* (2020): In 1990, when we had only a handful of TV channels in Denmark, and where the main broadcaster, DR, was not too keen on airing American content, something suddenly happened. *Twin Peaks* came around, and all but changed my life. As a young child, it traumatized me and gave me weekly nightmares about mirrors and grey-haired men, but it also fascinated me and hit me with its uncanny mood, its surreal storylines and absurd moments, however little of it I actually understood. It never left me and continued to grow on/with me. And today, after writing three books, numerous articles and two documentary episodes about it, I still cannot claim to fully understand it, let alone to be done with it. It continued to thrill, astound and amaze, and I suspect it will always be a thing of wonder for me, an object of interest, an alluring enigma and a warm place to return to. It changed everything for me, even if it might not, in fact, have changed the face of television, it is still a rather unique piece of art in the entertainment industry.

Ben, Andreas, & Bryon in 2018

Chapter 16

Season 2: Episode 14
"Lonely Souls"
Aired: November 10, 1990
Written by Mark Frost
Directed by David Lynch

The Log-line

The Giant tells Cooper it is happening again, and Maddy Ferguson is killed.

Behind the Curtain

Episode 14 was the episode that finally revealed who killed Laura Palmer. Some believe the killer shouldn't be revealed. "What killed *Twin Peaks* originally," Lynch elaborates, "'Who killed Laura Palmer?' was a question that we did not ever really want to answer, and that Laura Palmer mystery was the goose that laid these little golden eggs. And then at a certain point, we were told we needed to wrap that up and it never really got going again after that. I always felt, even if it only happened mentally and emotionally, the story goes on" (*The Cincinnati Enquirer*, May 21, 2017, page V17).

Ken Scherer: I think if you want to talk about why this show didn't succeed in those days is because Mark and David would say repeatedly, we don't know the ending. We don't know who killed Laura Palmer. And we don't want to solve it. We really don't. We love the mystery of it all and there was a very tense meeting at ABC where they kept saying, "You have to solve it; you have to solve it." It was not the story those two guys wanted to tell.

Bob Engels: In my mind, it wasn't so much about solving the mystery, but I guess it was. We had known [Leland was the murderer] for most of the year during the show. About five of us knew.

Ray Wise (Leland Palmer): It was the day before we actually shot the reveal scene. You know, I look in the mirror and I see BOB, and then I put on my rubber gloves and then Maddy comes and I take her all the way back to Missoula, Montana. Actually, she was beaten to death by three different people that day. By Richard Beymer who played Ben Horne, by me, and by Frank Silva, who played BOB, because David didn't want anybody to know who the killer was, not even the crew. So poor [Sheryl Lee]—15, 16 hours of getting beaten to death by three different guys.

I get called into this room. I see in this room Sheryl Lee sitting there with Mark Frost, Richard Beymer, David Lynch, they're all sitting cross-legged on the floor in this dark room ... I didn't want to be the killer, you know. It can be anybody else. Ben Horne looks good to me. I had my own little baby daughter. She was, like, two years old at the time and the whole idea of being the murderer of my daughter on the show just didn't sit right with me. In fact, I had some bad nights. At one point, I even considered not doing it, not doing the reveal show.

And then he proceeded to say, "But Ray, it's going to be a beautiful thing." And he went on to explain how it was going to happen; how I was going to die and I would be looking down on a long terrible tunnel. And at the end of that tunnel would be a white light and standing in that white light would be my daughter, Laura. I get weird every time I even talk about it. But, I felt relieved. I felt a great weight had been taken off my chest because I didn't want to be the killer. I said, "Okay, let's do it, man. Let's go." (*Courtesy of* FWWM *event*)

Richard Beymer (Ben Horne): David said, "We made a decision and you're going to do this, but we don't want anyone to know, so we're going to play it like you are the killer, Richard, and then were going to do the scene with Ray and [then with Frank]." I was first, which was kind of fun because that sort of set the blocking of the scene. I don't find it difficult being evil. It's fun doing all of that.

Julee Cruise on singing "Rockin' Back Inside My Heart" at the Roadhouse: David said I moved too much. I said, "Why didn't you tell me? I mean, come on. Let me learn." That's why [Donna] is mouthing that, because I was moving too much. David likes accidents. (*Courtesy of* The Red Room Podcast *Ep125*)

Dana Ashbrook (Bobby Briggs): I think I just went by [the set] and I just wanted to hang out with David. That's the way it works over there. You hang out long enough, they're going [to put you into the show].

Ray Wise: When I was killing [Sheryl Lee] as Maddy, we laughed in between takes. That was the main way to keep our sanity. It was a great release.

Sheryl Lee (Laura Palmer): It had to be choreographed for safety and stunts and everything just so perfectly. And I was working with such great actors that I knew I was in really good hands. So you have the whole technical part of it that has to be sort of hit exactly. And then, this emotion with it. Your adrenaline carries you through those days. It isn't until the next day when you try to get out of bed, you can't, you realize, "Wow, that was a doozy!"

Ray Wise: I didn't actually hit her. It was a close-up shot of me and I was punching a pillow actually because it sure looked like I was hitting her. We all went through the same action. They all pushed her face into the wall and they all punched her when she was on the couch. We all did the same stuff.

Richard Beymer: I was pleased [I was not the killer] because I knew that the killer wasn't going to be in the show much longer.

Scott Frost: It was just one of the most amazing television episodes I've ever seen. I remember watching it with some people and I hadn't seen a cut of it until it was broadcast. The whole room was just kind of shattered by it, just shaken. It was truly disturbing in a way that you just never see on network television, back then anyway. It was the kind of thing that would have been really cool if we could have kept that kind of edge going for most of that second season. But I don't know if the network would have allowed that.

Brings Back Some Memories

Ben: Everything was pointing in the direction of Ben Horne at this point. It was a red herring. This was the first episode that we both sat down together and watched the entire episode together. I got to see your reaction to finding out who killed Laura Palmer. It was pretty special. You had no idea the killer was Leland Palmer!

Bryon: I couldn't believe my eyes seeing him as the killer. I really thought it would be Ben Horne. Doesn't Ben Horne kinda look like an evil owl?

Ben: Before Maddy is killed she mentioned the smell of burnt engine oil. In Episode 8 when Cooper questioned Jacoby about Jacques Renault's death, Jacoby mentions a peculiar smell of scorched engine oil and again in Episode 10 under hypnosis, he mentions the smell at Easter park when he is beaten, and then he realizes Leland Palmer killed Jacques. At the time, I couldn't say how the scorched engine oil smell would lead to Leland/BOB being the killer and eventually lead to the pool of oil near the entrance to the Black Lodge.

Favorite Quotes and Scenes

Ben: My favorite quote is from the Log Lady, "We don't know what will happen, or when, but there are owls in the Roadhouse." It's so fitting that the message is being delivered by Margaret Lanterman and her log.

Bryon: My favorite quote comes from the Giant, "It is happening again." This quote and scene bring us back to a very mysterious time in *Twin Peaks*. The way everything unfolded and how Cooper is starting to put together all the pieces, but is in the wrong place to be able to do anything.

Bryon and **Ben:** Our favorite scene is Cooper at the Roadhouse listening to the angelic sounds of Julee Cruise, The Giant appearing and giving Cooper a message, and Maddy is murdered at the hands of her Uncle. It is David Lynch at his best. He is able to ease us into the scene and then hit us hard with the brutal murder. Thirty years later, this scene is still powerful and disturbing.

Ben: ABC had promoted this episode as the episode we would learn who killed Laura Palmer. So my first time watching this episode live on ABC, I'm asking myself how the heck are we going to find out who killed Laura Palmer with 10 minutes left of the show and Cooper is just sitting around the Roadhouse listening to music and eating peanuts? Then all of a sudden the music stops, and Cooper sees the Giant, and we see Leland kill Maddy.

Bryon: I think I said, "No, he's not the killer. Leland's not the killer. No!" when we watched that episode together. It was the last person you would ever think it could be. But in hindsight, it makes sense now because when Leland killed Jacques, we didn't blink an eye. That should have been a big red flag.

Community Commentary

Laura Stewart (Assistant Editor-in-Chief, 25YL): I was 10 when I first watched *Twin Peaks*. It's been with me since my earliest memories. First, when I was a child watching with my dad, a rare time just he and I, precious memories they are. Then later I revisited it in my teens, and I understood the context and the spirituality of it so much more. It became almost a way

of life to me then, almost every event in my life could be adorned with a quote from the show. My life mirrored Laura Palmer's at times. At others, I was Donna. Nowadays, I feel more like Norma.

Laura Stewart and Michael Horse

It's funny how this TV show has traveled with me. For a long while, it kind of disappeared from 'me,' then *The Return* was announced and a spark was reignited. I took a chance offered by the good people at 25YL to write about the show each week. Fast forward 2 years and I'm the Assistant Editor-in-Chief of a very successful media and entertainment website. I'm doing what I love, with the people I love. I began writing because of *Twin Peaks*. It helped me get over the death of my best friend. *Twin Peaks* fixed my heart.

Chapter 17

Season 2: Episode 15
"Drive with a Dead Girl"
Aired: November 17, 1990
Written by Scott Frost
Directed by Caleb Deschanel

The Log-line
Ben and Jerry Horne flashback to Louise Dombrowski dancing on the hooked rug with a flashlight and Leland takes his death bag for a ride.

Behind the Curtain

Caleb Deschanel: In *The Shining*, when Shelley Duvall goes and finds out that Jack Nicholson has been writing his novel, she wants to see what he's writing. You find out [it is], "All work and no play makes Jack a dull boy," for like thousands of pages perfectly lined up on the page. It's like you're always trying to find some visual elements to show that someone's totally insane. To me, just having all these golf balls being hit by Leland and not even thinking about breaking windows or anything and then when Donna and James come in, they just think it's a little goofy thing. They have no idea how insane it really is. Then when you see Maddy or at least part of her hand bloody in the bag when he puts the golf club in, suddenly it completes the image and the idea.

Scott Frost: It was kind of a natural for me to [write an episode] because I had [Cooper's] voice in my head pretty thoroughly at that point. [Scott Frost had written the script to *Diane: Twin Peaks Tapes of Agent Cooper* cassette tape and would go on to write *The Autobiography of F.B.I. Special Agent Dale Cooper: My Life, My Tapes book*].

I have some very fond memories of that episode. Louise Dombrowski doing the flashlight dance on the hooked rug. I hadn't actually written a flashback in the script. Caleb Deschanel directed it. He's one of the great cinematographers to ever live and I think he came up with the idea of doing a flashback.

Caleb Deschanel: The whole thing with the flashback was that it was just kind of flat when they were just talking about Louise Dombrowski. So I sort of had this idea to do it and David thought it was great and Mark thought it was great. It was something where you had to sort of set it up and cast the little boys and then cast the girl as Louise Dombrowski. As a matter of convenience and the fact that Emily Fincher [sister of film director David Fincher] happen to also be there at the office and was a good dancer and was cute and all the things that you wanted in a babysitter for these 10-year-olds who are sorta getting some inkling of being interested in a girl for the first time.

Ray Wise: In my head, I just did whatever I had to do to get ready for the next scene. Sometimes it meant I had to go off in a corner, in a dark corner and just stare at the corner, get away from everybody and everything. Other times, I could be a little lighter about it and walk around and sing a song. And Leland had a lot of light moments. He sure loved to sing. (*Courtesy of* FWWM *event*)

Caleb Deschanel: Ray Wise was just so amazing in that episode. I just really love working with him in that. There's this sort of wonderful scene where Harry and Cooper come in and they see him dancing like Fred Astaire in the hotel. When they tell him about Ben, they sort of think he's very upset about it. So when you see them from behind, you feel he's upset, but when you're on his face, you see this diabolical look and you realize he's laughing and playing off against the emotion of one being laughter and one thinking that he's very upset about Ben being accused of killing Laura Palmer.

Scott Frost: It all had been pretty mysterious up until the episode before that. And then suddenly Leland is in the world so BOB has got to go with him. It just seemed natural to be driving down the road with [Maddy] stuffed in a golf bag singing "Surrey With The Fringe On Top." I think Ray had a good time getting a little a musical number as I remember.

Caleb Deschanel: I think [Leland is] the killer and I think he's possessed. I think the killer that he sees in [the mirror], it's like having an alter ego. It's somebody who exists in him. It's like somebody having dual personalities. He definitely is the killer. I think that's what's sort of wonderful about him. He's so charming. When he gets stopped by [Truman and Cooper] and he says, "Oh, I'm sorry, I guess I was thinking about Ben." Yeah right.

Scott Frost: I think to make it real, you had to write it in a way that BOB was the evil that's in all men. It's not that he's an actual physical presence. When things go off the rails, he's what's waiting for anybody. That makes it more human.

Brings Back Some Memories

Bryon: Dale Cooper seems to be a little off his game during this episode. He seems to be a little confused. Getting to see Leland Palmer play the killer was a lot of fun for this episode. I see BOB coming and going into Leland's body and Leland playing two roles; the father who is mourning the loss of his child, but when BOB takes over, a heartless psychopath. To this day, I still firmly believe that Leland, the father, had really no inkling of what he did. I see BOB as this parasite that used his body as a vessel to kill and to do horrible things.

Ben: I question whether Leland knew what he was doing when he committed all the heinous acts. From a mythology standpoint, it's interesting to have the evil spirit BOB take possession of Leland when awful things happen, but does this let Leland off the hook and basically say "the Devil made me do it"? He can't be blamed for raping and killing his daughter? And what about Sarah Palmer?

Bryon: David Lynch likes to tackle the dark side of the nuclear family. Typically the mother is supposed to stay home and take care of the kids while the father is off working and supporting them with his job to pay the bills. This dynamic gives Leland all the power over Sarah. It didn't help that Leland was drugging her when he did those things to Laura.

Favorite Quotes and Scenes

Ben and **Bryon:** Our favorite scene is Sheriff Truman and Dale Cooper walking down the hallway in the Great Northern and seeing Leland Palmer dancing like Fred Astaire in the common room.

Ben: Ray Wise is just a fantastic actor who can sing, dance, and his emotions can turn on a dime. We have always seen him as this loving husband who has been grieving for this daughter and to see him so menacing looking when he thought no one was around was shocking. We see a whole new side to Leland.

Bryon: This scene reminds me of when Leland held the picture of BOB under his nose in front of Cooper and Harry a couple of episodes ago. I feel BOB gets a thrill out of being right in front of them the whole time.

Ben: Also in this episode, Leland is stopped by Truman and Cooper for reckless driving. Leland actually opens the trunk to show Cooper his golf clubs as if he wanted to also show him the dead body of Maddy in the truck too. When Truman and Cooper leave, Leland looks into the mirror and we see BOB looking back. You normally think the bad things happen only during the night, but BOB could strike at any time.

Bryon: My favorite quote comes from Jerry Horne who says, "Ben, as your attorney, your friend, and your brother, I strongly suggest that you get yourself a better lawyer." This is after Jerry Horne gets roasted by Dale Cooper about his law degree and Ben seems to not have a good alibi on the night Laura was murdered. Jerry is way over his head and he knows he can't help his brother so the best advice he has is don't count on me to defend you.

Ben: My favorite quote comes from Sheriff Harry Truman, "I've had enough of the dreams, the visions, the dwarves, the giants, Tibet, and the rest of the hocus pocus." What I like is that the Truman/Cooper relationship is being challenged, but Cooper backs off and supports Truman.

Community Commentary

Connor Ratliff: When Season 1 of *Twin Peaks* first aired, I had play rehearsal on Thursday nights and I couldn't watch it. I was in 8th grade, and I probably wouldn't have tuned in anyway, if it weren't for one of the younger adults in the play talking about it. They taped every episode and loaned them to me once the play was over, and I watched those VHS tapes all summer long. *Twin Peaks* would remain special to me as the decades passed. *Fire Walk with Me* felt like it was truly the end, and *The Missing Pieces* felt like a minor miracle, a tiny time machine that took me back to a place that no longer existed. The first whispers of Season 3 felt so improbable that they weren't worth getting my hopes up, and the 18 new hours defied every expectation I had.

Chapter 18

Season 2: Episode 16
"Arbitrary Law"
Aired: December 1, 1990
Written by Mark Frost, Harley Peyton & Robert Engels
Directed by Tim Hunter

The Log-line

Cooper takes 24 hours to be sure that Laura Palmer's murderer is caught.

Behind the Curtain

Tim Hunter: My father was a blacklisted writer during the McCarthy era. And I had to keep it secret when he was working on TV shows under an assumed name because the FBI would show up at the door. I've always been pretty good at keeping my mouth shut when the situation required it.

Tony Krantz: The clarion called by ABC as to who killed Laura Palmer came and they wanted to figure that out and to resolve it. And David and Mark were adamant that the minute that they resolve who killed Laura Palmer, the series is over. They were 100% right about that. It's interesting, the Bob Iger autobiography that just came out, he actually reflects on that debate and he sort of says that David may have been right. It was never meant that the murder of Laura Palmer would overtake the series, the country, popular imagination the way that it did. It was always supposed to be sort of an exciting incident, the murder of Laura Palmer.

Tim Hunter: David was always able to do stuff in his own natural way without pushing it. A couple of times, I would push things a bit like BOB in the mirror in that episode Leland is dancing with Lara Flynn Boyle. I looked at the next episode that David did and he had done something much creepier with just a slight gesture. And he made me realize how good David is and how unique he is and how in a couple of places I had pushed stuff a little too far to get the effect I wanted, whereas David just tossed off this stuff.

Ray Wise: Tim Hunter directed and the water sprinkling down on me and Kyle was great. It was redeeming for me as a human being, not only as an actor. And so it made it all alright. I never had BOB in my mind. It was always Leland and when that old switch went off and he became something else, it was him. And whether it was another part of his brain kicking in or whatever you want to call it, I did not ever think about BOB. At the end of the last episode when I die, I become aware of everything that I've done as BOB. What a big surprise it was for Leland. (*Courtesy of* FWWM *event*)

Tim Hunter: I pride myself a little bit in TV that I've had a pretty high percentage of director's cuts. They had been more or less approved as is and put on the air the way I gave it to them. The producers almost invariably have to trim out a minute or two. But beyond that, I've had a pretty rewarding history of not having to have had scenes re-cut or restructured.

Ray Wise: I was never glad to leave the show. I didn't want to leave town. I love these people. (*Courtesy of* FWWM *event*)

Kyle MacLachlan: All the signs were kind of pointing towards Leland, but no one was really sure. And then we get the script and say, yes, that's what it was. That is very difficult to imagine that. The idea of this possession, and then it turned into a different thing that he was actually released from this awful torture. Oh, OK. There's something bigger out there that is doing this, that's even more dangerous and more frightening. Which was a track that went into *Fire Walk with Me* and then ultimately came out in Season 3.

Favorite Quotes and Scenes

Bryon: My favorite scene is when Leland gets the phone call about Maddy not making it home, while Donna overhears the conversation. We get to see Leland yet again going towards a dark place in this scene. BOB has become very emboldened by his last kill and seemingly getting away with it, that pushes him to strike again, this time at Donna. If we look at this scene from a BOB perspective, it makes perfect sense he would strike at another girl that seems to trigger the memories of Laura, from having Laura's sunglasses on and lighting up a cigarette in the house, all the things she used to do. Such an intense scene and I honestly thought Donna was going to die.

Ben: My favorite scene has to be the death of Leland Palmer. As Leland is dying, Cooper comforts him. This is just a very powerful scene with amazing acting by Ray Wise and Kyle MacLachlan. I just love all the emotions and story development that happens in this one scene.

Bryon: That scene just solidifies for me that the real Leland was clueless to all those horrific acts he had done over the years. We witness the real Leland heartbroken about what he has done to Laura. Before he passes away, he sees the light, and in that light is Laura calling for him and forgiving him. This is just heartbreaking to watch. All these emotions are wrapped up into one.

Ben: Leland mentions how Laura is smiling and this reminds me of the ending of *Fire Walk with Me* with Laura smiling in the white light with angels surrounding her. After all that she has gone through, I want to believe she is at peace.

Bryon: My favorite quote is when BOB says, "Leland's a babe in the woods, with a large hole where his conscience used to be. When I go, children, I will pull that ripcord and you watch Leland remember. Watch him!" We have been seeing a man being toyed with by this parasite. Do we really want to witness Leland realizing he killed his own daughter? Of course not, but this horror will finally come to an end when the truth is revealed. BOB would have kept killing, but Agent Cooper put a stop to that.

Ben: Leland also says, "He opened me, and I invited him, and he came inside me." If it physically happened, did Leland get sexually abused as a child? Maybe by a neighbor or, God forbid, his grandfather during the summers at the lake house? Did Leland continue the cycle of abuse?

My favorite quote comes from Agent Albert Rosenfield, "Maybe that's all BOB is—the evil that men do." I think it is easier for the viewers (and even Ray Wise the actor) to deal with Laura Palmer being abused and killed by an evil spirit than by her own father who is supposed to protect her and care for her. Child abuse is happening every day and Lynch/Frost made it a little easier to discuss with BOB carrying out the horrific acts.

Community Commentary

Andy Bentley (Designed *Twin Peaks Unwrapped* Podcast logo): I struggled through several iterations of this. Would I profess my love for dear Dale Cooper? Confess my struggle to understand that "Laura is the one"? Or lay out a conspiracy string board explaining just what happened in those final two episodes? I finally decided it's the feeling of sharing this wonderful and strange show that is worth putting pen to paper. Like Ben and Bryon, I have always watched *Twin Peaks* with a co-pilot. I've enjoyed the show with roommates and girlfriends and am currently watching two episodes a week with my mom.

It's a joy to experience the twists and turns anew in their eyes. And then there's the fan community at large. I've met so many kind and generous people through the love of this show. These are the memories that will endure. Oh and that llama huffing in Cooper's face.

Chapter 19

**Season 2: Episode 17
"Dispute Between Brothers"
Aired: December 8, 1990
Written by Tricia Brock
Directed by Tina Rathborne**

The Log-line

The townspeople attend the wake of Leland Palmer, and Cooper and Major Briggs go camping in the woods.

Behind the Curtain

With the Laura Palmer case resolved, Lynch/Frost had to come up with new ideas. "A hundred different stories are left. The murder of Laura has always been just the tip of the iceberg. It was never designed to carry the series. We'll come up with stories that are equally compelling. There will be more mysteries." -Mark Frost ("Meanwhile, Back at 'Twin Peaks,'" *The Los Angeles Times*, Wednesday, May 23, 1990)

Tina Rathborne (Director of ep. 3 and 17): The really interesting things that happened were in the first season. The first season we were in the Valley in this warehouse, we were all on top of each other. There wasn't enough space to do anything. The costumes were mounded on each other. It was down and dirty, but in the best way. There was a lot of camaraderie. It was kind of a feeling of, we're all in this together, and by the time we got to the second season there was a lot more money, it had become famous. It became a very sterile working environment.

I think [Tricia Brock's] script was excellent. The fact is I don't know, as it says created by David Lynch and Mark Frost, how deeply they're involved in that second season in saying to the writer what they want from the script. The second episode I really didn't enjoy making, and I think you can tell. It's about a fight between [two brothers]? This is a very deep occasion. [But the Doc Hayward, Sarah Palmer and Cooper scene] is a very beautiful scene.

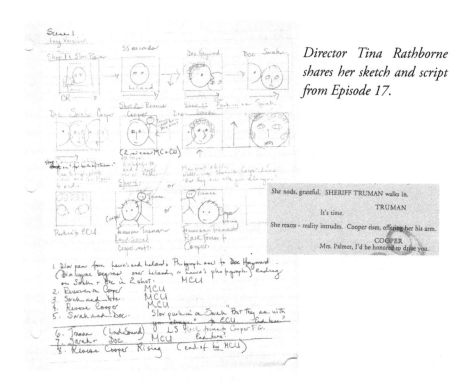

Director Tina Rathborne shares her sketch and script from Episode 17.

Eric Da Re (Leo Johnson): Now I'm a quadriplegic, slobbering physical being. At that point, the one thing I really didn't like about it was the continuity in the show was really starting to lose itself from scene to scene. And I felt that was a real dramatic stretch with my character for such a short time period. So I didn't enjoy really playing the character in that manner so much as well as I didn't like the fact that that's where the direction went. 'Cause I knew there's nowhere to really go from there. It was almost like it was designed to end. That was just part of the show ending. That's how I felt. And coincidentally, I think it really was. The whole character development from there on was, right up until the show got canceled, pretty much. I may have died at the end.

Ian Buchanan (Dick Tremayne): I loved working with Harry Goaz, my lovely friend Kimmy Robertson. We had our little triangle that was going [on], which wasn't a soap opera except it was kind of a very funny love triangle.

Tina Rathborne: It's very instinctive for me to dwell longer on an image. And so what was upsetting to me and Tony [Morgan] was the episode was much more held, the shot, and I felt [ABC] didn't like holding. So what we got back as notes, whereas I never got one note back on the first season, was cut that, cut that. So it was very depersonalized. Tony and I did the first cut of the [episode], [ABC] hugely re-edited it. The cut that we did I felt was much more emotional, much closer to the bone.

The first season just had more layers, emotional layers. This is what it felt like, that David was no longer connected with the second season. David's an artist and he's not a machine. I think he was probably no longer connected to it emotionally.

We bought the house next to him and it was a teardown. He wanted to make it into a studio and he let me live there because it was very expensive for me to stay in a hotel. And it was very sweet of him.

Sherilyn Fenn: [Roy London acting coach] said if you're going to be in a parade, you might as well lead it. They're trying to do what you're doing so we're moving in a different direction. I stopped wearing sweaters. I got a '40s-like business little jacket and started just moving in a different direction.

Tina Rathborne on the Green Butt Skunk: [Cooper is] going on a fishing trip. And I loved the fly, the beautiful fly that [Truman] had made for him. They must've been going trout fishing because flies have a hook inside and they're [made] really to be as beautiful as possible. In other words, they're works of art and tying flies is an art form. And I think it's part of what fishermen love about trout fishing. That's a very profound gift. I knew [about it] because I grew up fishing. So that was a jewel he was giving him.

Harley Peyton: The second season, it has its detractors. I would certainly say that the first season and up to the death of Leland Palmer, I think that run of episodes is as good as any television ever made. I really do believe that. And so the rest of that second season had a very hard act to follow.

Brings Back Some Memories

Ben: I know we said this last episode but this feels like the show is coming to an end. Where do you go from here? We see Cooper saying goodbye to everyone in the police station and then all of a sudden the FBI and a Canadian Mountie show up and suspend Cooper.

Bryon: I felt the second half of Season 2 was going to go into the White Lodge, not knowing it was going to introduce some new and wacky characters. I felt we could have ended the show after Cooper said his goodbyes and that would have made a fantastic ending. But this was being aired on network television in the early '90s and something like that would never happen as they needed a full 22-episode season, for better or worse.

Ben: The writers were trying to figure out a way to keep Cooper in Twin Peaks after the Laura Palmer case was solved. I did like that Harry makes Cooper an honorary Bookhouse Boy in this episode.

Bryon: Harry giving Cooper a Bookhouse Boys patch and telling him that he is one of them now is a beautiful moment.

Ben: It's too bad we didn't see more of the Bookhouse Boys' adventures.

Bryon: You'd think that would be the next logical step, but they went away from that.

Favorite Quotes and Scenes

Bryon: My favorite scene is Agent Cooper saying his goodbyes to Harry, Hawk, Andy, and Lucy. This is such a sweet and wonderful moment between Cooper and the Sheriff's Department. Of course, this would not be *Twin Peaks* without all this coming to an abrupt ending with Special Agent Roger showing up to open up an investigation against Cooper.

Ben: David Lynch never wanted to solve the mystery. I think Mark Frost now questions whether they should have even solved it. ABC demanded it because the ratings were dropping and people wanted answers.

Bryon: If the ratings were high, I feel they could have kept it going because they had the upper hand, but since the ratings were down they had no choice in the matter.

Ben: My favorite scene is Cooper and Major Briggs sitting around the campfire contemplating the nature of evil and broadening the *Twin Peaks* mythology with the introduction of the White Lodge.

In that same scene is my favorite quote from Major Briggs saying, "It is some men's fate to face great darkness. We each choose how to react. If the choice is fear, then we become vulnerable to darkness." How do we react to powerful forces of evil in the world? This is something Cooper will have to face towards the end of the season.

Bryon: My favorite quote comes from Dale Cooper, "There's nothing quite like urinating out in the open air." Cooper seems unsettled after being stripped of his badge and gun, but can still maintain his childlike enjoyment of peeing in the woods.

Community Commentary

Kirk Salopek: Like everything that Lynch does, the attention to detail and obscure subtlety is expounded most in his pairing of sound and picture. There aren't many directors out there that can do it like he does. Back in 2010, Silencio formed because we felt there was a real need to commemorate what he did sonically, but also give the listener a real-time, immersive experience. We were not the least bit concerned about putting our spin on things. It was really about getting it right and making the music sound just like it did in the films. Our time to be creative and pay respects to his influence came across in our original offerings, which audiences loved, and so did we.

Tom Wubker (*Chopping Wood Inside*: A *Twin Peaks* Podcast): I missed the first season of *Twin Peaks* even though I was aware of the show tangentially and already a confirmed disciple of the cinematic Lynch cult. A beautiful and mysterious girl owned my heart, my every thought. It was Laura (coincidentally) and I had no interest in school, sports, or network television. But the power of Lynch and Frost compels. Months later, I was loaned VHS tapes of the first season and watched the pilot and subsequent seven episodes in one night. In the morning, I told my mother I wasn't feeling well and stayed home from school. I binged the first season twice more that same day. I had never seen anything like *Twin Peaks*. It was a revelation. The mystery of 'Who Killed Laura Palmer' became an obsession. I wanted to be smart like Agent Cooper, cool like Bobby Briggs. I wanted to be a Horne brother! I had a strong desire to drink coffee and smoke cigarettes at the RR, even though I didn't drink coffee or smoke cigarettes. I fell in love with Audrey Horne, the music, the trees, the dreams and nightmares, the mystery and the weirdness. A beautiful and surreal television show owned my heart, my every thought. It was *Twin Peaks*.

Chapter 20

Season 2: Episode 18
"Masked Ball"
Aired: December 15, 1990
Written by Barry Pullman
Directed by Duwayne Dunham

The Log-line

Deputy Hawk explains the White and Black Lodges and DEA Agent Denise Bryson arrives in Twin Peaks to investigate Cooper.

Behind the Curtain

Harley Peyton: When Mark was doing *Storyville* [film], I was really number three I guess you could say. I then had to step up and try to run things as best as I could. And for the first time, god knows. If an actor wanted to talk about a script or whatever, I was the person who was doing that because Mark was not there. He was obviously reviewing every script and every outline from afar. I would come in and rewrite sometimes. That was a big year for me and a busy year for me because I ended up doing a lot of the show running towards the second half of the second season.

Charlotte Stewart: I was in the scene and it didn't make sense to me that Betty wouldn't know that [Major Briggs] had a secret life. She had to be a part of that. And so I said, "You know this dialogue doesn't make any sense?" And they said, "Well, we'll have to go talk to the writers." The writer came down and I said, "It seems to me Betty would know, not what specifically he was doing, but that it was secret and anything she knows, she can't talk about." And they went, "You're right." So that's how that scene ended up.

Caleb Deschanel: I don't think David had any idea how much work it was to do a show like that. He was interested in directing his own episodes. In the second year, I think Harley Peyton sort of took over as producer/writer on the thing and it became much more like old-fashioned TV where suddenly if you wanted to make a change, you couldn't just sort of do it. You'd never be changing anything seriously, but if an actor wanted to sort of change something slightly, you'd say, "Yeah, go ahead." It felt a little bit more restrictive than it did in the earlier days of doing this show.

Harley Peyton: [Transgender DEA Agent Denise Bryson] was a great character. It's the Eddie Izzard thing. It does seem a little ahead of its time.

Mark Frost (Co-Creator): Yeah, looking back it was kind of groundbreaking. We didn't try to make too big a deal about it. We had a character who had these concerns and these experiences and we just put it out there. I can't recall having seen it prior to that on network television shows.

David Duchovny (Denise Bryson): First of all, I was just so happy to be on *Twin Peaks* because I had watched the show the year before and I had known Sheryl Lee and was so amazed by the show. A big fan of David Lynch's and I just didn't want to fuck it up.

I guess from what I'd heard at the time and later, James Spader had come up with this character idea with Mark Frost. I think they were friends. This drug enforcement agent that went undercover as a transvestite for some reason and then liked it and decided to dress that way. So I guess Spader got busy and they just opened up auditions and I remember I went in there and I didn't dress to go in there. I just wore my clothes. And I brought a nail file. I thought it was pretty clever. I should have brought a nail file into more auditions. At that point, I was just going for any parts that I could and then I got this. I really was surprised that I got the part.

Harley Peyton: We had a lot of people come in to read for [Denise Bryson] and David was just amazing. You knew immediately that he was going to be the person that was going to play that part.

David Duchovny: Then I was like, "Well, what am I going to do?" I probably had a lot of ideas and then once I got into wardrobe and I did all of the makeup and the wig, I realized that the mask or the costume was going to say so much and that I could probably pull it back a little and just be comfortable and portray this person as having found their true face in a way. I just remember approaching it just as, "Okay if you're a person and you found your true face or the mask that fits, how open would that make you?" And then I just went into every scene trying to feel joyful and open, finally comfortable, comfortable in my skin and my clothes. So that was it. It was just kind of that feeling.

Harley Peyton: One of the nice things was that we could do whatever we wanted. So it wasn't like we didn't have a network kind of worrying about whether we were doing something that they didn't want to see. ABC sometimes gets criticized because there wasn't a third season. Nonetheless, the show is what it is because they gave us complete and utter creative freedom to write the show and make the show that we wanted to make and that doesn't happen anymore. ABC took a real leap of faith with the show back then.

Favorite Quotes and Scenes

Ben: Some of the best parts of the *Twin Peaks* storyline during this period are the local legends that are explored. It doesn't all fit together perfectly, but it gives viewers a deeper understanding that good and evil entities have been a part of the town for a very long time.

Bryon: *Twin Peaks* was ahead of its time back then with the Denise/Dennis character. They played it straight-laced and not for laughs. That is something they didn't do in the early nineties.

My favorite scene is when a malted whipped topping blows into Dick's face and a spinning diner chair sends Andy flying to the floor. I love how this plays out and yet again just shows how this show can go from one extreme to the next all in 45 minutes.

Ben: Many people say that this plotline is one of the worst of *Twin Peaks*. I'm glad you enjoyed that scene.

Bryon: Not all Little Nicky scenes are golden, but I felt this one is fun. A very Three Stooges feel.

Ben: My quote comes from Gordon Cole, "Let a smile be your umbrella." It's a great saying by Cole. During rough times, a smile will go a long way.

Community Commentary

Rosie (producer and host, *Diane* podcast): I first watched *Twin Peaks* alone in my bedroom around my thirteenth birthday, which would have been in 1997. It was long after the show had aired in the UK, but before I was using the internet regularly, so the only way I could find people to talk about the show with was by forcing friends to watch it. Luckily, the fusion of teenage gossip, murder mystery, magical elements, and extremely beautiful actors made it easy to get others on board. Now I produce a *Twin Peaks* podcast, *Diane*, and through this have come to feel like part of a much wider community of weirdos. The great thing about *Twin Peaks* fans is that they're never boring. It used to feel very lonely in these woods and now it's an absolute party.

Chapter 21

Season 2: Episode 19
"The Black Widow"
Aired: January 12, 1991
Written by Harley Peyton & Robert Engels
Directed by Caleb Deschanel

The Log-line

Cooper checks out Dead Dog Farm and Major Briggs returns to his family after being gone for two days.

Behind the Curtain

David Duchovny: I'd done a couple of bit parts of movies and I'd done *The Rapture* [film] a little before this, but this was my first television role. I remember using Nair on the hair on my legs. And I won't forget that smell either. It's kind of like burning everything off of your body. An interesting product to have on the shelves. The clothes, the pantyhose, and stuff were uncomfortable.

Remembering back to shooting the first few, way back when in Season 2, I just remember Kyle MacLachlan was so nice and just really supportive, not just of the work I was doing but of me as a person. I have found Kyle to be, even though we're not in touch, I have found him to be one of the genuinely sweet, good people in Hollywood and I enjoyed working with Michael Horse. I was just so thrilled to be there.

Charlotte Stewart on Major Briggs returning to Betty: I think it's one of the few times in the whole series that you see that there was a love story [between Betty and Major Briggs]. You don't have to spell it out. You can see it in the way [Betty Briggs] was worrying and frantic that he was gone. But there was so much she didn't know about what Major Briggs did. It was all very secretive, but you could see the love there.

Sherilyn Fenn: On-screen chemistry can be very different from offscreen chemistry. Kyle and I were friends. We didn't have what I would call chemistry, but when Special Agent Dale Cooper and Audrey Horne came together, something happened. It just did. And at a certain point, David said, "Are you in love with Kyle?" And I was like, "God no. Not even a little. At all. But Audrey thinks he's the bee's knees."

Harley Peyton: Obvious she was crazy about him. When we were talking about the second season, [part of the plan was] following a relationship between Cooper and Audrey, and who knows where it would have gone or how it would have been or even how romantic it would have been, but based on that, the question was just how would we kind of deal with that and what would we do with it? And that was going to be a big part of the second season, but I think Kyle just didn't want to do it. He didn't think it felt right.

Kyle MacLachlan: It was sort of a charming little diversion for Coop and [Audrey] was obviously fascinated with him, infatuated with him. I thought that was great, but I said this really can't continue. She's in high school. I know it's sort of alluring and interesting, but we can't really make this a part of it.

Sherilyn Fenn: I was really, really upset that they moved me away from Dale Cooper.

Kyle MacLachlan: They resisted a little bit, but I said I'm pretty adamant about it. So they ultimately kind of wrote around that and it didn't end up being sort of the Audrey/Cooper Romance. I didn't feel it was right for the character, for the story. Right or wrong, those were the choices that were made at the time. He's got such a strong moral compass and to see that bend in the face of, albeit, a very lovely and attractive and sexy young woman, I think we lose some Cooper there.

Harley Peyton: The reason that actors will do anything for [David Lynch] is pretty much he'll do anything for them. And so on a lot of television shows, by the way, this was my opinion, you would just say to Kyle, "No you're doing it. We're not going to screw up the second season because you have this problem."

Mark and I have these discussions and at one point that seemed to be where we were headed, but as it turned out, no, we decided not to do it. That was really one of the few times in the whole process where I really felt like, well that may have been a wrong turn because it did take away a rather substantial storyline that we wanted to follow in the second season.

Favorite Quotes and Scenes

Ben: My favorite scene is Audrey bringing photos to Cooper and him saying she may have saved his life. I loved this idea of Audrey rescuing Cooper when he is in trouble. Also when Denise comes by, Audrey seems both to be jealous of and to have respect for Denise. Maybe if the show hadn't been canceled, Audrey would have pursued a career in the FBI in a future season.

Bryon: It was a missed opportunity not making Audrey an FBI agent in Season 3. We saw, especially in Season 1, that she was kind of a Nancy Drew type, trying to help Cooper solve the Laura Palmer case

Ben: As Audrey leaves Cooper's room, she gives him a kiss on the lips. This will be the last time they have a real moment together, which is a shame.

My favorite quote comes after Cooper thinks Denise would not like girls anymore. Denise Bryson expresses, "Coop, I may be wearing a dress, but I still put my panties on one leg at a time." I take that to mean that she may be a woman, but she still likes women. Just because she is transgender does not suggest what her sexual orientation is. It's a great line and it shows Denise hasn't really changed that much.

Bryon: My favorite scene involves this wonderfully filmed scene of Dale Cooper talking to Diane. A closeup profile shot of Cooper, front-lit from the window across from his bed. We go from a close-up of his mouth to the newspaper of Windom Earl's next move to a profile shot of Cooper's face while holding his trusty tape recorder. This has a very noir feel to it.

My favorite quote is from Big Ed Hurley: "I'm living my life, Norma. I just don't like it much." This is the love triangle that matters to me: Hank, Big Ed, and Norma. We finally see Ed and Norma reconnecting at the Double R. This is the only side plotline I'm really invested in at this point.

Ben: Big Ed and Norma are so wonderful together. We root for them to be together.

Community Commentary

Mark O'Brien: I'm an original *Twin Peaks* kid. I first discovered the show when I was 11 in 1991 when it was on BBC 2 in the UK on Tuesday nights at 9 pm. The first episode I watched was Episode 14 with the big reveal, but it was also a great first episode to view as it showcased all the elements of the show— the funny, the sad, the good and the evil, the night and the day, and the wind and the trees including Julee Cruise singing on stage at the Roadhouse. Then *The Return* was announced and I finally made the pilgrimage to Snoqualmie and North Bend and met a *Twin Peaks* family of fans, including the guys who wrote this book. The *Twin Peaks* community really is a whole damn fine town of wonderful people!

Harry Goaz and Mark O'Brien

Chapter 22

Season 2: Episode 20
"Checkmate"
Aired: January 19, 1991
Written by Harley Peyton
Directed by Todd Holland

The Log-line

Jean Renault holds Cooper hostage.

Behind the Curtain

Sabrina Sutherland: Mark Frost was really the person who ran the second season and he was there and Harley Peyton, I think, was considered the showrunner. It really was Mark who was running it with him, kind of the overseer of Harley and Bob Engels. Those were the main three I remember. And then David came in for his shows.

Harley Peyton: Mark came out of television, he'd done television prior. He knew how a television show needed to run. And David was coming from movies. He's much more about inspiration at the moment. So the kind of linear thinking, well we can't really do this here because in three episodes we're doing that over there, that's just not something that David's thinking about. He's thinking in much larger strokes or oddly enough, in even smaller ones.

There was this weird period where Mark went off to direct *Storyville*. I was the number two guy and so suddenly I was in charge or in charge as much as I needed to be. I was in constant communication with Mark, who was shooting down in New Orleans. I think they had like a 21-day schedule, so he was gone for a while, but the fact of the matter is, I was left to make certain decisions and David was not pleased by a couple of them.

Todd Holland: At the beginning of Season 2, David and Mark were very much there and by the end of Season 2, less so. Mark was [doing] *Storyville*. David was doing art shows in the east, in Japan. As far as I remember that time, we didn't see them much by Episode [20]. Harley Peyton largely took over by the end. They really were consulting, but they weren't around. (*Courtesy of The Red Room Podcast Ep125*)

Harley Peyton: There's this weird urban legend that David was there in Season 1 and gone in Season 2 and that's just not true. David's office is right across the way from mine and, actually, to me, the real absence in that season, although I'm sure Todd may be right about Japan, was Mark because Mark went off to direct a movie. I know he probably wishes he hadn't done that now, in the focus of time.

Tony Krantz: I remember going to a restaurant, it was called Muse. It was a restaurant that David, Mark, and I would go to all the time at night, or David and I would just go by ourselves. David was one of my dearest friends. We'd have Thanksgiving together. We were very, very close in those days. And I remember the three of us having dinner at Muse. I said, "You guys are much stronger together than you are apart. The success that you've had has been legion. We need you guys to grasp hands and work together, and that's really the secret of the relationship." I remember literally grabbing both their hands and having them hold each other's hands across the table.

Harley Peyton: Todd called me one night and this was my midnight phone call and he said, "I just got off the phone with David and he has all these notes, but my whole day is set for tomorrow morning. I can't really shoot what I planned because of the things that he was talking to me about." I said, "Shoot your day exactly like you planned it. I'll handle this." Then I talked to Mark, who I think was probably then in New Orleans, and said, "David can't give notes at 11:00 at night, the night before we're shooting. It makes it impossible for production." And he said, "Fine. No problem. I'll take care of it." [laughs] I got a phone call from David the next day, which I remember to this day, he was not too happy. This was before meditation I guess.

Who can blame him? Suddenly, there I am, sort of saying "No, you can't give notes the night before we're shooting something." So believe me, he was there and very active.

Ken Scherer: Mark went off and made a movie, so I was commuting back and forth. I was going to *Storyville* down in New Orleans on production with Mark, and I was trying to keep David happy. David once described me in a public meeting as a camp counselor. Towards the end, I really felt like I was the marriage counselor.

Todd Holland: I kind of felt pressured 'cause the first opening [Episode 11, Leland interrogation] was so successful. I remember the whole deep space thing was me. And it was more trying too hard. When the first one was so organic, that the second one felt less so, but they still went for it.

Eric Da Re: There was no background really of [Leo] or where he came from, how he met Shelly. I guess it didn't matter at that point, but to get to where they did so quickly in two seasons with the character was just too much, too fast. The thing that killed me, because I wasn't there when they were shooting it, was when Nadine Hurley got superhuman strength. I was like, "Uh-oh, it's going somewhere else."

Todd Holland: That episode went on location; we got out to the Dead Dog Farm and all that. But the first one [directed] felt so tight and so clear, and we're so embedded in the Laura Palmer narrative that it just felt so dreadfully compelling and I always thought that [Episode 20] just lost steam.

David Duchovny: I just have a memory of meeting [David Lynch] at the *Twin Peaks* wrap party way back when. We met and I said, "Nice to meet you." He said something like, "I'm so glad I didn't have any scenes with you because you would have stolen the scene." I was like, "Oh yeah, thanks."

Twin Peaks is so totally transformative of the medium. I don't want to say *The X-Files* came out of it, but *The X-Files* is kind of a straight version, in a way, of *Twin Peaks* , and from *The X-Files* television changes as well. It's such a generative kind of show, even though there were only two years, and then the third. When I look back, I got to be in *Twin Peaks* and *The X-Files* and *Larry Sanders*, and I feel like I couldn't have done better in terms of television.

Favorite Quotes and Scenes

Bryon: My favorite quote comes from Norma: "You're the last thing I think of when I go to sleep at night and the first thought on my mind in the morning." The reason I picked this quote is that this is a turning point for Big Ed and Norma. It looks like they can finally be together, or so they think.

Ben and **Bryon:** Our favorite scene is with Renault having Cooper captured at gunpoint at Dead Dog Farm and a standoff with the Twin Peaks Sheriff Department outside.

Bryon: Jean Renault, played by Michael Parks, gives us a fantastic performance that will definitely be missed after this episode. Before Jean Renault meets his demise, he gives us an interesting monologue about his thoughts on Dale Cooper.

Ben: Yeah that's my favorite quote. "So if you die, maybe you will be the last to die. Maybe you brought the ... the nightmare with you, and maybe the nightmare will die with you."

There is darkness in Cooper's life, but he is not a bad person. Bad things follow Dale Cooper, from his childhood (*My Life, My Tapes*), to the death of Caroline, and into Twin Peaks. It's clear though that Cooper and Renault have different interpretations of good and evil. Cooper's idea of heaven is coffee and cherry pie, while Jean's world of heaven is selling drugs, going to One-Eyed Jacks, and not getting caught. Now he is not happy that the law has caught up with him and destroyed the corrupt world he made for himself.

Bryon: A fantastic scene that made you wish Jean Renault lasted longer so as a foil to Dale Cooper.

Community Commentary

David Wirch: Of course, I love the characters and stories in *Twin Peaks*, but the supernatural scenes have been especially inspiring to me over the years. The iconic Red Room, the Lodge spirits, even creamed corn. I first watched *Twin Peaks* at a formative age, and it undoubtedly played an important role in how I learned to enjoy and create art. I just love it!

Chapter 23

Season 2: Episode 21
"Double Play"
Aired: February 2, 1991
Written by Scott Frost
Directed by Uli Edel

The Log-line

Jean Renault holds Cooper hostage.

Behind the Curtain

Scott Frost: I remember [that episode] was directed by Uli Edel who was a really talented independent filmmaker. Did some pretty interesting films.

Uli Edel (Director): I had just arrived in Hollywood from Germany and lived at the Chateau Marmont Hotel when I ran into David Lynch in the lobby. We had met years before in Munich when I worked on the German trailers for *Dune*. David: What are you doing in Hollywood? Me: My movie *Last Exit to Brooklyn* is opening. David: Are you staying for longer? Me: If I'll find a gig. David: Direct a *Twin Peaks* episode for me. That is how I got my first job in Hollywood.

A day before we started shooting, Diane Keaton suddenly stood in my office and asked if she could watch me direct. She was scheduled to do the next episode and was quite nervous and unsure if she could complete it in the limited time frame. I was of course surprised. "Diane, you've worked with Francis Ford Coppola, Georg Roy Hill, Richard Brooks, and Woody Allen. What more can you learn from me?" She told me she wanted to see how, within seven days, anybody could accomplish an entire *Twin Peaks* episode. She'd sit on a chair in the corner and of course not disturb me. Of course, I felt honored; Diane Keaton wanting to observe me at work.

My first shooting day was an office with a dead man sitting at his desk. Special Agent Cooper had just discovered him in the episode before, which was directed by Todd Holland.

In the middle of the set though, there also lay a huge stag head. That wasn't in the script.

I asked the AD why it was there. He told me with a smile that Todd had already established the stag head on the desk and therefore it had to remain there. "You got pranked by Todd! Now you have to somehow incorporate the stag head into the story." But how? Diane Keaton, watching me from her chair in the back, was wondering as well how I would deal with this. I had to make a decision quickly, the clock was ticking. I told Kyle and his policemen to "Pursue your investigation as planned and ignore the stag head as if it isn't there." That's how I shot the entire scene and to this day people ask me, "Why doesn't anyone see the stuffed stag head on that desk?" I always answer: "That's the *Twin Peaks* effect!"

Kyle MacLachlan on his brother Craig MacLachlan: [My brother] was in LA and kind of looking for something to do, and he's incredibly well-organized and good with people. I'm not quite sure how he got involved, but he was a PA on the set for *Twin Peaks*, which is kind of the low man on the totem pole, but he took that in stride and he's very capable. Had he just wanted to continue a career in film and that kind of side of things, he would've done very well. Probably would be a first AD by now. But he was doing it more just for fun. And so they thought it would be kind of kooky to have him in it. At the time he had super, super long hair 'cause he had just finished his work with a band. They stuck him in a chair and made him a victim of Windom Earle. He loved it. He had a great time.

He would wrangle all the actors, trying to get them to the set on time. And he had his hardest time with Michael Ontkean [Sheriff Harry Truman]. Ontkean would finish the scene and before they were turning around he would like make a beeline for his trailer and ended up taking off all of the sheriff's gear. He had a gun, and the hat ... and then they'd call him back to set and he'd come to the door and he'd be dressed in his t-shirt and underwear. Craig would be like, "Mike, we gotta get back to the set, man, come on." Somehow Craig was able to finagle him and get him back in time.

Scott Frost: So much of the work of an episode is just getting that structural flow from scene to scene working. I just knew the characters. I never really had a concern about the sort of backstory, making sure all that worked. It was just about making a coherent piece of cinema, in a sense.

[*The Civil War*, documentary miniseries by Ken Burns in 1990] took the country by the throat and said, watch this. And I don't think any of us were any different. It sort of fit into [Ben Horne's] kind of strange meltdown [laughs]. It got a little goofy, but I think that was part of the inspiration.

Bob Engels: I wanted to get [Richard] Beymer and Russ Tamblyn to sing together 'cause they hadn't done it since *West Side Story* [film]. They both said no, they're not going to do it. And then they both did it.

Dana Ashbrook: Once the whole Cooper [and Audrey relationship] thing got derailed, I think they maybe for a second they thought [about hooking Bobby and Audrey together]. I think they were just kind of trying all sorts of stuff at that point. It seemed like they were going for that for a couple of episodes and then it just petered off. I never really got to the bottom of it.

Sherilyn Fenn: No they were not going to do that. They just didn't know what to do with Bobby and they wanted him around more. He's my buddy. I love him so much, but no, they weren't going to hook us up at all.

Scott Frost: The camera just ate up Sherilyn Fenn, and she was such a little sex bomb that you couldn't place any one of those young men in a room with her and not have that be an element.

Harley Peyton: Windom Earle must have made his first appearance in a script I wrote because that's when you get to name characters usually. I named him. It's a combination of the names, one actor and one character. There was a minor league movie actor named William Windom; Windom being his last name. Who knows, maybe I saw an old movie on TV that night. And Humphrey Bogart in *High Sierra*, his character's name is Mad Dog Roy Earle. Out of that just came Windom Earle. I just took one name and put it with the other and it really felt right. And obviously, Mark went, "Oh cool, let's do that." And of course, the actor who played the part was so tremendous. He's actually a good friend of Bob Engels.

Bob Engels: Ken Welsh, I've known forever. That was my idea to cast Ken.

Kenneth Welsh: It so happened I was making a TV movie in Los Angeles. My ex-wife, Donna, called me up and said, "Kenny, Bob Engels is working on a new series." Bob and Donna were students at the University of Minnesota when I was working at the Guthrie Theater there in 1973. And so we were all good friends. I knew Bob very well and she said, "Kenny, you have to call Bob." So I did; I called Bob and he said, "Ken, funny you should call. There's this great part that's coming up on the series and it's totally right for you. Can you come on the set and meet a few people?" So I go out to the set and David wasn't there. I never met him until much later. Mark Frost was there. I met Mark, and I met the wardrobe lady. And that was it. And Bob said, "Well, you're hired. And you start next week." I said, "Ah, yeah, I guess so." I had no idea about the series. I'd never seen it. I looked through [the script] a little bit and I thought this character looks interesting. So that's how I got the part.

Favorite Quotes and Scenes

Ben and **Bryon:** Our favorite scene is Agent Cooper opening up to Truman about the baggage he brought to Twin Peaks. We learn Cooper fell in love with Caroline, Windom Earle's wife, who he was supposed to protect. Cooper believes Windom Earle killed her.

Ben: My favorite quote is from Major Briggs: "I will be in the shadows if you need me." Cooper has an ally in Major Briggs. In Season 3, Major Briggs will still provide support to Cooper, but from another time and place.

Bryon: My favorite quote comes from Norma Jennings: "It's time I started correcting some mistakes I've made." Sitting in the Double R Diner, Big Ed and Norma express their love for each other, free from Nadine and Hank. We can now see one of the best love stories in *Twin Peaks* blossom before our very eyes. I just love that quote and these two together.

Community Commentary

Rob King: *Twin Peaks* is a series that came to me through its ads in its original run and its homage in *Northern Exposure*. That is to say, it came to me in fragments and a lot of waiting. It spoke to me through girlfriends, one in 1997 who would speak to me of Bobby, Leo, and Laura. She introduced me to *Wild at Heart*. Another girlfriend in 2000 would ruin me on *Fire Walk with Me*. That very week, I found a used VHS cassette of the international pilot, which left me thoroughly confused and enraptured until the release of the Artisan

DVD set for Season 1, which would then leave me waiting for Season 2 five or six years later. Mysterious how it wanted to introduce itself to me over the years—tenacious, really. That I associate my introduction to it through young love, I now realize, will always be cool.

Chapter 24

Season 2: Episode 22
"Slaves and Masters"
Aired: February 9, 1991
Written by Harley Peyton & Robert Engels
Directed by Diane Keaton

The Log-line
Ben Horne's Civil War reenactment concludes.

Behind the Curtain
Robert Bauer (Johnny Horne): Diane [Keaton], it was like being directed by Annie Hall. [She was] sort of fluid and fun and giggly and laughy and just on board with all of it. She was just sweet and lovely and she knew what she was after. Also, just an artist, top to toe, and was all about the exploration and feeling things out. I just remember laughing a lot that day.

Harley Peyton: Diane Keaton obviously is Diane Keaton. So that was sort of a big deal. There were certain directors who came in and did an extraordinary job executing the way the scripts had been written and they would bring certain things to them, but really what was significant about her work was just how much visual interest she brought to it. All those guys sitting at the bar in their identical uniforms. Everybody wanted to direct episodes. We had a lot of episodes that needed directing and she was a really happy addition to the show.

Kenneth Welsh: The script indicated that Windom played the flute. So I told Bob [Engels], "I play the Shakuhachi flute, which is a Japanese flute made from bamboo. If we can make a rubber version of that, I can beat the shit out of [Leo] with it." He said, "Great idea!"

So I get on the phone with Angelo Badalamenti. He's in New York. I'm in LA. He says, "Ken, give me the notes on your Shakuhachi." So I played whatever the notes are. And he goes to his piano right on the spot and comes up with this melody. He says, "Can you play this?" And I play it. Then I went off to the sound man. We recorded it four or five times and we had something. Then I beat [Leo] up with the rubber Shakuhachi. But they didn't use it, unfortunately. No, they use the synthesizer instead. I was disappointed.

I met David when Diane Keaton was directing. I was dressed in this sort of weird plaid outfit playing the sort of Greek character and David comes by and he said, "No, that's wrong." She said, "What?" [He said] "No that's wrong. Windom should be dressed in a black, worn-out, torn FBI outfit. Black suit." Then he's gone. I never saw him again until the final episode.

Robert Bauer: I got lost in the second [season]. I literally stopped reading the scripts because I was like, I don't fucking know what's happening. I read the script. I don't know what's happening. I tried to get through what I could, and then I would get to my scenes and go, okay.

Tony Krantz: It became like this Russian novel of character after character sprawling out in a sort of unending way. And all the core characters were never really dealt with. There were no storylines interweaving the series regulars. It was always about what we can do that's new and where we can take a story.

You look at a show like *Succession* ... You're really dealing with all the core characters. You fall in love with the characters and you can't wait to see what's next and you tune in to the next episode as a result. There was no interest that was created from a story point of view where people just got fed up with it. It's like quirky and weird and I don't even know who this character is. It was basic storytelling 101 that was missed and it's frankly harder to write stories about your core characters because you've got to interweave them and it's complicated. It's easier to just forget about them and just write new stuff. And that was, I think, the biggest reason why the show failed.

Harley Peyton: There was definitely the Audrey spinoff idea because I think, in a weird way, that ended up being *Mulholland Drive* [film]. They had a story for her. They had a whole thing that they wanted to do.

Ken Scherer: There was a wonderful concept which David would later exercise which was called *Mulholland Drive* and that conversation began: "What if we took [Audrey] and put her out of *Twin Peaks* and she moves to Hollywood?"

Tony Krantz: I had this very novel idea to mix movies and television. Had *Twin Peaks* succeeded, what would have happened? What our plan was, was that there would be a cliffhanger at the end of Season 2, which would be an Audrey Horne cliffhanger which would then tell the story of Audrey's arrival in Hollywood, a story around Hollywood for her that would be a movie that David would direct, that would come out in the summer between the second and third season. Then, *Mulholland Drive* would spin off into its own series and the third year as the Hollywood story of Audrey Horne. But when *Twin Peaks* failed in the second season, all of that went out the window.

Sherilyn Fenn: We had dinner with my longtime manager, [David Lynch], and his agent Tony Krantz. They said they wanted to do a spinoff where Audrey goes to Hollywood and it was called *Mulholland Drive* and again, me being young and dumb, I said, "Well, do people do that? What's it about? Is Agent Cooper in it? I don't understand."

Ken Scherer: Where Mark wanted to take it was: "How do we extend *Twin Peaks*?" But David was very protective of the concept. These are hard decisions that creative partners make all the time and some [are] more successful than others.

Sherilyn Fenn: It never ended up happening. Well, it did turn into a movie later, but I wasn't asked to join, but life went on.

Tony Krantz: But the idea of a Hollywood story with David was something that I always wanted to do. I love the idea of Audrey Horne and *Mulholland Drive*. So it took me ten years to convince David to do it after the demise of *Twin Peaks*. He didn't want to go into TV, and he blamed the medium rather than the show.

Brings Back Some Memories

Ben: This episode was directed by Diane Keaton and is a bit controversial for some because of her over-stylized directing. The wacky characters and the tone of the episode did not stay true to *Twin Peaks*. I, personally, liked Keaton's style for these reasons. She brought in her own perspective to the *Twin Peaks* world including things like extreme close-ups of chess pieces and strange characters who speak and move in unison. I thought it was humorous and a fresh take on the show.

Bryon: I think Diane Keaton did a fantastic job directing this episode. It felt like a Lynch-directed episode and Keaton deserves the credit in giving this episode a different style. This was my favorite episode of the second half of Season 2. We get more subplots while wrapping up others and focusing on Windom Earle. We kind of get a network television version of John Doe (Kevin Spacey's character in *Seven*). I could see Earle putting a head in a box if this was not aired on the ABC network. He has this devilish, sinister feel to him. I think he could have been a lot worse if it wasn't for network censors.

Favorite Quotes and Scenes

Ben: My favorite scene is with Agent Albert Rosenfield updating Harry and Cooper. He enters the conference room and tells Bobby to "Get a life, punk," gives Harry a bear hug (they are friends now), and tells Cooper that Gordon Cole is "worried about Coop." Miguel Ferrer is just an amazing actor and knows how to play Albert as sarcastic, serious, and funny.

Ben and **Bryon:** Our favorite quote is from Albert Rosenfield, "Coop, about the uniform ... replacing the quiet elegance of the dark suit and tie with the casual indifference of these muted earth tones is a form of fashion suicide, but, call me crazy—on you, it works."

Bryon: I have learned over my time doing the *Twin Peaks Unwrapped* podcast that David Lynch didn't like Dale Cooper in flannel but in all honesty, he pulls it off.

Ben: I love Cooper in his black suit. It is his classic look, but it's fun to see Cooper become a local townsperson for awhile.

Bryon: My favorite scene is Windom Earle controlling Leo Johnson to write mysterious letters to Shelly, Donna, and Audrey. There is some irony in Leo Johnson becoming a victim after he was controlling and abusive to Shelly. I don't think any fan of this show feels bad about what is happening to Leo at this point.

Ben: He's getting a taste of his own medicine. That's kharma.

Community Commentary

Andrew Blossom (Organizer, The Great Southern): When *Twin Peaks* first aired, I was a kid. Something of a media-savvy kid. The phenomenon definitely caught my attention—I remember the all-black newspaper ads and Homer pretending to understand the show on *The Simpsons*. My parents watched *Twin Peaks*, at least during its first season, and I very distinctly recall being told to leave the room when it came on. Because I was devoted to video stores, it wasn't long before I found David Lynch that way: *Eraserhead, Dune.* And when the collective *Twin Peaks* came out on VHS, that was it. I was wholly, utterly in love. That VHS set began with the European version of the pilot, whose extra ending was strange, beautiful, melancholy, somber—solving the mystery of Laura Palmer's death without providing any kind of concrete answer, setting up the template for what followed. It opened up worlds to me. In the many years since, I've watched *Twin Peaks* and *Fire Walk with Me* countless times. Each time, it feels like going home. This is one reason I'm grateful for *The Return*—in addition to the sheer brilliance of its making, it shows us that home was always more complicated than we ever understood.

David Bushman, Arthur Smith, Pieter Dom, Scott Ryan, Brad Dukes, Charlotte Stewart And John Thorne, at The Great Southern in 2016.

Chapter 25

Season 2: Episode 23
"The Condemned Woman"
Aired: February 16, 1991
Written by Tricia Brock
Directed by Lesli Linka Glatter

The Log-line

Agent Cooper and Sheriff Truman confront Josie Packard and the Great Northern's nightstand drawer knob becomes haunted.

Behind the Curtain

Lesli Linka Glatter: The first two [episodes] I did were before you found out who Laura Palmer's murderer was. And then I think the show shifted quite a lot after you found that out. And I did one more episode afterward and that was a different experience. That was a different vibe.

Todd Holland: I watched Lesli Linka Glatter's episode on network TV and forgot what would come up next. Then I see Josie morphs into a nightstand knob. I called Lesli up and was like "What the fuck was that?" and she goes, "I don't know."

They didn't tell you anything. They said, "Here's what you're doing." And you did it. It really is remarkable for a series where you're so working in the blind and there wasn't a writer sitting beside you every second to help make sure you didn't veer off of the narrative. Nowadays, there would be somebody there who had a bigger sense of the picture, but the directors only knew what was on the page. You knew what was behind you and what was on the page. You had no idea what the next episode was indicating or what it was going to be. It made it fun. (*Courtesy of* The Red Room Podcast *Ep125*)

Harley Peyton: For David, I think, it was if Joan doesn't want to do [*Twin Peaks*], then Joan doesn't have to do it. That wouldn't really be the way things would be done usually. On most TV shows, "Okay you want to leave the show? You're going to be here for the rest of the season, then you can leave." We all know examples of actors being killed because they weren't happy. That certainly happens, but I think in this case there was a freer attitude, I think, amongst everyone that allowed for that. And so as a writer, you just had to sort of field it and do your best job. In other words, if you knew that certain characters were going to be gone or wouldn't be available or were doing something else, you just had to write around that and then sometimes just hope for the best.

Joan Chen's letter to David Lynch before the start of Season 3 as Josie Packard:

Dear David,

I write to you from the wooden drawer knob in which I have been trapped for the past two decades, yearning restlessly for an escape. I hear voices whispering the rumor of a return to my body, and I implore you, O Creator, to let me come back. It seems that the possibilities of who I shall become are as infinite as your fecund imagination.

From my oubliette within the chest of drawers, I can sometimes see bodies fumbling, sweating and convulsing with lust, and I long for my physical form—once strong and lithe, now old and shriveled, or perhaps plump and fertile with age like a rosehip to rose.

Oftentimes I think of Judy, my twin sister. I imagine her wandering drunkenly into the room holding the drawers which imprison me, incinerating suddenly due to the sheer volume and flammability of the alcohol in her veins. In my mind's eye, I see her burning; I admire the bright color of the flames spreading to the drawers, the air breathing back the energy that was once her spirit. We could inhabit one body together, just as we had done as mere cells in our mother's womb. Once again, our two souls could crowd one vessel, forcing us to struggle for mine—or could it?—as my being invades Judy's body like a parasite.

Would the physical universe overwhelm me? Would the exhale of a housefly compound into dissonant chords, lunging anguished and unrestrained at my eardrums? Would each microbe terrify me, leave me with nowhere to hide, nowhere to run from the insolent bubbling of nature in its purest form, like Petri dishes pungent with life, proliferating perpetually, bursting with unbridled being? Or would all the living things on earth pale in comparison to the countless lost souls caught between worlds, their cries trilling chromatically, enchantingly, in ways that are neither human nor holy?

Do you hear me now—as a rustling in the curtains, murmur in a crowd, an echo without an origin? My time in purgatory has been served, don't you think? Isn't it time I at least get to meet my maker one last time?

Yours,

Josie

Joan Chen (Josie Packard) on why she wrote the letter: I just wanted to bring a smile to [David Lynch's] face when he read the letter.

Chris Mulkey (Hank Jennings): It was 1991 and I was standing by our extensive craft service table in the studio in Van Nuys. Sherilyn Fenn, eating a red vine, looked deep into my eyes and whispered, "Hank, do you believe in the devil?" Melting a little inside, Hank replied, "Yes I do!"

Sherilyn Fenn: Billy Zane. He's a very nice person, but it wasn't right because [the Audrey and Cooper relationship] came organically.

Brings Back Some Memories

Ben: When this episode originally aired, I missed it because I went to a high school dance. For two years, I considered this to be a lost episode until Season 2 came out on VHS. The worst part about missing this episode was that *Twin Peaks* went on hiatus for six weeks after this episode.

Bryon: I was and still am confused about why we got BOB and the Little Man From Another Place showing up on the bed after Josie's death. I felt the writers were just reusing things from the past rather than coming up with something new and different. It almost feels like they broke their own rules on how the Red Room works. Also, the mystery of Josie going into the drawer pull still baffles me. It was a great episode overall, but kind of an odd ending. I feel the writers wanted to remind us of the Red Room because we had veered away from the supernatural elements of the show. I'm still trying to figure out Josie in the wooden drawer pull to this day.

Ben: I agree. You only saw the Little Man From Another Place in the Red Room and it seemed off to see the little man and BOB in the Great Northern.

Favorite Quotes and Scenes

Ben: My favorite scene is the showdown between Harry and Josie. Up to this point, Harry has blindly loved Josie, not understanding that she was manipulating him. With Josie pointing a gun at Cooper, Harry must come to the realization that Josie is not the person he thought she was. Michael Ontkean shouting "Put down the gun!" was intense. A great performance.

Bryon: My favorite scene is Nadine coming home from school and telling Big

Ed that she and Mike are in love. This confession from Nadine is so heartfelt and moving from her, but in the end, this allows Big Ed to finally be with Norma. You can see how relieved Big Ed is hearing this news of her wanting to break up with him.

Ben: My favorite quote is from Andrew Packard who proclaims to Thomas Eckhardt, "I'm alive!" A funny line, but also kind of ridiculous like the whole Josie Packard/Andrew Packard/Thomas Eckhardt storyline.

Bryon: My favorite quote comes from Big Ed: "Norma Jennings, I've loved you every day for the past twenty years. I dream about you every night. It's time for us to be together. Will you marry me?" It was great watching Big Ed march into the Double R and go right behind the counter and take Norma Jennings in his arms and proclaim his love for her right in front of Shelly. A sweet moment between the two, and a romance I think every *Twin Peaks* fan is rooting for. This is my favorite side plot. It's simple and you are just rooting for these two.

Ben: These two care about each other so much that they actually gave up on the thought of being together because they knew that was the right thing to do. Norma understood that Big Ed had a responsibility with Nadine and Big Ed knew that Norma had to deal with Hank.

Bryon: They both had hurdles to overcome and the stars finally aligned for both for a moment.

Community Commentary

Brad Dukes (Author of *Reflections: An Oral history of Twin Peaks, The Blue Rose Magazine*): One of the best things that ever happened to me was discovering *Twin Peaks* at the age of nine. I was captivated from the first image I saw, and that electric feeling of true wonder has yet to leave me as a man thirty years later. *Twin Peaks* is more than a TV show or a movie. More than a continuing story. It is the nightmare I don't want to wake up from.

Chapter 26

Season 2: Episode 24
"Wounds and Scars"
Aired: March 28, 1991
Written by Barry Pullman
Directed by James Foley

The Log-line

Sheriff Truman mourns the death of Josie, and a pine weasel interrupts the Stop Ghostwood Fashion Show.

Behind the Curtain

Ian Buchanan: The pine weasel [episode] I liked. I had no idea what to expect from that day. No idea how it would work. So I think I got lucky with whoever directed it.

Mary Jo Deschanel: The one thing I insisted, I didn't really care about much in terms of a contract, I said I wanted a wheelchair to practice with in my house. So there was a really funny incident. I had the wheelchair in the house and I would get in just to practice how to maneuver the electric wheelchair. I didn't want to not know how to do it, obviously. My children were at home and it was kind of a crazy household. Lots of things always going on in the house, a lot of people coming in and out. And I remember one time I was in the wheelchair and some people came in. I don't know why they were there, but it wasn't someone I knew and they didn't know me and I was in the wheelchair, and they said hello and I didn't think anything of it. And then at some point, I got up out of the wheelchair to go do something and the look on their faces!

The campaign to save *Twin Peaks*/COOP (Citizens Opposing the Offing of Peaks).

Michael Cuputo (Co-founder of COOP): Keith Poston was the one who got me to watch [*Twin Peaks*]. I thought it was probably pretty remarkable for a lot of people. We were both writers on [the Jack Kemp] campaign for president.

Michael Cuputo and David Lynch.

Keith Poston (Co-founder of COOP): *Twin Peaks* did get some mainstream popularity. It was kind of this edgy, odd thing.

We really didn't envision it to be some national campaign. We both had public relations so it really kind of started out as, well we had a group of friends who were pretty upset, bummed out that the show was on hiatus. Mike and I, neither one of us did entertainment PR, we were both more political guys. Let's find out who all the people are at *Variety, Entertainment Weekly,* and *USA Today* and let's put together this organization that we'll say is headquartered here. I don't remember who the very first story was, but I remember a couple of our really big ones. Tom Shales and *The Washington Post* wrote a pretty extensive piece. *USA Today* covered us regularly.

Michael Cuputo: Keith, when somebody asked you, "What do you think of Bob Iger?" you said...

Keith Poston: You remind me today of a small Mexican chihuahua.

Michael Cuputo: In two and a half weeks, we gathered the names and addresses and telephone numbers of 10,000 people, and that was via U.S. mail. Can you imagine what we could have done if we had the internet at our fingertips?

Keith Poston: David Lynch called me at my office. I can still remember that day when I picked up the phone and it was like, "Keith, David Lynch here. I want to tell you what a great job I think y'all are doing." And I'm sitting there thinking, "Aww, fuck you, Mike!" I started laughing. After about a minute where I first said, "Drop it Cuputo. I'm busy," or something, [David Lynch] kept talking, and then Mark Frost was on the phone too, and at that point, I was kinda like, "Holy shit!"

Once we successfully came back, they were like, "Look, we want to say thanks to you guys. What do think about if we have some people come out?" We got Jacoby and Leo, as well as Ken Scherer, who was the head of the studio.

Ken Scherer: There was a bar in DC, which was one of my favorite nights. It was sold out and it was the night that the show [returned from being on hiatus] so it was on the local TV.

Eric Da Re: I flew [to Washington DC]. That was also the night my father [actor Aldo Ray] died.

Johanna Ray: Eric was told when he was on the plane.

Eric Da Re: They actually pulled the plane in right before we're going to take off to see if I wanted to get off 'cause he just passed away. It was weird going out there and having all that happen at the same time. I remember getting to the hotel and turning the TV on. Boom. [The news of my father's passing was] on every news channel. I think it was kind of actually nice seeing that he was not forgotten. I didn't get off the plane 'cause I know that that's what my father would want. You got a commitment and you take care of it. Life is what it is and we all know this happens, so take care of your responsibilities. That's the way he was. So I'll try to make him proud of me.

Brings Back Some Memories

Ben: Back in 1991, I thought the show had been canceled, but after a six-week hiatus, the show returned and was back to Thursday nights like it was in the first season. Heather Graham joins the show as Annie, a love interest for Cooper, and at this point in her career, she was an unknown. Being a fan of the Cooper/Audrey relationship, I wasn't sure about Annie and Cooper. But since Audrey moved on with John Justice Wheeler, it made sense that Cooper would find a love interest.

Bryon: I'm a fan of the Annie and Dale love story.

Favorite Quotes and Scenes

Bryon: My favorite scene is with Dale Cooper sitting at the Double R Diner, drinking coffee and reading his book but having a new waitress, Annie (Norma's sister), greet him in a way that seems to catch him off guard. He seems to be smitten at first glance. He is so taken by Annie that he ignores any strange feelings from Windom Earle dressed as a biker staring at him across the diner. We now know that when Cooper falls in love, this can cloud his natural judgment of his current surroundings.

My favorite quote comes from Deputy Tommy 'Hawk' Hill about Truman. "I've never seen him like this. It was like taking a hike to your favorite spot and finding a hole where the lake used to be." I love this metaphor Hawk uses to describe Harry's love for Josie. The lake feeds the forest and allows everything to grow and live, and that is Harry's heart feeding his body. But once that lake is gone, it is game over for the rest of him. Josie fed that heart and kept Harry going and now he has nothing to live for, and we watch him break down.

Ben: When Cooper talks about Josie's strange death and how it may have to do with what he saw (Little Man and Bob in the Great Northern), Hawk says, "Maybe we better just whistle on our way past the graveyard." Hawk is very in-tune with the mystical parts of Twin Peaks, but he didn't want to touch these supernatural elements. My favorite scene is between Cooper and a depressed, drunk Harry Truman. Cooper listens to his friend in pain and comforts him as he deals with the loss of Josie. It's a wonderful bromance moment.

Community Commentary

Sean Glass: *Twin Peaks* is too big to sum up. My most impactful anecdote though... When I was far too young, I was exposed to this weird world via awkwardly catching the original Red Room sequence while my grandmother watched. I did not understand, yet I got hooked. At the time, 10-years-old-ish, I had a best friend who was the Laura Palmer of my world and community. I understood something that allowed her to open up to me in ways she could not others. Today, I understand I was utilizing the education I received from the character, helping my version avoid the same traps. To this day, there is no more dualistic character, none better drawn. If you ask me, she is simply the most impactful character in the history of storytelling. And *Twin Peaks: The Return* is the greatest set of moving images ever.

Chapter 27

Season 2: Episode 25
"On the Wings of Love"
Aired: April 4, 1991
Written by Harley Peyton & Robert Engels
Directed by Duwayne Dunham

The Log-line

FBI Deputy Director Gordon Cole can hear Shelly Johnson; Cooper, and the sheriff's officers go spelunking in Owl Cave.

Behind the Curtain

Brenda Strong (Miss Jones): It was a true creative adventure for me, and from the start as a girl from the mountains of Oregon, I felt right at home in *Twin Peaks*. A fan of the show going in, getting to work with the caliber of the directors David Lynch assembled was like a master class for a young actor and, with David Warner as a partner in crime, I was in proverbial actor heaven. From being directed by Diane Keaton to James Foley, we got to live in the universe of David's vision and to bring ourselves fully to exploring what wasn't on the page (although learning to speak Afrikaans proved a bit challenging for both David Warner and me).

Finally, attempting to kill the Sheriff was one of those scenes for the record books: part sadism, part seduction, but life-altering and affirming all at once. Such delicious fun to be able to play with such creative and wonderful folk. Getting to play "Jones" the assassin was a dream job. Thank you, David Lynch!

Harley Peyton: [Cooper and Audrey's] connection was great. They worked wonderfully together as actors. I think it was a missed opportunity. Then we had to move her off toward the Billy Zane story, which actually I wrote a lot of and really enjoyed. Then we brought in Heather Graham's character [Annie Blackburn], and that was the story that Cooper did. I feel like that was fine, but it's one of those things I would have loved to had a chance to write [Cooper and Audrey developing a relationship], given how I sort of got it rolling in that third episode.

Heather Graham (Annie Blackburn): I loved working on *Twin Peaks*. I was a huge fan of the show and I had a big crush on Agent Cooper. I was so excited to work with Kyle MacLachlan and David Lynch.

Kenneth Welsh: I always had access to the scripts, actually more than most people because Bob [Engels] was my buddy. When I was your basic Windom, I was in black. Then I decided, as Bob let me do, to play different characters with Windom. [He would say], "In this episode, you're up at the counter at the diner," and I said, "Okay, I'll be a fat biker." I got to choose whatever I wore. I would go in with ideas like that English guy and I thought, "Okay, let's put him in tweed and then I think he should be smoking a pipe…" and blah, blah, like that. I would make this shit up and [wardrobe] would come up with the perfect outfit. I totally trusted the wardrobe.

Mary Jo Deschanel: One thing that was sort of difficult was that I could never know the backstory of why I was in a wheelchair. I remember asking about it and it was like they just laughed and they said, well, we have so many different scenarios that are possible [laughs]. So it was kind of revealed later. I sort of had to have in my mind, as an actress you have to have your own story, but I sort of had to have it a little bit loose. Almost like someone maybe with a faulty memory or not knowing exactly what happened 'cause it could have been completely psychosomatic. I didn't know what it was because they didn't tell me. They had many ideas, but they didn't know which way they were going to go. It just felt like that was who she was. I don't think I thought of myself as being in a wheelchair. I was just like that was my reality.

The Autobiography of F.B.I. Special Agent Dale Cooper: My Life, My Tapes

Ken Scherer: [Mark Frost] was really excited about the Agent Cooper book that his brother Scott wrote. That was a fun project.

Scott Frost: I think I may have finished it before I wrote the first [episode] because that was one of the more insane writing projects I'd ever had. 'Cause I literally had thirty days to write it. It's one of those things where you jump out the door of the airplane and you hope you have a parachute, but you have no idea.

I think part of it was that the cassette tape was pretty successful and it just seemed like such a natural thing in terms of Cooper to flesh that out more. I think that was part of it in terms of my involvement with it. I sort of was his voice at that point to some degree. At least in terms of writing anything in long-form. And everybody else was busy working on scripts. I wasn't, so I was the last person standing.

[For research] I sort of made the grand tour [of Philadelphia]. It was kind of ridiculous cause it was one of those Hollywood comes to Philadelphia things. Ken Scherer came with me 'cause he knew [the area]. So I was being chauffeured around in a limousine and going to all these different places and my main memory is going to get a really terrible Philly cheesesteak sandwich.

Ken Scherer: It was really cool traveling with Scott and imagining the early life path of a young Agent Cooper.

Scott Frost: We went to the Hoover building in DC, and then we went down and spent the afternoon at the Academy and met a couple of behavioral science guys and generally just got the tour, went out, and shot some weapons on the range and that kind of stuff.

Ken Scherer: The one clear memory I have, as someone who does not like guns, was when the FBI took Scott to the gun range so he could target practice. I think it was at a time that they were changing the type of firearms agents were using. Scott was pretty good at it and then they asked me if I wanted to shoot. It was the first and last time I have shot a gun. Let's just say that at that moment my manhood was severely called into question with my inability to hit the target.

Scott Frost: It turned out that there were a lot of fans of *Twin Peaks* at the FBI, which was really funny 'cause there was little about Dale's process that had anything to do with reality.

Ken Scherer: Watching Scott as a writer get into the very being of the character that Mark and David had created and Kyle gave life to was an amazing experience. The experience gave me a greater appreciation for writers and the worlds they create.

Scott Frost: I had a breakfast with David, probably at Du-par's or someplace, and he sorta went through what he wanted, which in typical Lynch fashion: [speaking as Lynch] "Well, I want a thing about asparagus." Ok. [As Lynch again] "He's got to do an investigation into asparagus." That was sort of the approach David would take. Those sorta quirky things. The idea was to give Diane a presence [in the book] which helped to support this quirky thing that Cooper had going with his little tape recorder.

There was an actor [Roger Rees] who's done a lot of stuff for years, and he kind of has a look a little bit like Cooper. Mark decided, "He'd be a great older brother. We gotta put him in the book." Even though there was no place for a brother yet. It was one of the things that didn't pan out [in the TV series]. I suppose the Windom Earle stuff was really the stuff that had to be weaved in 'cause that was where much of the story went that second season.

Favorite Quotes and Scenes

Ben: My favorite scene is at the Double R diner where you get Gordon Cole meeting Shelly Johnson for the first time. Even though he is hard of hearing, he can miraculously hear Shelly perfectly. Also Cooper tells Annie this really corny penguin joke. Two charming moments in well-executed scenes.

Bryon: My favorite quote: "My socks are on fire!" is a line that will stick with me forever and I seem to use it at least once a week. This is just one of my all-time favorite scenes from *Twin Peaks*. We get to see David Lynch have a great time playing Gordon Cole, who, all of a sudden, can hear Shelly Johnson. This whole scene plays out wonderfully between the two.

Ben: My favorite line comes from Cooper, "Harry, I have no idea where this will lead us, but I have a definite feeling it will be a place both wonderful and strange." This is a classic line from *Twin Peaks*. We, too, as fans watching the show have no idea where *Twin Peaks* will go, but I bet it will be both wonderful and strange.

Bryon: It can be the tagline for the entire show.

Community Commentary

Pete Glessman: I was fully committed to avoiding the *Twin Peaks* hype in 1990. As an alleged late teen connoisseur of the unconventional, the show was too trendy and mainstream for me. I recall seeing a *Twin Peaks* "relationship web" in a national magazine article detailing the phenomenon while I was in a doctor's office and I don't think I could have flung the magazine back on the table any faster or with more disdain. Things changed when I visited my fiancée's house after work during the ABC summer reruns. I saw "Laura" calling Dr. Jacoby from the gazebo while Angelo Badalamenti's masterful soundtrack set the tone, and I was immediately captivated. With my future mother-in-law telling me to shut up and watch, all I desperately wanted to know was how someone who had been dead and wrapped in plastic could be making this eerie phone call from beyond the grave.

Chapter 28

Season 2: Episode 26
"Variations on Relations"
Aired: April 11, 1991
Written by: Mark Frost & Harley Peyton
Directed by Jonathan Sanger

The Log-line

FBI Deputy Director Gordon Cole kisses Shelly Johnson; Windom Earle kills another victim and places the pawn in the Easter Park gazebo.

Behind the Curtain

Mary Jo Deschanel on Donna discovering her Mom's secrets: When [children are] small, they look at their parents as sort of the absolute authority. And [you] sort of think about your parents in one way and then no matter what the story is, it's different as you get older. And you realize, oh, they're human beings and they have their whole lives and secrets—or not even necessarily secrets, but just things you didn't realize or struggles that you didn't know because you're a child, and you shouldn't know that really. How much they're maybe struggling or depressed or whatever. Then you usually come to terms as you grow up at some point and then you see them as full human beings and then you can have all sorts of very different relationships.

Ian Buchanan: The wine tasting I really liked, 'cause I think it was Dick at his finest, being a dick.

Twin Peaks: An Access Guide to the Town

Ken Scherer: The guide to *Twin Peaks* was all about Mark [Frost] because he had met [Richard Saul Wurman] in San Francisco. Richard was the guy who was producing, in those days, all the guidebooks to Paris, the guide book to London and all that kind of stuff. He was a fan of the show and somehow he and Mark connected and he said, "Let's do a real guide to Twin Peaks."

Richard Saul Wurman (Co-author of *Twin Peaks: An Access Guide to the Town*): I know you have questions for me, but I would like to start off with what seems like a simple-minded question. How did you find me? I did *Twin Peaks Access* a number of years ago, but it's one of the oddest things I've done in my life. If you've taken the trouble to Google me, it doesn't have a major place in my curriculum vitae. This was a one-off strange experience to do this book, which was triple and quadruple jokes on itself.

This is the only actual piece of work I've done in 60 years that I was asked to do. It wasn't my initial idea. It was just some people who were hyping something and the show was being hyped and they thought it would be funny. They knew I loved to do zany things, so they came to me.

Ken Scherer: [Richard] had the template. He had the creativity and he wasn't wedded to it as much as Harley and Bob Engels.

Richard Saul Wurman: It was done by my office. We did all the layouts; we did all the artwork. Michael Everett worked for me, he was the art director, and the credits up there were David [Lynch] and Mark [Frost]. They didn't have anything to do with it. David took some of the photos, but it was difficult getting things out of them. Some of the [*Twin Peaks*] writers contributed ideas and most of them came out of Michael Everett and myself.

Harley Peyton: Mark announced we were going to do this. We loved the idea.

Ken Scherer: And so we would literally sit in a room and this was why it was so much fun for me because, the rest of the time, creatively I was not involved nor should have been, but this was the one creative piece where we all just said, "Look, we've got to get this book done and we know it's kind of at the end of the run but let's have fun with it because it will last beyond the show."

Harley Peyton: We were assigned different sections of the access book. Now that doesn't mean they weren't rewritten or put together. I couldn't really speak to that because it happened in the middle of production. [I] spent like an afternoon putting some things together and then sent it along. And to be perfectly honest, I couldn't tell you if that had changed a great deal by the time they came to the publication, but I remember loving it, certainly.

Richard Saul Wurman: Mark was very pleasant to work with. He was much more open than Lynch. I think you would find this interesting because we cannibalized all this stuff we could possibly cannibalize from everybody. It's a whole book of marginalia basically. It's all footnotes.

Ken Scherer: [We would] just make some great shit up. And then people like Harley and Bob Engels and maybe Mark to some degree and Scott Frost would kind of add pieces to it based on the character development.

Richard Saul Wurman: We were trying to mirror the show and take it to an even odder place. When we showed that hand with fingers cut off, it didn't appear in the show. We just made up that joke. That was all.

I love maps. That's why there's a bunch of maps in there. We did all the maps from scratch. Nothing is meaningful in the whole thing. I also redid the phone books in California called the smart yellow pages. That's why we have that phone book thing. David Lynch took the photo on the cover.

Ken Scherer: It was the pie on the cover. He loves that picture. There was no discussion about what the cover should be, ever.

Richard Saul Wurman: [David] took the photos of the taxi cab section of the book. They're all meant to be fuzzy and out of focus. Everything's meant to look very unprofessional. And then the opening letter to the book, a letter from the mayor, is to me and gives me permission to do this book.

Ken Scherer: My brother, who was not well at the time and has since passed on, is profiled in the book because I wanted to do a tribute to him. So the photo of the football team is a picture of my brother's team the year they won the state championship. And my dad passed away, so I did a little thing remembering him in the book. For me, that book is very, very personal and I loved it because I actually had something to do with it.

Richard Saul Wurman: When I did this, I was also doing a lot of work in Japan and they all had it in Japanese. It was translated into about ten different languages, this book. And when I was in Japan, they would say, "Oh, *Twin Peaks!*" Probably was six months [to put the book together].

Mark Frost: [For *The Secret History of Twin Peaks*] I did go back to the *Access Guide* because we had created some of that geography and timeline in that book. So I felt it was wise to build on that and use it as a stepping stone.

Favorite Quotes and Scenes

Ben: My favorite scene is Gordon Cole kissing Shelly Johnson at the Double R, and Bobby walks in shocked by the embrace.

Bryon: Yeah that's my favorite quote: Gordon Cole: [shouting as usual] "YOU ARE WITNESSING A FRONT THREE-QUARTER VIEW OF TWO ADULTS SHARING A TENDER MOMENT."

My favorite scene is with Dale Cooper in Harry's office putting the pieces together of the ripped up poem Windom Earle sent to Donna, Shelly, and Audrey. We are getting the old Cooper back and he is in top form.

Ben: My favorite quote comes from Cooper and Annie in a boat in Easter Park: Annie: I lived in my head, mostly.
Cooper: That's not a bad neighborhood.
I like this quote for the dreamy atmosphere. Annie wasn't the popular girl. She kept to herself, seemed to be a deep thinker, and had some strange and troubling thoughts. We know she tried to commit suicide. Even though they have only known each other for a short time, she feels comfortable sharing with Cooper. The quote also makes me think about if *Twin Peaks* is just someone's dream with strange neighbors filling their head.

Community Commentary

Rikki Robinson: I first discovered *Twin Peaks* when I was fourteen and Season 1 premiered on ABC. My dad would watch and I would watch with him and then we'd often discuss the episodes. My dad had always enjoyed a good whodunnit and *Twin Peaks* was unlike anything we had seen before. Season 1 was, simply put, the best television we'd experienced, my dad and I—my mom never got as into it like my dad and I. When Season 2 started, we were super excited but our excitement diminished at the same rate as the quality of the show. Then, in August of 1992, *Fire Walk with Me* debuted in the cinemas. My dad and mom were out of town so I went to see it by myself and to this day *FWWM* is EVERYTHING. I was ecstatic to have a Season 3 and it felt like an extension of *Fire Walk with Me* and, I believe, it forever changed television in the best of ways. I wish my dad would have still been alive to watch *The Return* because he would have loved it so much.

Chapter 29

Season 2: Episode 27
"The Path to the Black Lodge"
Aired: April 18, 1991
Written by Harley Peyton & Robert Engels
Directed by Stephen Gyllenhaal

The Log-line

Windom Earle captures Major Briggs, and Audrey Horne stops John Justice Wheeler's plane from taking off.

Behind the Curtain

Kenneth Welsh: We had great directors on that show. Stephen Gyllenhaal, he did one of the best episodes, I thought.

Stephen Gyllenhaal (Director of episode 27): It's been 30 years. *Twin Peaks* remains a kind of high (and low) point in the work that I've done in movies and TV. High because *Twin Peaks* was so stunningly beautiful, poetic and cinematic at the most profound level. Low, because it went so deep. Has anything touched the depths of what it is to be human in America? I don't think so. It was as if we were all sent off in David's spacecraft/submarine. His vision was always propelling the direction, but he also gave us so much freedom to explore the worlds he laid out for us.

As a director, I have never felt so free and inspired—showing up on the set each day almost felt like floating in space or deep under the sea. And to know that so many others felt the same way who worked on or watched *Twin Peaks* speaks to something miraculous about the human race.

Willie Garson: I remember going in for the role of Heavy Metal Roadie, and as I was starting to lose my hair and could only think about hair and rock-and-roll, I thought there was no way I'd be right for this. Johanna Ray, the casting director, was an early fan and would cast me the next year as Lee Harvey Oswald in one of Propaganda's (Lynch's production company) first films, *Ruby*. Anyway, all I did to prepare was take some hair gel and mess the hell out of my hair and drove over. There were all these punked-out rock looking kids in the waiting room, and I thought "no way." When I went in, I said to them, "I have to be honest. You have this role 20 times over in the waiting room. It's just not me." And I don't remember if it was Harley, or whoever in the room said, "Well, that's why we're *Twin Peaks*. You're hired."

At the shoot, the character is very scared and starts to cry during his interrogation, and I remember Steve Gyllenhaal, the director, when the time came, yelling at me, "Cry! Cry now!" which is as bad as someone asking you to "be funny," on cue. Impossible. Anyway, we got it quickly (ironically, I wear a backward baseball hat, you know, as heavy metal roadies do), and of course the show looked gorgeous and mysterious and dark, and I was completely thrilled to be on it.

Stephen Gyllenhaal on how he came up with the idea of characters' hands shaking unexpectedly: I think it was two things, one conscious, the other less so. Something about fear, the shaking. It was bewildering to have this just take over a part of a character. I remember feeling it was capturing something that was so David Lynch. We are not in control of our deepest aspects. The other is more an understanding that I have now about the fact that below the molecular level of explaining what constructs us is the discovery that it is all energy, i.e., quantum mechanics.

Why did I come up with that idea, then? Because David forced us while making that show to move down a path toward the unconscious. The definition of the unconscious, I guess, is that which we haven't yet made conscious. So really, it was David who came up with it!

Billy Zane (John Justice Wheeler): Leave it to David Lynch to cast against type by hiring the crazy guy from *Dead Calm* as the straightest fella in the Peaks. Love him and Mark for that because it was those white-hat hero, classic Hollywood characters of moral compass that actors like Gary Cooper and Clark Gable and John Wayne played that inspired me most and made me want to pursue a career as a film actor.

You play a bad guy on a boat once and that's what you spend a career trying to sink, so to speak. I'm just grateful to have had the opportunity to contribute to that indelible world, with its level of artistry, mystery, sexiness and dark humor as one as noble and confidently square as John Justice Wheeler. It was wise messaging for the early '90s by David and Mark at a time when all media was getting edgier, more violent, more explicit from cinema to music lyrics. J.J.'s dignity, philanthropy, and romantic overtures that even inspired a serenade were rewarded with the profound and surprising privilege of making love to Audrey Horne for her first time, on his private jet, yet still retain his good-guy status. Now, that is gangster!

Tim Hunter: Consistently hanging over the *Twin Peaks* production was the question and threat of what the network would do to the show and whether or not they would cancel it. There was always the knowledge that ABC didn't really get the show. As much as the working atmosphere was incredibly special, I think everybody would say that there was this sort of sword hanging over it as to how long the network was going to keep it going.

Harley Peyton: We were all sort of waiting to see if there was going to be a third season. I know that Mark and David went to ABC and this was one of those few times where there was that sort of contact. They went to ABC, sat down with them, and said, "We have a plan for a third season and here's what we want to do."

Brings Back Some Memories

Bryon: I pretty much nailed the BOB and host thing during this episode. I felt he needed a new host so he could continue killing. I also felt the owl could move the spirit between two worlds, but it would still need a host. I thought the people who had the shaking hands were sensitive to what was happening around them (electricity). I felt they could have spaced all that out over Season 2 rather than just put it all in at the end. But despite all that, I really loved this episode.

Ben: I do like the fact that you only have a certain amount of time these spirits are able to come out into the world.

Bryon: I always thought the electricity and the owls were how they moved around, so the planet stuff never did anything for me. I like the circle and the burnt oil smell, that stuff is interesting, but I felt they were muddying up the water a bit much at the end with the planets.

Ben: I'm guessing it had to be Mark Frost who added this aligning of the planets. He probably saw that little Saturn planet lamp in the Red Room and wanted to tie that into the mythology as well. Personally, I eat this stuff up.

After this episode, there was uncertainty about whether the show would come back. Basically, *Twin Peaks* had been canceled. Although, the last two episodes were shot, and ABC decided to air them as a Monday night movie of the week in June of 1991.

Favorite Quotes and Scenes

Bryon: My favorite scene is with Cooper going into the Double R Diner and having some coffee with Annie Blackburn. They both confess they cannot stop thinking about each other in cute ways. The camera slowly moves away exposing more and more of the diner around them. The music is slowly drowned out by a sinister darkness. Is this foreshadowing of spilled blood?

Ben: My favorite quote is with Annie and Cooper. "Hear the other side; see *the* other side." Annie is saying that she should take a chance. Somebody who has been shy and really hasn't been part of this community is going to take a chance and be more active.

Bryon: My favorite quote is from Special Agent Dale Cooper: "Gentlemen, when Windom Earle arrived in Twin Peaks, I assumed he had come for vengeance, for me, but I miscalculated. He's been after something else all along: the Black Lodge." I love this quote because it shows that Dale Cooper is back and better than ever. It's a great little speech that Cooper gives to Harry and Major Briggs.

Ben: People's hands shaking through the whole episode really drew me in, and the episode ends with BOB's hand coming out of the Red Room at the Sycamore Trees. It's a short scene, but it's my favorite moment of the episode, with the red drapes reflected in the circle. Visually stunning. We mentioned before how these characters from the Red Room showing up on the bed after Josie dies felt weird and out of place. With no dialogue, just seeing BOB's hand coming out of the woods surrounded by the sycamore trees and the red curtains feels so right. BOB had returned.

Community Commentary

Jeremiah Beaver (TakeTheRing.com): In 1995, I was a sophomore in a rural Indiana high school who liked to hang out at a local music shop. Having become friends with the proverbial guy-at-the-counter, and after discussing *Blue Velvet* and David Lynch, he said I definitely needed to see *Twin Peaks* as soon as possible—demanding that I rent the pilot episode, but it was rented out; however, they had *Fire Walk with Me*. For better or worse, my guy said to watch it. And so, the *Twin Peaks* journey began, completely out of order and without context. I saw the pilot shortly thereafter and saved up my after-school job money for the VHS box set of the series. I was riveted and remain so to this day. *Twin Peaks* became an endless game to play in my mind, an unsolvable mystery in which every question answered unearths another. I can go down the rabbit hole of history, come up with an atomic meta-theory or just enjoy memorable moments with great characters in a TV show that continues to inspire audiences worldwide. But I'll never forget the exhilarating feeling of awe, wonder, and confusion while watching *FWWM* for the first time. That's what *Twin Peaks* means to me; it's what I've held in my heart, and it's what I'm still feeling after *The Return* so many years later.

Chapter 30

**Season 2: Episode 28
"Miss Twin Peaks"
Aired: June 10, 1991
Written by James Foley
Directed by Tim Hunter**

The Log-line

Twin Peaks residents participate in the Miss Twin Peaks Contest pageant, and Windom Earle makes an appearance.

Behind the Curtain

Ken Scherer on the relationship with ABC: I think the relationship was good in the beginning. [ABC President Bob Iger] was the one who saw this show. But unfortunately, those around him who are kind of responsible for the day to day running of the network didn't really believe in the show, and they didn't believe in the show because they didn't own it. David and Mark own the show outright. We weren't getting the promotion we thought we deserved.

Tim Hunter: Everybody knew the show had been canceled. David was coming back to do the last episode. Nobody had any idea what it would be like. And at that point, the spirit of the show had dampened. Some of the actors become more cynical. I was excited to go back and do that penultimate episode because I'd had such a great experience on the show. The challenge on that one was because the cameraman had slowed down so much. When I got there, they told me that I was only going to be able to get, like, 60 shots a day, and that boils down to like two setups a page. Normally, you could easily get 40 or more setups a day. I asked to see the production reports of the shows that had gone before and indeed the number of setups that were being shot in a day had just gone down drastically. So I had to figure out how I was going to do the show with a lot fewer shots than what I was used to getting. I decided that

I would run Ozu film *Tokyo Story*, which I ran for myself and just got into a kind of a minimalist frame of mind.

The show had also gotten a bit soapy. I always thought of the episode as my Japanese style Falcon Crest. It was a different show. It was the Windom Earle story rather than the Laura Palmer story.

[Windom Earle's] black teeth are from me. And that was an homage to Japanese cinema because I had watched Ozu and Mizoguchi before directing the episode. So that was an inside gag for me as an homage to Japanese films that I watched before doing the episode. If you look at those Mizoguchi geisha films that are so wonderful, *The Life of Oharu*, and other films in that period. I guess it was fashionable in those days to black the teeth out.

Robyn Lively (Lana Budding Milford): Playing Lana Budding Milford was a career highlight! I felt so honored to join the extraordinary cast of a show that was so ahead of its time and one I was personally obsessed with! Fun fact: Lana wasn't written as southern. It was a character choice I decided on as I was reading the audition material. For ME, it was an obvious choice. The dialogue just popped from the page as southern. I knew I had to be confident in the choice and go for it! A gamble for sure, but one that fortunately paid off! I couldn't have loved the experience more! I only wish it had lasted longer. David Lynch and Mark Frost are true geniuses! *Twin Peaks*, forever in my heart.

Kimmy Robertson (Lucy Moran): I was a dancer for 35 years, for heaven's sake. A ballet dancer. I was in a company for ten years called American Folk Ballet. And I was doing that until I started doing *Twin Peaks*.

The Pink Room: David Lynch Burlesque, Photo by Sachyn Mital

I was at my desk on the set, and [David Lynch and Mark Frost] were down the hallway, like if you were looking down from my desk, straight down the hall. They were down there sort of twittering back and forth like two old aunties. And they kept looking at me giggling, turning their backs to me, looking back at me, giggling, turning their backs and I was like, "Oh no, what am I going to have to do now?" [laughs] They literally came up as they walked, it was almost like their knees were tied together. They even walk like aunties and they said, "We have something we want you to do," and I went, "I knew it!" Then they said, "You want to do a dance?" And I said, "What kind of dance?" And they said, "Well, dancing the talent portion in the Miss Twin Peaks Contest." And I said, "Okay?! Do you want to be like, (this is funny because I've asked this question for other things that I've done), real dancing or Disney dancing?" [They said] "You know, Disney dance." "Okay, I'll do it then." They said just use your music, whatever you want, and we'll have Angelo make up something that goes to the dance. So I did choreograph that to "Mack the Knife." I did choreograph it to be corny and like uplift people rather than a *So You Think You Can Dance* kind of thing. And then the split at the end, everybody was worried about me because I was pregnant, you know. They forget that is not really happening.

Tony Krantz: *Twin Peaks* was a remarkable thing. It was a beautiful thing as David would say. It was a rocket ship that rose super-duper high and came crashing down in many ways just as quickly. The demise of *Twin Peaks* is a bit of a cautionary tale about needing to not make the form conform to you, but you're working within the form of a show that needs to give a mass audience satisfying episodes.

Tim Hunter: Certainly we were given a fair amount of stylistic freedom, and I felt some of the later one-shot directors sort of used it as a springboard for some directorial overachieving at times. I remember in the [Roadhouse] at one point, they were packing up and I had them carry the mounted [deer] across the frame, that sort of thing.

You just knew that David Lynch was going to do something that was more abstract and personal and phantasmagorical and somatic [for Episode 29]. I always felt they used me to some extent as a utility man on that show. In one case, I think I came in after David and I felt that my purpose was to kind of reorient the story and get everything kind of clear again in the audience's mind. And then there were those times where I went right before David and

I felt that my function was to kind of clarify the story. Get the story into focus in the minds of the audience so that David could then come in and do whatever the hell it was he wanted to do.

Favorite Quotes and Scenes

Ben and **Bryon:** Our favorite scene of this episode has to be all of the Miss Twin Peaks Contest.

Ben: I think Audrey Horne had the best Miss Twin Peaks speech and should have won. "When something you love is in danger, you must fight to save it or lose it forever." I take the message really to be directed at Cooper and losing Annie forever.

Ben and **Bryon:** Our favorite quote comes from Major Briggs, "Fear and love open the door." It's a great concept that this spiritual world feeds on love and fear. Fear would open the door to the Black Lodge and love would open the door to the White Lodge.

Community Commentary

Courtenay Stallings (Author of *Laura's Ghost*, Sr. Editor of *The Blue Rose*):
I first discovered *Twin Peaks* in high school. I rarely watched TV at the time, so it's amazing I ever caught an episode. Initially, I loved the melodramatic soap opera elements to the show, and, of course, the mystery of who killed Laura Palmer. What really sparked my interest was the surreal dream-like world of the Red Room. I'd never seen anything like it—a dream world broadcast from my parents' 1980s Zenith TV. Laura Palmer is my favorite character, which is interesting because she is deceased for the entirety of the television show. Here's the homecoming queen who is beautiful and seemingly perfect, but she's filled with secrets. Laura appeals to me because her story is one of spiritual redemption — she never allows BOB in and meets her guardian angel in the end. Now, my love for *Twin Peaks* has evolved into my passion for writing about it — in academic journals, blogs, the *Blue Rose Magazine* and my book exploring Laura Palmer: *Laura's Ghost: Women Speak About Twin Peaks.*

Chapter 31

Season 2: Episode 29
"Beyond Life and Death"
Aired: June 10, 1991
Written by Mark Frost, Harley Peyton & Robert Engels
Directed by David Lynch

The Log-line

Agent Cooper enters the Black Lodge and encounters familiar faces.

Behind the Curtain

Richard Beymer: It was the last episode. The episode took, what? It took eight days to make it, so we always had a weekend in there. Since it was a big cast and all, generally I had two to three days to work on the show. I had done my time, and there was a feeling that this might be the last show and we'd never had any photographers on the set. I mean, some people came down from the production office, I guess, and took some pictures, but there were no professional

photographers that came in like on movie sets. I told David, "I like still photography and no one's doing this. How about if I just start covering this?" He said, "Get your camera."

Photo by Richard Beymer.

Harley Peyton: [Episode 29 is] a script that Mark and myself and Bob all worked on. I think our intention when we were first putting together the second season finale was we wanted [lots of cliffhangers] again, in particular, to convince ABC to come back for a third season.

I remembered the word filtering back from the set was like, "Oh Dave, he's gone crazy. He's doing all these things and changing all these things." My inclination at the moment was, "Oh, how dare he, that's ridiculous. David's finally lost his mind." Then I saw the episode, and I think it's one of the best episodes of television I've ever seen. It's hard to complain with that, but that kind of inspiration is just difficult to do on a weekly basis. Particularly when you're telling a serial story.

That's sort of what could be frustrating sometimes when I'm working with David, that he's going to go his own way and there are certain things that will happen that'll take you by complete surprise, but most of the time what results is every bit worth it.

Kenneth Welsh: When I did work with David finally in the last episode [Season 2], he was so cool because he'd just change the dialogue, "Windom, I don't think you should say what's in the script right here. So what I want you to do is turn around, look out the back window of the truck and say to Heather, 'Oh look, 12 rainbow trout.' Just like that, okay." At that point, I knew Windom so well. I felt the character so much that I thought, "Great! Throw it at me, man. I'll do it." I trust this guy. He wrote this shit. And it was fun because it wouldn't be that big a deal. It wouldn't be like he's throwing a big soliloquy at you. It was just a couple of lines. He was always really supportive.

Then he said, "All right, when you're walking towards the woods, you have the flashlight in your hand. When she speaks, turn it on her. When you're speaking, turn it on you. That's how we'll light this scene. All right, these actors are great. Let's go." And then we went down into the Lodge, the Red Room.

Mary Jo Deschanel: It was right after the big sort of beauty contest, Miss Twin Peaks, there was a scene the next morning, and I went and I'm thinking because everyone was up really late and all these things happened and it was a traumatic night, I thought we would all be in the same clothes from the night before. When I went into makeup and hair I said, "Oh, I thought we were going to do this." "Oh, no, no, we're not. This is what we're doing." So

I get the makeup, we have the wardrobe and get my hair and then we go to have a group rehearsal. Everybody's ready. Everyone's spent the two hours or whatever getting ready and everyone's ready except for the final thing. And I said to David, "Oh, I'm surprised. I thought we would be in the stuff from the night before and it would be like that." He just looked at me, he said, "Oh, okay." And then everybody is back to makeup, to wardrobe. A comment like that and he went, "Oh, that's a good idea." In television no one's listening to you that much. You certainly don't have that power or even if you wanted to, you would not take the time to do that because it costs them a lot of time. [But] that's David.

Kenneth Welsh: [Cooper] was consciously pursued from this crazy angry man who never achieved what his goal was, but kept killing people along the way. That was a great character. My two favorite characters are Windom Earle and the character I played in Lodge 49.

We did ADR [Automated Dialogue Replacement] for the speaking backward. [David] called me at home and I recorded it, in those days, on my cassette recorder. I kept the cassette because I wanted to have it as, like, a relic. At a certain point, it disappeared. I could not find it. Figure that one out. It's in the Black Lodge, man.

Harley Peyton: I wish I could remember it more perfectly, but my feeling is that I was on my way to work and just thinking, "Jesus, I know what the end should be." And I got there to find out that, of course, Mark already knew what the end should be. And that we both individually had had the same idea. And for all I know David did too. Who knows? Given everything we'd done and the way that BOB had been set up, it was sort of the perfect way to go out. There's BOB in the mirror.

Mary Jo Deschanel: It really was an amazing show. It really was groundbreaking when it came out, and you felt like things were possible that you never thought could be possible in this sort of creative way. They certainly broke all these rules in terms of getting around censorship and all of that, which is pretty cool.

Lesli Linka Glatter: It was an extraordinary game-changing series on every level because there was room to have visual storytelling. I think TV is back to that now in the last 10 years. We are making movies for TV. Whether it's an hour or two hours or whatever length you have to tell the cinematic story. It was a visual storytelling experience.

David Duchovny: I was selfishly sad when the show got canceled after the second year. I really felt like there was a real character there that could have existed in that world in a significant way. So I was kind of bummed.

Dana Ashbrook: I think every job I've gotten since [*Twin Peaks*] probably has something to do with the fact that I was on *Twin Peaks*. I've made lifelong friends, and it's opened up the whole world for me.

Robert Bauer: *Twin Peaks* was a great experience, but the real value that I could take out of *Twin Peaks* is my friendship with Dana.

Scott Frost: Anytime you get to work on a series and have had a good time, that's something, because I've seen more times than not, it's not always a good time.

Eric Da Re: After the show ended, I continued to work, but I'd never had to read for anything I went on. I was just hired, which is really unusual for somebody who wasn't an actor. Not to go and read on stuff, but it was all for the same or worse characters. It was all villains. Not all of it, but generally that's what it was. Directors and producers were upset that when they met me on the set that I wasn't Leo; that I was, in fact, Eric, and I'm a separate person.

Tim Hunter: Certainly the show has had a long life and it was wonderful to be a part of it way back then. I still have my crew shirt and my hat.

Ray Wise: [Sheryl Lee] gave me a picture of herself in the fourth grade. And I put in my wallet when we did the pilot and I kept that picture in my back pocket for the entire series. She was with me the whole time and then I gave the picture back.

Ken Scherer: I'd always heard, as I was working at AFI and other places, and you hear it today, you become a family and there's an environment, and boy that was true of *Twin Peaks*. It was such a great place to go every day. People were just in it, and David and Mark had the sense of building a family and with David, still to this day, he tries to work with all of the same people. I see Kyle two, three times a year at various events, and it's always a warm hug and greeting and we reminisce for a few minutes and then kinda move on. But that's the environment that David created, and Mark.

Tony Krantz: It would be a mistake to dwell on the negativity of the demise of *Twin Peaks*. It is much more interesting to talk about the fact that it was the first. It was David Lynch who is an American treasure coming in and doing something that was so interesting. All the shows that we see now are not necessarily a result of *Twin Peaks*, but *Twin Peaks* was the first, and then there ware many other shows that became, slowly, the result of *Twin Peaks*.

Scott Frost: For a brief moment, a little lightning got caught in a bottle, and it was a fun ride.

Lara Flynn Boyle (Donna Hayward): It was a dreamy time.

Brings Back Some Memories

Ben: Back in 1991, I recorded the two-episode movie on VHS. I still have it to this day because I have such wonderful memories of watching the amazing Episode 29, directed by David Lynch. I had never seen anything quite like that on TV. I thought all my questions would be answered, but they left the viewers hanging with the biggest cliffhanger ever: Cooper possessed by BOB. It was heart-wrenching and a punch to the gut. Good was supposed to defeat evil. I was never going to see *Twin Peaks* again, and this is how things were going to be left?!

Bryon: A great ending to a fantastic show. So many great moments, characters and classic lines. A journey I'll never forget, not only because it was a great show, but because I got to experience it with you and meet such a welcoming community along the way.

Ben: In one version of the *Ronnie Rocket* film script [unproduced 1977 film by David Lynch], a conversation is overheard by a "Girl" speaking to a "Guy." The Girl says, "I got idea, man ... you take me for a walk (she moves closer to the guy) under the sycamore trees (closer) the dark trees that blow, baby. In the dark trees I'll see you and you'll see me." The Guy says, "I'll twist your neck."

The words spoken by the girl would be reused to create the "Sycamore Trees" song in the Red Room.

Our podcast on Episode 29 went out the week of the 25th anniversary of that episode and we also just so happened to celebrate with our friends, at the Great Southern *Twin Peaks* fest that weekend. It was a really special time.

Favorite Quotes and Scenes

Ben and **Bryon:** How can you not pick the Red Room scene as your favorite in this episode? Basically, the whole second half of this episode is my favorite scene. The moment we get to see Dale Cooper enter the Black Lodge is nothing I have ever seen on television. The talking backward, seeing Laura Palmer, the Giant, the Little Man, all come together.

Bryon: My favorite quote comes from The Man From Another Place talking backward, with subtitles, "Wow, Bob, Wow. Fire walk with me."

Ben: We heard this line all the way back in the pilot, and of course it is the poem the One-Armed Man says. Yet again, Lynch brings this back full circle. It's almost like Lynch's greatest hits. It's all the things he's done in the past, and now he mixes it up and brings it back in a new way.

Bryon: He does so seamlessly.

Ben: My favorite quote comes from Laura Palmer, "I'll see you again in 25 years." I think as a die-hard fan, hearing that quote from Laura Palmer made me want to believe that someday in some way *Twin Peaks* would come back.

Community Commentary

Damon Lindelof (Executive Producer and Writer of *Watchmen*, *The Leftovers*, and *Lost*): I would not have a career if *Twin Peaks* never existed. From the moment Laura washed ashore, my imagination was on fire ... a fire I would walk with through every episode (and a movie) as I was alternately mystified, horrified and tickled pink. Words can't describe how immensely grateful I am for this show ... in a landscape littered with sameness, it remains one of the most unique pieces of art ever to emerge from a television screen and I will love it forever.

COOP

Citizens Opposing the Offing of Peaks

H. Keith Poston
National President

Michael Caputo
National Director

June 5, 1991

Dear COOP member:

As you are surely well aware, ABC's fall line up was announced late last month. Painfully absent from the schedule was Twin Peaks, network television's sole creative exercise. However, it is not time to mourn the death of Agent Cooper---not yet.

Unfortunately, Lynch/Frost has exhausted all options in their attempt to keep Peaks on the air in forthcoming seasons. ABC-TV dropped the ball, and no other network stepped forward to pick up the financial slack. Without the proper investment, the production company did not want to drastically cut back on quality just to put out the show on TV.

David Lynch has assured both of us that the antics of the small northwestern logging town will live on. Where, they are not quite certain yet, but Peaks could be destined for the movie houses. Lynch/Frost will have more information in a few weeks, and promises COOP members will be among the first to know the details. We all know just what Lynch is capable of on the big screen, so there is a ray of hope on the horizon. Hopefully, we in COOP can all be of help.

Please note the change in address for The Great Northern. Direct all correspondence to the new Lee Highway venue for COOP. Next, <u>please take a moment today to jot down a few names and addresses of your friends who are Twin Peaks fans and drop them in the mail to us</u>. We need to get as many people involved in our effort to support the work of Lynch/Frost Productions as possible. We need your input.

We would also like to express our thanks to Star Pics, the makers of the *Twin Peaks Collectible CardArt*, for paying for the stamps, envelopes and photocopying for this mailing. It was time for us to contact you and bring you up to date, but we literally had no money. Many of you had asked us how to find these rarities, so check the enclosed flyer. According to David Lynch, "The cards are mighty cool."

Your work and dedication to creativity brought back Twin Peaks from the first hiatus. Your dissatisfaction with typical TV fare is well known; we have really made a difference. Our voices were heard from New York to Hollywood. We cannot thank each one of you enough.

So, stay tuned. When we hear anything, you will be the first to know.

Sincerely,

Keith & Michael

Letter courtesy of C.O.O.P.

Chapter 32

Twin Peaks: Fire Walk With Me
Released in the U.S. on August 28, 1992
Written by David Lynch and Bob Engels
Directed by David Lynch

The Log-line
The FBI investigates the death of Teresa Banks, and the last seven days of Laura Palmer's life unfold.

Behind the Curtain
Ken Scherer: The hard thing about any creative process is there is no formula, and you can't even then dissect the ingredients in many cases. They're two very distinct different men in Mark and David. Mark, his real genius is words and story, and David's real genius is images. And so when you put those two things together, you can have the potential of coming up with *Twin Peaks* for sure. That's why the movie, in my humble opinion, was less successful and certainly, I think, less satisfying to a lot of people who really enjoy the original series. It lacked the kind of discipline of storytelling that Mark brings to the screen. I'm not sure David would agree, but that's my opinion.

Tony Krantz: I was the guy who put together the deals that represented Bob Engels. David looked at him as the new Mark Frost. Bob was a very good guy. David could work with him in a way that he couldn't with Mark.

Bob Engels (Writer): I was working on the show and that really was my first TV experience. David and I got along great. As Dave would say, "Ike and Mike." He asked me if I would like to write a script with him, but it wasn't

Twin Peaks. I think it was *Started in Heaven* or *Dream of the Bovine,* I'm not sure which. And we'd work at David's house.

One day, he came from a meeting with Ciby 2000 and he said, "We're going to write a *Twin Peaks* movie," and we just started. We just jumped in, and it sort of turned into what it is. It's a prequel and a sequel. That kind of was the idea, that it would cover everything, before and after, which it kind of does. I think he didn't feel like he was done with a series.

[On if the book *The Secret Diary of Laura Palmer* influenced the film] We all knew what was going to be in the diary, but no, it all comes from David. But [the book and film] kind of match up.

Ken Scherer: What you have are two distinct creators who have established this world. It would be like if Benioff and [Weiss] who did *Game of Thrones* started arguing. These two men created this exceptionally incredible story. And now they were finding their creative juices going in different directions. It was never personal. I witnessed the fact that they were able to come back together. David is an artist, and sometimes artists get bored and want to do something. When you have a partner that you have to kind of answer to creatively who's not with you in the same kind of direction, it gets tense. And so that started happening, and I think Kyle knew enough because he's a smart guy, that a movie that didn't have both of them attached could be risky.

Bob Engels: Kyle at first didn't want to do the movie, as I recall, and we said well then Chris Isaak will. It's pretty simple. Somewhere in the course of getting everything ready to go, Kyle reconsidered. That made it a change [to the story], which was just kind of cool.

Ken Scherer: I think David's friendship with Kyle was so incredibly tight and remains that way, that Kyle was able to be brought back in. Then we found the funding for it through the relationship David was developing on his own with a French company that had given him a big chunk of money to make three movies. Thanks to CAA [Tony Krantz worked for] and others, we were able to set it up with distribution from New Line, which seemed like the right partner. So I think people said, Well, maybe this is a kind of a way to say goodbye." I mean, the real hardship is when you have to end the show so abruptly, both creatively where you didn't get to finish your story, but also to the family idea. People were losing jobs and scrambling and all that kind of stuff. So you try to make up for some of that and the movie was another way to kind of do that.

Bob Engels: You get all the regulars in [the film], everybody has a scene and then the first couple of drafts, everybody was in it.

Sherilyn Fenn: I went and did *Of Mice and Men* [film] so I didn't do *FWWM*. I was already contractually obligated and frankly I was gladly obligated to work with those people. David was mad. "We can't replace you in the movie."

Bob Engels: When David shot it, everybody had a scene. And then we cut lots of stuff out. And the first draft was huge. I guess it was probably 180 pages.

David, at one point, wanted to do an intermission and then whoever it was, I think it was Bob Ramey, who was the money guy behind this part of it in America, said, "No, you can't do that because we got to be able to show this movie five times in a day." The time was not going to work out.

Gary Bullock (Sheriff Cable): It was the first movie part I got when I moved to Hollywood, fortunate enough to get an agent very quickly. It was probably the most unique audition I'd ever done because we never read anything from the script. It was a sort of talk about this and that and the other thing, and I think we talked about the character. I certainly was familiar with the character because I come from the south and he was, as far as I'm concerned, he was just a redneck asshole sort of guy. He was protecting his bailiwick and all that sort of thing. And it was pretty simple to me. But any rate, it was really pleasant.

Ricky Aiello (Deputy Cliff Howard): I wasn't a fan of David's. I didn't really know his work. I never really saw *Twin Peaks*. Joanna Ray, who was the casting director, had a picture. I don't know if I met David, but I never read for him. So at the time in my career, I was carrying a lot of New York cops, gangsters, a lot of energy. So when I got to the set, the first scene that we played was in the trailer with Harry Dean Stanton, Chris Isaak, me, and I think Kiefer (Sutherland) was there. It never made it to the movie. They cut it. I went in there and I started doing my thing like I do east coast, cop gangster, a lot of energy. So I'm thinking they cast me from my picture, they must know what I do. Obviously, he's not happy and he comes to talk to me, and I'm paraphrasing, he says something like, "I want you to pause so badly, so much. I want you to be uncomfortable." Meaning that the pace was too quick. In the moment I learned a little bit about acting. I mean he wasn't groundbreaking, but [David] taught me to think about other things than just spurting the words out. When I saw the movie, I saw his style. I thought he was a genius and I don't use that word a lot. He could make you laugh, cry, and scared the shit out in the same 30 seconds. I mean, he is special.

Gary Bullock: When I first arrived, the first thing they wanted to do was take the still shot that is on the wall in the sheriff's office. They made up this fake newspaper piece. So we went out to some park there. They just ran me out somewhere, set up, and they said, "Here's the piece of steel." And it was already prebent of course because it was real rebar. I heard the story about how they had to bend it because nobody there could do it. Nobody could possibly do it. It's one of those things that is really impossible to do. Here I am this tall, thin skinny guy bending over a piece of steel rebar. Well, it's just ridiculous, of course. I've tried to make up things in my head like, "Okay, he has the magic arts or he's learned something in the east." Some bullshit to explain this thing. They told me they actually use the lift on one of the trucks to actually bend the bar.

When we're actually doing the scene, all of those rebars sitting around were stunt rebars and you can tie them in knots. I have a picture of myself with one tied in a knot.

One thought that I pitched at one point, and it was purely tongue in cheek, Sheriff Cable, after having his butt handed to him, decided to quit law enforcement and wrote romance novels, which is what I had already written. So I just simply pattern to my own life.

Ricky Aiello: About '89 I did a movie [*The Preppie Murder*], and I was at the screening and Chris Isaak had a song in the movie. They introduced him and I'd never heard of him. But when I heard "Wicked Game" in the movie, I became an instant fan. Then I found out a few years later I'm going to work with him. And I'd been around a lot of people and I was more impressed with him than just about anyone else I've ever met. Not only that, but he called me in my hotel and he said, "Can we rehearse?" It was his first movie, I believe, and he really wanted to get it right. I just respected the hell out of him for that.

Gary Bullock: David's just laid back as they come, and the only direction he gave me that stuck with me all of these years, this is on dialogue, he says, "Okay, slow down. Slow way, way down. When it gets to feel like it's so uncomfortably slow, that's about right." You think about the pace of the show, the way Angelo Badalamenti's music [is] behind it, and this kind of heartbeat kind of boom ... boom. It all just fit together. He said, "You don't realize, I'm hearing the music in my head while you're doing this." I was a fan of the show to start with, so I kind of grew into the pace. Everything is so slow and deliberate. Everybody, particularly Kyle MacLachlan, was like take your time and let all the words count, and whatever comes out it's just beautiful that way. I quite enjoyed it.

Bob Engels: [David Bowie] was a way to get [Kyle MacLachlan] back in the movie. I don't recall anything other than that. David [Lynch]'s assistant, Debbie Trutnik, would always come in when we were writing and joke about what part David Bowie was going to have in the movie. So then we added a part for him.

At the time of the David Bowie announcement that he was going to be in the film, he mentioned David Lynch had plans for more films. "There's a sequel he's already written, and my character re-emerges in Part 2 in quite a grand proportions, so he wants to introduce me in this one." (Detroit Free Press· 12 Sept 1991) We don't believe a sequel script was ever written, but we're sure David Lynch, Mark Frost, and Bob Engels had ideas for more films.

Carlton Lee Russell (Jumping Man): After many years in Social Services, I needed a break. *FWWM* was my first SAG movie. I understood that someone else had the role but had been let go. I was determined to do the best job possible. I can tell you that it was one of the best experiences in my acting life. As I was being wrapped, David called all of the crew together and informed them that it was my first role. I got a big round of applause from the entire cast and crew. Great memory!

Bob Engels: Most of the time when you see [Michael Anderson] on-screen, my wife Jill is somewhere just off-camera feeding him the backward lines. A lot of the stuff where he's, like, looking up. He's actually listening to Jill say his line. She would always say Kcor stel. It's her idea [to put "Let's Rock" on Agent Desmond's car windshield].

Dana Ashbrook: I was doing the shuffle in the pilot. I kinda did a shuffle backward and right before I got to the door, I turned around and walked through the door and [David Lynch] said, "No, no, no. Just keep shuffling straight back to New York." And made it a little more complicated. And then he wanted me to do this shuffle back thing again in *Fire Walk with Me*. It was sort of the thing I was doing, and he kind of perfected it.

Moira Kelly (Donna Hayward): When I was cast in *Fire Walk With Me*, I was psyched and sick to my stomach. It was the same feeling you get when you're the new kid at school. You're coming in an outsider. This was a cast and crew that had been working together for years, and a character established by another actress. So I was a bit nervous. But from the first day, I felt right at home. David infused the set with comfort and freedom to explore without inhibition. You had to be willing to be "all in," and he created the right environment for that to happen. I think Dale Cooper said it best: "I have no idea where this will lead us. But I have a definite feeling it will be a place both wonderful and strange." Working with David will always be one of the highlights of my career. I can't thank him enough for letting me come and play.

Sheryl Lee (Laura Palmer): I did extensive research, especially once I knew that we were going to do the film, and I also was in brilliant hands with David as a director. I had genius people playing my parents, Grace [Zabriskie] and Ray [Wise].

Ben & Bryon at the Palmer House in 2017.

I need to also give credit to the two people who wrote wonderful complex female characters.

As a woman, to be even able to read a script that has a female character that is that complex, and that layered, and has that many sides to her… that is a gift just to even get to read a script like that because they're not as common as we wish they were. When I played Laura, I knew her story. I knew her story inside and out. Like I said, I did extensive research. But as I've gotten older now, three decades older and a parent, I don't know that it's changed, so much as it's deepened and expanded in me, is my heartbreak of how often Laura's story happens in real life every single day to so many people. And I don't understand how those statistics from 30 years ago to now have not gone down. And that's a question for our whole world. (*Courtesy of* FWWM *event*)

Ray Wise: What Sheryl went through. That was an amazing tour de force. That performance.

Sheryl Lee: I couldn't have done it without you.

Ray Wise: We tried to keep it light in between takes. Tried to hug each other a lot and joke a little bit, then get back to the serious stuff. We managed to keep our sanity throughout all of it.

Eric Da Re on filming the cabin scene with Sheryl Lee: It was horrible because I had no idea what I was doing. And I love Sheryl Lee. She was one of the first people [I met]. We became very, very close. At that point, she had been through everything with her character. I really felt like I was raping her and it was so unnatural and so awful feeling. She was Laura at that point. It wasn't her, really. It was very strange. In fact, we talked about it recently and she agreed 100%. She knew exactly what I was talking about. If it made any impression, it probably made the right one for the film. Literally, I thought after the scene, I don't know if I can ever look at her again. I don't know if I could carry on the way we were before. It was that weird. It was that awkward.

Bob Engels: We talked a lot about the redemption of Laura. And I think that's where the angel came from. That idea is to lift her up literally.

Ricky Aiello: It was nice to be part of it 'cause it's one of those things on my resume that people take notice of. *Twin Peaks*, everyone knows. Even if they're not fans, they know.

Bob Engels: I think what is cool about the movie is that it covers so much stuff.

Ray Wise: When that movie opened in Cannes, at the festival, the audience actually booed it. David walked out after a few minutes and the booing continued. But then every passing year, the movie kept getting better and better. It didn't change, but it kept getting better and better and better until now. Well for my money, I think it's one of David's masterpieces.

Bob Engels: Kind of remarkable how it holds up. Like all good movies, you can watch them and watch them and watch them. It strikes me as so remarkable how popular it is.

Bryon, Joel Bocko & Ben with Eric Da Re, Sherilyn Fenn & Ray Wise in 2019.

Brings Back Some Memories

Ben: In June 1991, Lynch/Frost Productions considered continuing *Twin Peaks* by means of films. Mark Frost stated, "If the movie works, I suppose there's an opportunity to do, like, a *Star Trek* movie every couple of years, if that's what we want to do" (*Star Tribune* 28 Jun 1991). In an alternative universe maybe we could have gotten ten *Twin Peaks* films by now?

I was very concerned about how good *Fire Walk with Me* would be back in 1992. Newspapers said Mark Frost was not going to be involved and it was going to be released in theaters in August of 1992. This is a month considered by many to be a "dump month." A time when subpar movies are put out after the big blockbuster movies have been released and movie audiences less frequently go to the theater.

I went to see it opening weekend. It was a Saturday afternoon. The theater was not packed, but the people that were there seemed very excited to see it. When Kyle MacLachlan's name came up during the open credits, everyone cheered. As soon as I saw the blue screen and Angelo Badalamenti music playing and then the smashing of the television, I knew the movie would not let me down and it didn't. There was so much to love about the film from Lynch's directing, Badalamenti's music, the amazing acting, and the expansion of *Twin Peaks* mythology. Sheryl Lee's performance was unbelievable with the range of emotions that she went through. It's a very dark and difficult movie to watch, at times. They hit on taboo subject matters that can be very hard to watch, but still, it's a brilliant film.

Bryon: After my first watch, I felt that Chet Desmond and Sam Stanley were cool, and I wanted more of them, but once we got back to *Twin Peaks* and Laura's story started, I forgot all about that first 20 minutes of the movie. I was so captivated by her story. Now after seeing this film a handful of times, I could not fathom *FWWM* without those first 20 minutes. It has meaning and brings it all together, after seeing it multiple times.

Ben: What I love about this film is that it extends and elaborates on some of the symbolism and mythology in the original series. The Little Man From Another Place says, "I'm the arm and I sound like this [whooping noise]." And he later stands by the one-arm man as his arm and they denounce BOB. I thought that was a nice touch.

Bryon: When he makes that noise, it's like the electricity noise when we see the power line pole. That is how I always felt the spirits moved about, through these power lines.

Ben: There is also a new meaning behind the Palmers' ceiling fan. Throughout the series, the Palmer house fan was shown closeup with no real context. In *FWWM*, Leland Palmer turns on that fan when he is preparing to abuse Laura. This puts a whole new outlook on something that we thought was just a random shot of the ceiling fan.

Bryon: This movie is a great bookend to *Twin Peaks*. It's a prequel, it's a sequel all wrapped up into one movie.

Ben: And somehow it resolved the *Twin Peaks* story in its own way. Maybe Dale Cooper was meant to be stuck in the Red Room to console Laura Palmer?

Favorite Quotes and Scenes

Bryon: This movie is a rollercoaster ride of emotion from the oddball pairing of Special Agent Chet Desmond and Sam Stanley to the downward spiral of Laura Palmer's life and eventual death. David Lynch paints such a dark atmosphere over the Palmer household that you are just emotionally spent once the final credits roll. My favorite quote: Donna: Do you think that if you were falling in space ... that you would slow down after a while, or go faster and faster? Laura: Faster and faster. And for a long time, you wouldn't feel anything. And then you'd burst into fire. Forever. And the angels wouldn't help you because they've all gone away.

This line of dialogue feels like foreshadowing into Laura Palmer's life. She is caught in this tailspin of drugs, sex, and abuse, and she does not know how to get herself out of it. She is willing to let herself go and burst into flames if she has to, just to escape this hell that she is in.

I felt that last night was to say her last goodbye to James and then she planned to get fucked up and possibly overdose. I don't think she knew she was going to die by the hands of her father. I think that was a total shock.

Ben: My favorite quote is: Jeffries: Well now, I'm not gonna talk about Judy. In fact, we're not gonna talk about Judy at all, we're gonna keep her out of it. One of the big mysteries of *FWWM* was, "Who was Judy?" Phillip Jeffries doesn't want to talk about her in front of Cooper. It seems to me he thinks Cooper is the doppelgänger/BOB/ Mr. C. Judy seems important to the bigger mysteries and this is reinforced with the monkey saying Judy at the end of the film. In *Wrapped In Plastic* #58, Bob Engels confirms one idea was to make Judy Josie Packard's sister, but this never made it into the final script version or the film. I always like the theory that Judy was really Laura Palmer. That maybe Laura, incognito as Judy, was assisting from the afterlife.

My favorite scene has to be the ending with Cooper by Laura's side in the Red Room and the angels show up. Somehow David Lynch was able to make a happy ending for Laura Palmer and Dale Cooper in a film that dealt with incest and death. I don't know how he pulls it off, but it works. I like the idea of the Red Room not having a chronological timeline. Cooper can be in the Red Room at the same time Laura has just died. How do you top that ending? That is like the ultimate ending for *Twin Peaks*.

Bryon: You give us *The Return* and go in a whole new direction.

Community Commentary

Joel Bocko (Journey Through Twin Peaks): I first attempted to watch *Twin Peaks* at the tail end of a long "dark age" when it was difficult to see on home video. I rented the first hour-long episode before the pilot and wasn't sure if it was for me, nor how involved David Lynch really was, until the terrifying moment when Sarah Palmer gasps and we cut to BOB out of nowhere. The episode after that, from the Hornes eating their dinner in awkward silence to the Man From Another Place dancing in the Red Room, hooked me completely. Unfortunately, I had to wait a couple more years for the Gold Box edition before I could properly watch the series! As someone more accustomed to the rhythm and texture of feature films, I was fascinated and frustrated by *Twin Peaks*; while I loved its sense of ongoing mystery and rich atmospheric setting, I was disappointed when the show seemed to abandon both of those qualities in the back half—at least until David Lynch stepped back in for the unforgettable finale.

I didn't quite know what to expect from the prequel movie. I had heard it was controversial but was intrigued by the return to the powerful Laura material of the earlier episodes and the promise of a potentially richer, darker, deeper cinematic style. What I discovered was one of the most troubling and powerful experiences I've ever felt in a movie. Thanks, not only to Lynch's fearless plunge into material the series had only dared to whisper about, but also to Sheryl Lee's unparalleled performance, drenched in empathy and incredible awareness. For years, I found it hard to reconcile these two *Twin Peaks*—the alluring, maddeningly uneven TV series and the upsetting, unflinching film--and I wondered if they could ever be brought together. Only while watching *The Missing Pieces* [on their own, not integrated into the movie] was I reminded of the subtle connective tissue between these two dramatically different worlds: Laura and the town, film and TV, pure Lynch, and a team of creators working in and around his sensibility. Much of my own subsequent work was borne out of this discovery, one which will continue to fuel this fan's fire for years to come.

Courtesy of Aaron Cohen.

Courtesy of David Wirch.

Courtesy of Pete & Kim Glessman.

Chapter 33

Getting Back To Twin Peaks

Catherine Coulson: David does often say there are a lot of stories left to be told about the town of Twin Peaks, but I'm not sure that he would ever want to revisit those same people. (*Q&A at* Twin Peaks *UK Festival 2012*)

Jay Aaseng (Past Assistant to David Lynch, Drunk in Season 3): The whole time I was working for [David Lynch] there were several opportunities [to return to the world of *Twin Peaks*]. People coming to him with various different things. I think at some point somebody wanted to do a graphic novel or a comic book series.

Harley Peyton on returning to *Twin Peaks*: I've kept in touch with Mark [Frost] in particular over the years and every once in a while we would talk about it and is such a thing possible. I at one point suggested that we do a comic book in the way Joss Whedon did with *Buffy* and *Angel*. We had those conversations, but the real missing piece was with David. David would never really do it. And I think Mark wasn't really certain that he wanted to revisit [*Twin Peaks*] either.

Jay Aaseng: Maybe it just wasn't the project for [David Lynch]. He would often just kinda say it was not a world he was ready to plunge back into. He kind of felt like he was done with it, at least at the time. I certainly believe that probably is how he felt, but at some point, that was obviously rekindled.

Mark Frost: It started with my calling David and saying I think I might have a way to get back to *Twin Peaks*. We had lunch in August of 2012 at Musso & Frank's and enough came out of the conversation to pick up the thread and start following it.

My recollection is that one of the things we did first was actually watched the final episode together and there's that moment where Laura turns to Cooper in the Red Room and says, "I'll see you again in 25 years." That was certainly the moment when the spark plug ignited.

We started talking on a regular basis and nine months to a year, I think, before we actually started writing anything. I don't live in LA anymore. I live about 75 miles north. So we're both comfortable with Skype as a means of communication. So that's what we ended up using and it worked out really well. There was a lot of really fruitful discussion and laying the groundwork for what was to come and that's how it all began.

Sabrina Sutherland (Executive Producer): I really got involved towards the middle of 2013. David and Mark had been working prior to that and writing. So I came in and David explained to me exactly what they were thinking, what they had written down so far and then kind of what they were hoping to do. And I had to create a budget and a schedule based on that. Kind of like a projection of what it possibly could be so that people would say whether or not they would want to support something like that.

You have to figure out how to do everything. It was still in David's head, most of this stuff. So, like, the effects and those kinds of things. Those were visuals that David had in his head and it wasn't even on a written page. Trying to estimate what that might be is definitely a challenge. But it's not just effects. I mean it's everything. Any vehicles, the clothing, the locations and what would be built, what would be practical. It's a lot of stuff to think about. I just would work with David on everything and then having to find out if those locations were even feasible.

Kyle MacLachlan: David and I are neighbors and we are friends. When I'm in Los Angeles I always would bring up, sort of obliquely, the idea of going back to *Twin Peaks*. And he was always sort of a cagey and wasn't really connecting.

Years go by and then [September 2014], he reaches out to me and sort of says he needs to talk to me about something. I knew that there was something brewing, but I had no idea that it was going to be *Twin Peaks*. He said he couldn't speak with me over the phone; it needed to be in person. He was going to be in New York in a couple of days. So we made a meeting place where he was staying, and I went over to see him, and we sat down and he just said to me, "How would you feel about going back to Twin Peaks?" And I said to him, "You know, David, I never really left Twin Peaks." That's all he really needed to hear was that I was back in. Then, he didn't really elaborate but said there were going to be some things that were going to be really challenging and nothing really specific. And I said, "That sounds great."

Debbie Zoller (Makeup Department Head): I kind of knew that something was brewing about five years prior because I got these emails from Sabrina, from David, asking me some very specific questions. And I didn't know it was *Twin Peaks*. I didn't know what the project was. I just knew that there was something brewing. And then I, just like everybody else, read it on Twitter.

Harley Peyton: I saw the tweet about the "gum coming back in style," and my phone rang almost immediately and it was Mark saying, "I just wanted to let you know," and then he explained to me what was happening. And he was very sweet because the point of the call was, "David and I wrote all the scripts together. Had we not, you would have been the first person to call to write some," which is very nice to hear. That's just based on our being friends more than anything else.

> **David Lynch** ✓
> @DAVID_LYNCH
> Dear Twitter Friends: That gum you like is going to come back in style!
> #damngoodcoffee
> 11:30 AM - 3 Oct 2014

> **Mark Frost** ✓
> @mfrost11
> Dear Twitter Friends: That gum you like is going to come back in style.
> #damngoodcoffee
> 11:30 AM - 3 Oct 2014

Debbie Zoller: I think I was at work and I jumped out of my chair and ran outside and called Sabrina immediately, "Is there something that you need to tell me?" She started laughing and then I started laughing, and she [said], "Yes, but give us a few minutes cause we're just sorting some things out."

Kyle MacLachlan: When I was back in LA, [David] would give me certain hours. They weren't episodes, they were just "hours." We never referred to them as episodes. Certain "hours," to read it, look through, just to give me a sense. He would hand me a script over at his house and I would go off to a little exterior location. I'd sit and I'd read the material and I'd come back and hand them back the scripts. It was very compelling and interesting and confusing and exciting and all the things that we finally actually brought it to life. It became clear to me really quickly that the demand on my work was going to be extreme because of the characters.

Catherine Coulson: David called me in the fall [of 2014] and said he was going to do *Twin Peaks* for Showtime and was I interested? I said, "Yes," and he said, "Well, details to follow."

Announcement on Mark Frost writing a new Twin Peaks *book:*
FLATIRON BOOKS TO PUBLISH "THE SECRET LIVES OF TWIN PEAKS" BY SHOW CO-CREATOR MARK FROST (New York—October 16, 2014) Bob Miller, Flatiron Books president and publisher, announced today that the Macmillan division will publish *The Secret Lives of Twin Peaks*, a novel that reveals what has happened to the people of that iconic fictional town since we last saw them 25 years ago and offers a deeper glimpse into the central mystery that was only touched on by the original series. The book is written by New York Times bestselling author Mark Frost, co-creator and executive producer of the series with David Lynch.

Sabrina Sutherland: David and I went on a scout early on at the end of 2014. He and I went up to Washington to see what was there and we had the most wonderful people who took us around. We were able to look at everything that had been in the original and *Fire Walk with Me*. And then, also, we're looking at things that David thought could be in the new series. We did that well before we even started pre-production just to see what was there.

Duwayne Dunham: When David first mentioned the project to me, he said it's gonna be nine hours. And I laughed and said, "Yeah, I know you. Nine will be ten, eleven, twelve." And then he laughed and said, "Or thirteen or fourteen."

Catherine Coulson: And then it kind of fell through for a while because Showtime didn't want to do it the way David did.

David Lynch
April 5, 2015 · 🌐

Dear Facebook Friends, Showtime did not pull the plug on Twin Peaks. After 1 year and 4 months of negotiations, I left because not enough money was offered to do the script the way I felt it needed to be done. This weekend I started to call actors to let them know I would not be directing. Twin Peaks may still be very much alive at Showtime. I love the world of Twin Peaks and wish things could have worked out differently.

Sherilyn Fenn: He called on Easter and said, "I'm out." I said, "What do you mean you're out? If you're out, I'm out, I'm not doing it without you."

Kimmy Robertson: He called me and I was at my sister's, and I literally kind of fell to my knees in the backyard when he said he couldn't do it. And that made me so mad that [the cast] just called each other like at the same time.

Showtime statement: "We were saddened to read David Lynch's statement today since we believed we were working towards solutions with David and his reps on the few remaining deal points. Showtime also loves the world of *Twin Peaks*, and we continue to hold out hope that we can bring it back in all its glory with both of its extraordinary creators, David Lynch and Mark Frost, at its helm."

Kimmy Robertson: I know Kyle has said that he's waited so long to work with him again, and we all waited. And we would do anything for him.

Kyle MacLachlan: There's the creative side of things, and then there's the business side of things. And this was certainly the business side of things and that's where David was: working his way through it with all the folks at Showtime. I just trusted it and hoped that it would work out. I also knew that if it didn't work out, it would have been for very good reasons, being that David wouldn't have had the kind of control that he wanted and that he, at this particular point in his career, absolutely is entitled to. This is how he works. If we were going to go back and make *Twin Peaks*, he was going to make it the *Twin Peaks* he wanted to make. He was going to do everything, and Showtime had to go along with his vision.

Sherilyn Fenn: My understanding is that he had agreed to do nine [parts]. And then once he got into the world, he felt like nine wasn't enough, and he wanted to do twice as many and that meant twice as much money and they said no. And he said he's out. And then there was even talk that Mark and Kyle are still going to do it and that's when we got together. I said, "I'm not doing it. You know, I'm literally not doing it." I love Mark. I love Kyle. Sorry, but you can't lose the key component. I saw how the second season went. It wasn't pretty.

Kyle MacLachlan: I sort of stepped back and let that unfold. I didn't think, really, that my contribution at that time was something that was going to be helpful. So I just said yeah let them work it out and so that they're comfortable and then, hopefully, it will fall in favor of David and we'll be able to go forward.

Debbie Zoller: I was the same as every fan out there. I just had to be patient, and I knew in my heart and soul that I would be there. There was no question, but, again, I just had to be patient like everyone else.

Sherilyn Fenn: I called the other cast members. Mädchen is a computer whiz, and we had this idea. We got everybody on board.

Catherine Coulson: They got the idea to do [a YouTube video] that would go on social media.

Kimmy Robertson: It happened all over the world at the same time. Fans in other countries made their own "No, David, No *Twin Peaks.*"

Catherine Coulson: David said it really made a huge difference because it got so much response.

Kyle MacLachlan: David Nevins, who was the head of Showtime at that point, was very accommodating and really wanted David to have all that he needed. And so they were able to come to terms and the rest is history.

Debbie Zoller: I live around the corner from David Lynch, so it takes me ten minutes to get there. One day Sabrina called and said, "You need to be here now." I ran over to the house, and David was in his art studio. I gave him a big hug and we'd just sit and talk, paint and drink coffee, and he smoked and we just sat there and I said, "So we're going to do this?" And he goes, "Yeah, we're going to do this. Are you ready?" And I said, "Are you ready?"

Then, of course, I had to wait five months, but I was pretty much prepping during that whole time. I was allowed to read the script, but I had to be at his house to read it because they didn't have any production offices. Everything was based out of his house. So I would go and I would read a little bit and absorb that. Then I would go back and read a little bit more and absorb that because I was not allowed to have my own copy of the script. There were only, I think, five scripts total. Obviously, Scott, the first AD, had his, and the costume designer was allowed to have hers, but none of us were allowed to have our own copies. I had to memorize everything.

I must've read it five times backward and forwards because I had to have everything in my head so that I knew continuity to the best of my ability, and knew what I needed to prepare for.

Johanna Ray: I got to read the whole script, which David was constantly rewriting to the very end. Everybody who got to read a script had to read it at his house and leave it there. So that means half the time I couldn't remember all the characters because I didn't have the script in front of me. Then when I spoke to the agents, I couldn't tell them what the character was or what it was about. [I couldn't] say it's even *Twin Peaks* or David Lynch. I didn't have to say much because I've been doing it long enough that agents and managers trusted me enough that it would be a worthwhile project.

Karl Makinen (Inspector Randy Hollister): I guess my experience that best describes working on *Twin Peaks* is when I received the casting call to meet Johanna Ray. I asked my manager, "Are there any sides/copy to prepare?" She said, "No, we don't have anything, I guess they'll give it to you when you arrive." So when I get to the casting office and the Casting Director, Johanna Ray, asks me into the room and has a camera set up. So I sit down and she asks me, "So what did you eat today?" And I explained what I ate that day and I booked it. I wish all auditions were that easy. I loved the surreal experience of working/acting and be directed by David Lynch.

Jim Belushi (Bradley Mitchum): I was at a funeral for a friend of mine, older actor, and I was in my suit and tie and I got a call to show up at some odd address in Van Nuys. And I said, "What's it for?" He says, "I can't tell you." And I say, "Well is there a script?" He goes, "No." I said, "Well, what am I supposed to do?" He said, "You just go in and talk to 'em." I went, "All right. Whatever." So I showed up in my suit and tie sat on the couch. There were a couple of nice people there. They videotaped me and they asked me some questions and I just kind of talked and that was it. Then I got a call that I got the part in David Lynch's *Twin Peaks* and I went, "Was that the weird thing I did?" They said, "Yeah, that was the weird thing you did" [breaks into laughter].

Johanna Ray: I was casting all through production and the shoot. For instance, I had seven months pre-production to bring in actors, put them on tape for David (Lynch) to see and putting the conversations on tape, not a reading or an audition, just chatting with them so that David, when he looked at the tape, he could feel like he was in the same room with me at that time. He would take a long time studying each actor, listening to what they're saying, getting that inner sense of who they are. Worked for seven months doing that, and then it was a seven-month shoot, and basically I was still casting to the very end.

Filming started in September 2015

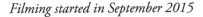
Photo courtesy of Sherilyn Fenn

Sherilyn Fenn: David will say, "Sherilyn Fenn stop tweeting." We were on set, I took one picture of me, literally, in my trailer. I tweeted. By the time I got to the set, I was called directly. "Sherilyn Fenn you can't tweet pictures." I'm like, "Good god. Why can't I tweet a picture?" '

Debbie Zoller on keeping the mystery alive: It was interesting and challenging in the very beginning, not having a script and having to memorize everything. And then finally, I was allowed to take some notes that I had to keep really tight to the chest and couldn't let anybody else see them. I was allowed to take photos, obviously, for continuity. I was allowed to take pictures for my own purposes, but nobody else was. So that became a bit difficult because if I needed a reference to something, I had to step outside and go look at my phone really quick. So because they didn't want phones on set, which I respect. Because honestly, if you're working on a set with David, the last thing you want is for people to be sitting there looking at their Facebook accounts and Twitter and everything. You should be relishing in the moment of being on set with him and experiencing that. I was actually kind of happy about the no phones on set situation, but if I forgot something, I would have to go to the production office. We had a little trailer and they had a safe and I would have to check out one of the scripts from the safe and somebody would sit there with me in the office so that I could look up the issue that I couldn't remember or the question that I had and then give it back to them.

Sabrina Sutherland: The hardest part between production and post was probably post. We were doing it like a feature film. We couldn't start on the process of music or mixing until everything was done being edited. You just didn't know where everything was going to be so you don't want to do it twice. David went through all of that before then he would go in, get all the music,

Instagram

madchenamick · 1h

© 2016 Mädchen Amick · whosay

♥ 932 likes

madchenamick #HappyTwinPeaksDay from #Shelly

do the mixing. Because we just didn't have enough time to do everything. We were color timing at night. We'd be working during the day and then David and I would go to the post facility at night to do the color correction and that, again, was being done as one big thing. We weren't starting to make tapes to be sent to Showtime until everything was done.

Mädchen Amick Posts a picture on Instagram of her in Double R Diner costume.

Duwayne Dunham: As David Lynch was shooting, I'd say, "I already have six hours on the shelf and you're nowhere near halfway through your schedule. I'm going to project we're going to be at 14 maybe even 15 hours." And I would keep adjusting. What never changed was a one-year timeline from the day David started shooting to the day we had to turn over a locked picture to Showtime. That date never changed, even though the movie ballooned to twice the size. I wasn't happy about it cause I told David, I said, "Look, if you're gonna shoot the whole thing, then I'm going to cut the whole thing." It just wasn't possible. And so we put a couple more editors on at the very end for specific material cause we weren't moving off that date. I kept saying, "Is that date etched in stone?" And David said, "It's etched in granite." So you say, "Ok. Well, we'll do it, but this is what it will take."

Showtime CEO **David Nevins** told the Television Critics Association on January 9, 2017 "We've seen the whole thing, it's the pure heroin version of David Lynch." (*Stuever*)

The Secret History of Twin Peaks: A Novel by Mark Frost

Mark Frost: I realized I was so engaged in running the show the first time that I never really had a chance to explore the town as a novelist. And, in fact, my career as a novelist really started post *Twin Peaks*. So it's a chance to use a different skill set and a way of expressing myself that is actually my preferred medium now. I wanted the ability to tell the story in a bunch of different voices. *Twin Peaks* is the story not just of one person or a few people. It's the story of the town.

It seemed, to me, the best way to accomplish that was to tell the story from this very subjective point of view. Meaning somebody could tell their story, then somebody else could tell theirs and we have people commenting on the stories. So it felt a little bit more like a historic mosaic that gave you a three-dimensional picture of the town that wasn't just a place and the people, but it was also the effect of time as a third dimension to see how the town developed and what people contributed to it and so forth. That was the approach they decided on.

[*On if all the* Twin Peaks *books are canon*] Canon is never a word that I use. The universe of the town and the people and the stories seem to me to be broad enough to encompass anything that comes along that's by one of the two primary creators. I have no trouble thinking of those books as part of our ongoing development of this universe, and I thought the book should actually continue in that vein.

To me, a book is, sort of, gifts you leave by the side of the road, and it's up to the person, the passerby, who picks it up and has a look to decide what it is and what they get from it. My hope would be that it gives you a read that is an experience that in its own rights stands alone, but one that also enriches and deepens your appreciation and knowledge of this world that so many people seem to like to visit.

Spencer Collantes, Pieter Dom, Eben Moore, Francie Sogno, Mark Frost, Bryon Kozaczka, Ben Durant and Murray Wasylnuk in 2016.

Chapter 34

Season 3: Part 1
"My Log Has a Message for You"
Aired: May 21, 2017
Written by Mark Frost & David Lynch
Directed by David Lynch

In Memory of CATHERINE COULSON

The Log-line

A man watches a glass box, and Cooper's doppelgänger, Mr. C, recruits help.

Behind the Curtain

Sabrina Sutherland: First let me just qualify one thing. The actual title of the show is just *Twin Peaks* and *The Return* is something that Showtime put on so that it could be distinguished in like the *TV Guide* or whatever, that it wasn't the original series; that it was the new series. It's really just *Twin Peaks*, but I guess people get confused somehow if "*The Return*" isn't added.

I think one of the best things that happened during production was, I was able to go through the script with David repeatedly, put together kind of a first draft of the schedule and then find out from him if he felt like he could do that much in that day. We would keep honing it down, honing it down before even Scott Cameron, the first AD, came on. Scott's really the one who then organizes the shoot, but because I was able to go through it with him so much before Scott even came on, it really helped us pinpoint how we could schedule everything and make it like clockwork.

Duwayne Dunham: David and I never sat down and reviewed a single scene. The only thing we ever looked at together was [when] we spent a lot of time sorting out the opening of the movie and tried a lot of different things. Sabrina was kind of concerned because we were spending a lot of time, but I kept saying, "Sabrina, don't worry. The scenes are in good shape. It's just you got to get this thing up and running and then we just can't change our mind and go back. We gotta make sure it's right." So it took a long time to get the first three hours sorted out.

Dean Hurley (Music Supervisor) on the *Twin Peaks* theme song: I don't think there was any idea to change it. It's an incredible theme, and I think with the new series, how it kind of catapults us 25 years later into a completely different vibe, that's one of the anchors that kind of keeps the through-line or the thread that feels *Twin Peaks*. It just sort of sets that off right at the start of the show. So every episode you get, kind of, this reset to anchor you into that original vibe, even though it's a vastly different beast. (*KEXP, Morgan Chosnyk*)

Kyle MacLachlan: Part of the joy of working with David is that we have such a shorthand. We've known each other for so many years. It's kinda crazy how long it's been, but you immediately slip back. It's like an old shoe. I slipped into that black suit pretty easily.

Richard Beymer on getting back into character: It wasn't easy, and that's not because of David. It was because of me as an actor. I wanted to find this person again, and I put it to sleep a long time ago and we didn't have that much [time], like a lot of actors didn't. I mean you had to hit the nail on the head immediately. There was no warming up. So that was a concern of mine. I would finish a scene and think, "That's just not Ben. I don't know what I'm doing here. This doesn't feel right." And then David would say, "No, no, it's good. It's good. Next one." So I said, "Okay, all right." What can you do? But I wasn't completely living it yet.

Duwayne Dunham: I was thrilled when I saw Bad Cooper for the first time, and that wonderful, strange music, and just his demeanor, and what he looked like.

Kyle MacLachlan: I recognized immediately that the character of Mr. C had to be absolutely the most dangerous person you've ever come across. As an actor, anytime you say, "Okay, he's the most dangerous person in the history of the world," your track? It's a little daunting. But I said, "You know what? We'll find our interpretation of that, David and I. We'll work together and we'll figure out what that is. What makes sense." It was a process.

You start with the script and what it tells you, what it gives you. That's always the best way. You have to read between the lines and figure out what the reality of that character might be, and what he might feel like given his circumstances of how long he's been in this dimension. And what does he like? What does he not like? Pretty simple. And then, as he's not of this world, how does he function in the world? So you start plugging in all these questions really, and they hopefully will give you answers. It's about creating not only the interior life but the exterior of the guy.

I look back at [the character] banging his head against the glass, and we evolved him quite a bit from just that, but then at the same time that's the beginning.

Nicole LaLiberté (Darya): Day one, I remember when my manager, Allan, called me with the news. I'd just finished shooting something. It was late, stars over the dark Pacific sea, and there I was, leaping in the air in an empty parking lot. "It's a rebirth!" he said. I felt trusted by David and that trust made all the difference.

Christopher Gray (Extras Casting Director): Working with David has always been a unique and surreal experience where we together journey to cast unforgettable faces that are perpetually memorable. Faces that captivate our viewers, thus shifting a mind-altering experience of reality up close. I love David's true-life casting process. It's the real deal.

Steven James Tingus (Silent Cabin Man #1): As a leader here in Hollywood on diversity and disability inclusion, I was surprised yet grateful to have received a phone call during the summer of 2016 from Christopher Gray, casting director for David Lynch. He said that David had come across my work here in Hollywood and wanted to know if I'd like to be in his Showtime *Twin Peaks: The Return* miniseries. I said yes and was asked for a phone video of my interest, and what disability inclusion means to me. Well, I got the part of Silent Cabin Man #1. It was an amazing experience, starting with arriving at a creepy log cabin set way up in the Culver City mountains.

David Lynch, writer/director, couldn't have been more welcoming and genuinely committed to disability inclusion as he was in the original TV series. I was teamed up with fellow actor Kyle MacLachlan, and being my first TV credit, I couldn't have asked for anything more. To have the opportunity to work with such established talent is a treat in itself, but to feel the camaraderie and authentic diverse inclusion was priceless. I pray that Mr. Lynch will invite me back for the next installment where I'll have a lot of lines and a dark character.

Debbie Zoller: A lot of the stuff was just kind of being created organically and at the last minute. And thankfully, I had a wonderful team of help who didn't mind working on the weekends. Basically, what would happen is Richard Redlefsen and I, he was my key, we'd be up in Washington and David would talk to me about a character and we would sculpt it and then ship it back down to Los Angeles to Vincent Van Dykes Effects lab. And then [Vincent Van Dyke Effect] would do the molding and make the prosthetics and then he would FedEx it back up to us. So things were very kind of last minute, yet at the same time, they weren't.

Photo courtesy of Debbie Zoller.

Vincent Van Dyke (Owner/Creative Director of Vincent Van Dyke Effects): Working on the new *Twin Peaks* was a dream-like experience. When Debbie Zoller approached us about the work, myself and crew were over the moon. Working on a David Lynch project is like none other, and the way you are pushed is completely unique as well. We are really proud of what we were able to contribute to such a magical show.

Geoffrey Gould (Forensic Photographer): They're really good at hiding stuff cause all I saw in the bed was the body. They didn't have the head on the pillow when I was in the room. So when I started the [part] I was like, "Oh that's surprising. That's interesting."

Kimmy Robertson on working with Harry Goaz (Andy Brennan) again: It was like being with a husband that you had divorced from that you didn't want a divorce from. He's so wonderful. Harry is, like, one of my favorite people on the planet. He's so nice. It was just magic to be with him.

Johanna Ray: David Lynch would be out filming and then he'd go home and he'd be writing new scenes, writing new characters. I don't know how he got any rest at all, but he knows exactly what he wants. The minute he steps on the set, he's totally prepared in his head. It's really amazing. Very impressive.

Sabrina Sutherland: David likes to experiment. So you're never locked into something. It's never this is what we're gonna do, A, B, C, D, because David will say, "Hey, I want to do Y today." Even though Scott Cameron was able to schedule us, and we kept on that schedule, David would want to add something new. And that was my one disappointment that I wasn't able to give him something every day because we were fighting time to get everything done.

Dep Kirkland (Police Chief Mike Boyd): There simply is no film (or in this case film disguised as television) set like it. A David Lynch set is more like a living organism. With David at its heart pumping out the life-blood (and the smoke, but we don't talk about that) into every arterial tributary. It's a living thing and even though there is no doubt who is the boss of the enterprise, you are constantly aware – from arrival on-site until you pull away – that you are in a familial, collaborative world. Part of that might be because of the decades that David has worked with the same key creatives. There is a shorthand and an economy of movement that is remarkable to witness. Even when a dispute arises, it is simply resolved – David somehow winning, again – through some grumbles and mumbles, all while the organism is adjusting and moving on. Some people have wondered about the fact that the man doesn't yell cut at the end of the written page but, instead, lets it run, sometimes for a while.

He doesn't tell me his secrets but, as an actor, my gut knows the answer. He's waiting to see what might happen. That small nugget of unspoken respect simply reminds us that he is one of us, on a shared journey to find the truth of the story. He is an artist's artist of the highest order.

Brings Back Some Memories

Ben: On May 21, 2017, Showtime aired parts one and two on TV, and parts three and four were available to stream that night. So I stayed up until one in the morning watching all four parts.

Bryon: I waited. I wanted something to look forward to that following week.

Ben: Having waited over 25 years for *Twin Peaks*, I just couldn't wait another week for more.

Favorite Quotes and Scenes

Ben and **Bryon:** Our favorite scene is the introduction of Mr. C, aka Evil Cooper, with the slowed-down version of "American Woman" by Muddy Magnolias. It was so sinister, dark and dirty sounding, and it really sets the mood perfectly for what we will be a lasting impression of Mr. C.

Ben: Kyle MacLachlan did an amazing job as Mr. C and that scene really made this episode.

Bryon: My favorite quote is from ???????, AKA The Fireman, who says to Dale Cooper, "You are far away." Looking back at this one particular line really helps me understand Season 3 more and more. The Fireman is giving us all the clues to Cooper's journey that we will see unfold in the next seventeen parts. But, "You are far away" explains why we will not see the real Dale Cooper until Part 16. This is Special Agent Dale Cooper's odyssey back from the Black Lodge to Twin Peaks.

Ben: We'll get the essence of Dale Cooper through living the daily life of Dougie Jones, but he is far away from the waking world.

My favorite quote comes from the Log Lady, "My log has a message for you. Something is missing and you have to find it." Laura Palmer goes missing from the Black Lodge and Cooper is told by her father, Leland Palmer, to find her. Cooper is missing in space and time and there are missing pages from Laura Palmer's secret diary. A big theme in Season 3 is about people and things missing and the need to find them.

Community Commentary

John Bernardy (25YearsLaterSite.com): I was one of those people who watched the Season 2 finale on TV back in 1991 when absolutely no one had any idea what was about to happen. Since that night, I've put an inordinate amount of thought into how Dale could get out of the Lodge, not once expecting to get a true answer. The only thing I wanted from the new series was to finally find out how Dale gets out. I didn't care about anything else. I knew it would be strange and confounding, and I didn't even care about who would be in it, or when, or for how long. That stuff would sort itself out. I trusted Lynch and Frost to take me on a journey again, and whatever that meant would be worth it. I wasn't even expecting a concrete ending. But I WAS expecting to see how Dale finally got out. And I don't think that happened. You keep a show in your heart for decades and you ask for ONE thing ... I may not have gotten my want, but Season 3 DID give us the template for HOW Dale could get out, and that's a lot of value right there. I may always love Seasons 1 and 2 more than Season 3, but as time moves on, Season 3 might end up being the most important.

Chapter 35

Season 3: Part 2
"The Stars Turn and a Time Presents Itself"
Aired: May 21, 2017
Written by Mark Frost & David Lynch
Directed by: David Lynch

In Memory of FRANK SILVA

The Log-line

After 25 years, Cooper speaks with Laura Palmer again in the Red Room.

Behind the Curtain

Nicole LaLiberté (Darya): The moment before "action." Everyone's awareness swimming in silence. Waiting patiently and attentively for the right moment to begin with all of one's light.

Stewart Strauss (Black Lodge Woodsman): The jail scene, which was me in Part 2, I had no idea when that was going to be used, if it would be used at all, and where it was supposed to be.

It's a day I'll never forget. Being in the actual location, the Los Angeles Police Museum in South Pasadena. It's a really cool place and it looks very much the way it did. At least those jail cells look dark, musty, dingy. Then add the lighting and what David and the crew did with it, and you know [it's] quite eerie. Just seeing myself in the jail cell at all before I disappeared, just the fact that I was there in David Lynch's world, in *Twin Peaks*, I was ecstatic.

Joe Adler (Roger): My time on *Twin Peaks* was unlike any other acting experience I've ever had, starting with the audition. As some may know, Lynch doesn't have actors read sides, he just watches taped conversations between actors and Johanna Ray. I remember leaving my audition wondering if my "conversation" went well. Eight months later he offered me a role. I then remember wondering what he would be like. He's always seemed so mysterious to me. Sure enough, he lived up to what I had created in my mind as being quite mysterious, but really lovely to work with. What I noticed most was how much the crew enjoyed working for him. That speaks volumes. Additionally, I felt very lucky to work with an all-time legendary character actor, Patrick Fischler. I had such a memorable experience being a part of this historic series.

Sheryl Lee: Working with David, working on this show, and working on this character, is a different way of working than a lot of other jobs. It requires a different part of my brain and a different skill set. For example, going to work in the Red Room. That's a very different part of creativity than going to play a doctor on a show. So neither one is harder or better or worse. It's just very different (Courtesy of *Fire Walk with Me* event with special guests Ray Wise & Sheryl Lee at Studio 35 Cinema & Drafthouse, July 19 - 21, 2019).

David Eubank (First Camera Assistant (A-camera)): It was a thrill being invited to work with David, Mark, Kyle and the entire family on *Twin Peaks: The Return*. Even though I was one of the new kids in town, I always felt welcomed and appreciated. To witness the excitement and love of so many original cast and crew members reuniting after 25 years, was a rare treat. Every day David creates his life and work with a painterly touch, which always inspires and invigorates those around him. So, working long hours at night, in the freezing cold, in a remote field … no problem. One of my most treasured takeaways from this experience, is having my 44-year Transcendental Meditation practice reawakened. I will never miss another day.

Nicole LaLiberté: On the set: Listening to the quiet mystery together, handing over the reins for "It" to live in exactly the way "It" wanted in each moment, with focus and infinite playfulness and mischief, made for the crème de la crème of dirt boxes.

Duwayne Dunham: David has a rhythm and a pace that he enjoys. He's worked long enough, and he's earned the right to have it be any way he wants it. So many things that I worked with him on in the past had time limitations. *Blue Velvet*, when we screened the first time, three hours and 57 minutes… The lights came on and David sat for a minute and then he turned to me and he said, "Wow, I really like it. I just have one problem." I was thinking, "Wow, this is easy." "For me to have final cut, it has to be less than two hours in length." So we had a big job ahead of us. *Wild at Heart*, we cut it way down. And then of course television has restraints on a certain number of commercials and they have to occur at certain places on the clock. And the ultimate running time is like 43 minutes and some odd seconds. You gotta be within those limitations or constraints. The more recent *Twin Peaks*, David didn't have that. And he didn't write it episodically. He wrote it as one giant continuous story. So part of the challenge was just to figure out using the script as the roadmap, where do these scenes fit? I think the time of each episode had to be between 52 and 60 minutes. It just was one of those things that kind of worked out that just about every episode ended at the Roadhouse with the musical number.

Dean Hurley (Music Supervisor): [The Roadhouse acts] were captured in a way where it was almost like a little mini-festival where they played their song, and the next act came on. It kinda was crafted in this way to create a lot of freedom in how David wanted to use them. (*Courtesy of KEXP, Morgan Chosnyk*)

Ben & Dean Hurley in 2018.

Duwayne Dunham: David, I think, shot I forget how many bands, maybe twelve bands in a day or two, something like that. And everybody did two or three songs.

I hired an editor who did a really terrific job and I said, "Here, your job is to take all of these songs and make it a music video." We're going to cut music videos and then I'll use that as a basis when I select a song that goes in a certain scene and we'll figure out how it plays within that scene or it plays on its own. That was a great thing.

Dean Hurley: I've been a Chromatics fan for a long time. I was just psyched to introduce David to them, who heard them. I was in touch with their manager and I played "Shadow" for David and it was pretty immediate that he said, "This is a great song. I love the band." When I play things for David, I like to kind of find web videos where there's a performance involved as opposed to just playing a song for him. Cause I want him to really get [it], especially for this when they're visually on camera and the energy and the look and everything sort of factors in, I want him to experience that. Showing performance videos of them and playing the song for him, everything sort of crystallizes and it's either a yes or no. I want him to fall in love with something. (*Courtesy of KEXP, Morgan Chosnyk*)

Favorite Quotes and Scenes

Bryon: My favorite scene is after William Hastings argues with his wife while he is locked up in a holding cell. He is left all alone holding his head in bewilderment on what has happened to his life. The camera pans to the right slowly to two holding cells over and we see a man in black just sitting and staring at the camera. He is covered head to toe in black soot with only the whites of his eyes showing any color. He slowly fades away with only his head still barely showing as it floats away. This scene grabbed my imagination. What did we just witness? What does this mean for Hastings? Is this the new evil Twin Peaks will have to face? I had so many questions and theories.

Ben: My favorite scene has to be in the Red Room with Agent Cooper and Laura Palmer facing off (pun intended). Laura predicted at the end of Season 2 that she would see him again in 25 years, and we get to witness their reunion. Somehow Lynch/Frost is able to amaze us once again in the Red Room. Besides the typical walking and talking backward, Laura exposes her face of light and is ripped away screaming from the Red Room. Truly a sight of awe.

Ben and **Bryon:** Our favorite quote in this part is from Shelly Briggs who says, "James is still cool. He's always been cool."

Dean Hurley: I guess that's a matter of contention among fans, you know, whether he is cool or not. (*KEXP, Morgan Chosnyk*)

Bryon: This line of dialogue hit the *Twin Peaks* community like wildfire. Everyone went from mocking James Hurley during Season 2 because of his melodramatic side plot--no fault of his own mind you, as we blame the writers on that one. But now we have Shelly Briggs saying to her friends and us the audience that James is cool and he always was cool. I think Lynch and Frost made James cool again in Season 3.

Ben: There is this nostalgic feeling you get when entering the Roadhouse and we hear the Chromatics playing "Shadow." They have a similar sound to the Roadhouse singer Julee Cruise. We hear the lyrics "For the last time," and it gave me the feeling that maybe these eighteen parts are the last we'll get of *Twin Peaks* and I should just enjoy every second of it.

Community Commentary

Jeff Lemire (Author of *Gideon Falls, Sweet Tooth*): There's nothing in the world I'm more passionate about than *Twin Peaks*, and the beauty of that is finding like-minded souls like *Twin Peaks Unwrapped* who keep the fire walking with me and all the *Peaks* community with their intelligent and heartfelt considerations of David Lynch's masterpiece.

Photo: Jeff Lemire's Cover for Blue Rose Magazine *Issue #5*

Chapter 36

Season 3: Part 3
"Call for Help"
Aired: May 28, 2017
Written by Mark Frost & David Lynch
Directed by David Lynch

In Memory of DON S. DAVIS and MIGUEL FERRER

The Log-line

Agent Cooper takes over the life of Dougie Jones and tries his luck at slot machines in the Silver Mustang Casino.

Behind the Curtain

Nae (Naido): I was a *Peakser* in Japan. It was a big movement. Mostly because of the unique characters portrayed and the sense of color in *Twin Peaks*. But even before that, the first cinema ticket I ever purchased was to the movie *Dune*.

Maybe I should keep this to myself, for not being considered weird, but here it goes. When I was meditating on a small island in the Mediterranean Sea I got a feeling and checked my naked body. I felt I needed to prepare. This vision was followed a few days later by a phone call from my manager in Los Angeles saying, can you come back.

Naido's room was really similar to my room in Greece. Arched ceiling like a monastery, fireplace, mauve atmosphere and even the lock on the French door leading to the balcony was the same.

The opportunity to play a torn, mysterious, shocking but still firm being as Naido, is something magical. It updated me as an actress.

Debbie Zoller: Naido's prosthetic was a huge collaboration between me, David, Richard, my key, Naido, as well, because she brings it to life. But David got in there with us with the sculpture, helping us figure out where the hills and valleys were in that sculpture. And then he also wanted the cuts in the sculpture very specific, and it wasn't until we did a test on her that he said I want you to add as if there was skin oozing out of those cuts. So that's how it comes together. And then he [said], "I want stitches, hand-laid in there. I want it to have stitches." Of course, then I realized I had to  hand lay the stitches on every piece and we had 20 of those pieces. That was a huge collaboration with all of us just trying to get that to look exactly how he envisioned it. And then there was a little bit of blood that David would like to add into those little cut pieces. I don't know how close you would see Naido's face, but if you freeze-frame on it, you'll see the detail. [I would say to David], "Hey, do you want to come and add this?" Some of the things we would do at the last minute on set and those were some of those things. So he always liked to get in there and he wanted it to have a little shine. So I was giving him the product we would use and he would take it on his fingers and he would make it shiny and stuff. If he could do the whole thing himself he would.

Nae was completely blind. I asked if we could have eye holes in it for her because I knew she would be in it for long periods of time, and (David Lynch) said, "Absolutely not. She's a professional actress. She will handle it. I have no doubt. Absolutely not, Debbie."

Nae: That role was not without its challenges; with three hours to put the makeup on and being blind for thirteen hours, driven around by Michael, who is David's personal assistant, in a wheelchair, it was one of the biggest challenges in my 30-year career.

Comparing the shooting schedule in Tokyo or Hollywood, it is the same everywhere, but the difference in *Twin Peaks* is the waiting time is because David Lynch was meditating. I loved this waiting time because I also do meditation. I understand how it assists with the creativity process.

Debbie Zoller: on Naido: What we would do is, [Nae Yuuki] would come to set, I would bring her into the trailer. The first day I showed her everything, where everything was, where she was going to be sitting. We showed her her trailer so she would have the image in her head of what the makeup trailer looked like, what her personal trailer looked like. So she knew how to find things, and then I would take her out to set and we would walk her out there so she could feel the ground, and feel and see everything so that all of her other senses would take over once that prosthetic piece was put on. And once she was in it, I always made sure either myself or Richard, or Michael, David's assistant, had a hand on her at all times. I got a wheelchair and I'd push her out into the set so that she didn't have to walk, but at least she had that image in her mind as she knew where she was going. She'd put herself in a very Zen place. She's [an] amazing actress. Nae is my hero because she brought that character to life like no one's business.

Sabrina Sutherland: Scott Cameron, who's the First AD, and myself, and David would meet pretty much every Sunday to review the next week's work. And this was when we'd hash out what we planned and if David was comfortable with it, what he wanted to see, and things like that. And during one meeting, he hadn't cast yet the guy who throws the bottle during [Audrey's dancing in Part 16]. So I said, "Scott, should do that." And Scott laughed and he says, "Yeah, well you should be Jackie, the floor attendant." So David said, "Okay." (*Courtesy of Tim Fuglei interview*)

Kyle MacLachlan (Agent Cooper/Dougie): The character of Dougie was also challenging but was a little bit quicker to play and a little more fun, obviously. I developed that with David as well.

[Dougie is] like a baby obviously. Everything in the world he experiences is for the first time. I debated how much of a memory he had, but I said, "No, he's got to have a memory." So once he does something kind of like a baby, you sort of remember; it becomes a pattern. It's like training a dog.

Sabrina Sutherland (Jackie, the Casino floor attendant): The very first take of Kyle was Dougie, and I know Kyle. When we're in the scene I come up to him and talk to him, and he turned and he spoke his line. I think the first take, I just kind of moved backward because he was something I didn't recognize at all. He was so in that character. He's so good. He's so versatile and just really amazing on all the characters that he does in *Twin Peaks*. I really think he did a hell of a performance, but when he hit me with that Dougie, I didn't know what to say; I kind of stuttered.

Kyle MacLachlan: It's always challenging because we're all friends. You've known each other for years. And you kind of have to pretend. I'm now relating to [Sabrina] in a different way than I would relate to her just in the day-to-day. For a moment, it's a little bit shocking to realize that the responses from me that she's used to, whether it's facial mannerism or language, are now different. I think it takes everybody, like, a beat to sort of figure that out.

Sabrina Sutherland: In the scene, I'm supposed to follow him down this corridor, kind of turn around a corner, and we're out of the shot and then Kyle looks at me and goes, "That's the first time you met Dougie, huh?"

Kyle, MacLachlan, Debbie Zoller, & Sabrina Sutherland

Photo courtesy of Debbie Zoller.

Debbie Zoller: [During pre-production] Basically my main focus was designing the different Kyle characters. Getting Agent Cooper done, and then figuring out from agent Cooper what his evil doppelgänger would be, and then figuring out Dougie, and then figuring out the other Dougie. So that was kind of what was milling around in my head for the most part in July and August 2015. And then I would meet with David. We would talk a little bit more as it got a little closer and then we did a camera test, and I had teeth made for Kyle. I had plumpers made for Kyle for the test. We had contact lenses; all things that we needed to test on him.

Dean Hurley: When David Lynch originally thought of this series, one of the directives was, "I want x amount of bands. I want a lot of bands to populate the Roadhouse." It's going to be like, every time you go back it's a different act. He had a lot of acts already and I was coming in to kind of supplement, throw things in front of him, get him to react to things, get them to fall in love with these new acts that I was finding. And one of them was The Cactus Blossoms which I [was] just kind of poking around the Internet [and] heard this group. And I was just pretty excited and I remember I was so excited that, like, I couldn't really contain myself. So when David came down and he's like, "What do you got? What are you listening to?" And I said, "What would you say if I told you we could get The Everly Brothers in this new season of *Twin Peaks*?" And he just looked at me. He was like [fucking A.] I played it for him and we went through several cuts of their album, which is phenomenal.

The thing with The Everly Brothers that has rarely happened throughout time is that you have to have the familial relationship of two brothers with vocal chords that are similar but just slightly off. And then when those chords come together, it creates the thing of that close voiced harmony that sounds so incredible. Like, the phrasing is tight, the tonality, the timbre tight, and it just creates this one singular voice from the two voices. It has to be family in order for that to happen, which hearing that is pretty thrilling. (*KEXP, Morgan Chosnyk*)

Favorite Quotes and Scenes

Ben: My favorite scene is Cooper entering the purple world. Lynch gives us a new and strange place to explore that is unlike anything we have ever seen. It seems to be a place between the Red Room and the real world. Cooper and Naido seem to be moving forward and backward in space and time. Watching it again, it seems like Naido knows Cooper.

Bryon: We find out later that Diane is Naido, so maybe she does recognize him by touch. This sort of mirrors Cooper and Diane having sex in the hotel in Part 18, when Diane is touching his face.

Ben and **Bryon:** Our favorite quote comes from Cooper as Dougie in Silver Mustang Casino when he plays a slot machine and he yells, "Hell-o-o-o!"

Bryon: The *Twin Peaks* community loves to refer to this.

Ben: It is just so funny.

Bryon: My scene has to do with Andy, Lucy, Hawk, and chocolate bunnies.

Deputy Chief Tommy 'Hawk' Hill: It's not about the bunny! Is it about the bunny? [Pause] No! It's not about the bunny.

This scene between Andy, Lucy, and Hawk is classic *Twin Peaks*. We see the chocolate bunnies from Laura Palmer's case file and one of the bunnies is missing. Lucy had bad gas, and to remedy that she ate one of the bunnies. She feels devastated that she had eaten it since this was evidence from an old case.

Ben: This goes back to the Log Lady mentioning to Hawk that something is missing and he has to find it and it has to do with his heritage. It's wonderful that Lynch/Frost brought Cooper's throwaway line in the pilot about holding chocolate bunnies into Season 3.

Community Commentary

JB Minton (Author of *A Skeleton Key To Twin Peaks*, Co-host of *The Red Room Podcast*): I was forced to watch *Twin Peaks* in 2010 and I wasn't all that impressed. The show was nearly 20 years old and wasn't even released on Blu-ray at the time. I was distracted by *Breaking Bad*, *The Walking Dead*, and *Mad Men*. I had never seen a David Lynch film either, so his name didn't impress me. But then time stretched out and *Twin Peaks* started working on me. I kind of wanted to go back and take another look, maybe, someday. And then *The Missing Pieces* came out and I could revisit the show on Blu-ray in beautifully restored high definition. I was interested again. And then those famous twin tweets dropped announcing that *Twin Peaks* would be returning for a Season 3. I was all in and I was not disappointed. In some ways, my lack of nostalgia about the original run was a benefit, as I went into Season 3 with zero expectations. I found Season 3 to be a transformative experience on the level of when I first read Henry Miller as a teenager. It consumed me and changed me, so much that I wrote a book about what Season 3 meant to me and what I think happened. And of course, the *Twin Peaks* community is what really keeps us coming back to the art.

Chapter 37

Season 3: Part 4
"...Brings Back Some Memories"
Aired: May 28, 2017
Written by Mark Frost & David Lynch
Directed by David Lynch

The Log-line

Cooper, as Dougie, makes himself at home. Gordon Cole meets with Bryson.

Behind the Curtain

Harley Peyton: It really came together in the fourth [part]. That was really worthwhile for me because I spent a lot of time going, "I'm digging this, it's brilliant. There's all this cool stuff happening, but it just didn't quite feel like *Twin Peaks* to me." *Twin Peaks* was always about the surreality of the normal, and the early [parts] felt like the surreality of David Lynch to me, which is an awesome thing. It's not a bad thing at all. It's great. But it was really the fourth [part] where I kinda went, "Oh, here we go!"

Ethan Suplee (Bill Shaker): [Quoting Harold Smith from Episode 12] "There are things you can't get anywhere... but we dream they can be found in other people." In reality, though, they only exist within the mind of Mr. Lynch.

Sabrina Sutherland: [As Jackie, the Casino floor attendant] David was testing me, maybe. He would throw things, change dialogue, things like that. For me, not being an actor, it was kind of hair raising because I was like, "Oh no, I can't even remember what I'm supposed to say. Now you're giving me something else to say," but it was all fun.

Brett Gelman (Supervisor Burns): I could go on and on about my very brief yet profound experience working on this show--working with my hero David Lynch, an artist whose films not only mean the world to me but completely changed how I think. His casting director Johanna Ray was my next-door neighbor at the time and is a very good friend. She brought me in to audition, and I was told that David had chosen me to play Burns. I couldn't believe it. I only worked for a few days, but upon even entering my trailer I felt a difference in energy than just moments before, in my car heading to set. I remember I was changing in my trailer and then BOOM. My trailer shook like crazy. I went outside and a car had run into it. And I don't mean a car belonging to someone associated with the shoot. A civilian's car. So strange. Yet, in a way, so perfect.

I got to set and was taken to meet [David Lynch]. I was so nervous. When I got to him he looked at my face with these bright shining eyes. He smiled this gigantic smile. "Hiiiiiiiiii!" he resonated in what is truly one of the best voices on the planet. All of my nervousness melted away. His presence felt safe. Not what you would assume. But it makes sense. Only someone so immediately comforting could get the people around him to dive into such intense material.

I started filming very late in the shoot but I remember the crew being so happy. At least they seemed that way. I think only because they knew that they were working on something that was beyond special. When I got to set I met Kyle MacLachlan, which was also a mind fuck for me. He was also so incredibly kind. I remember Kyle being in the strange trance that he was in. Mr. Lynch was sitting in this chair in this tiny office that was our set, with an unlit cigarette in his hand. After a few minutes, the First AD whispered something in his ear. Mr. Lynch perked up "Oh really?! You are a dear!" The AD's message became clear as David immediately lit up his cigarette. He gave us notes on the scene while he smoked, and I felt transported to another time. He gave me the intention of what he wanted from me and specific blocking of when and how he wanted me to lift the bag of money onto the table and push it to Kyle. It was choreography. Not just physical, but emotional, psychological choreography that you felt in the tone of that singular voice. Beyond specific. Beautiful dance steps to release yourself into.

He sat down next to MacLachlan who was, again, in this trance. He called him Kale. "Kale remember, just run your numbers. Run your numbers Kale." Kyle just nodded very subtly while he took Mr. Lynch's direction. I had no idea what the hell it meant, but I felt the note's poignancy. We did a rehearsal and I don't know if it was Lynch or me, but once he said action I felt the room change. I felt like the tone of the room had changed into that energy that you only experience when you watch David Lynch's work. It felt like a nightmare, but a nightmare you wanted to have. That you wanted to bask in. Now at the end of the scene, both Kyle and I are standing, and I tell him that we are watching him. Then he looks at my security camera on the ceiling and then I follow his gaze. It was a rehearsal of my close up and so David could only see my face and the back of Kyle's head. And when it came to the part where Kyle looked at the camera he sort of did it in a joking silly way. I thought, "Well if Kyle MacLachlan is joking around, who the fuck am I not to joke around with him?" So then I looked at the camera in a silly way. All of a sudden I heard a voice yelling from the other room. "NO NO NO! No horsing around! This is serious business here!" For some reason, even though I got the message loud and clear, there was something oddly comforting in getting yelled at by David Lynch. I mean if you're gonna get yelled at by someone, I recommend it being him.

I ain't no snitch so I didn't reveal that I had made the face because of Kyle. And Kyle made it up to me by giving me a little chuckle and a barely muttered "sorry" under his breath. We then did the take for real. No horsing around. Serious business, and at the end I guess I redeemed myself in my hero's eyes when he yelled even louder this time, "BEYHOOTIFUL!!" Holy shit! I just got a "beautiful" from David Lynch!

Every moment from this job feels like a story. That's what the man's mere presence does. Just watching him think is a story. Between takes, I talked with MacLachlan a bit. Again, just the nicest. We weren't sent full scripts so I had no idea what his storyline was. I remember saying to him that I couldn't wait to see what all of this meant. Kyle once again flashed that gorgeous subtle perfect smile. "Me too."

Jay Larson (Limo Driver): When I arrived to set, the Second AD asked if I wanted to meet David Lynch. I was like, "Ahhhh, yeah." He greeted me with a giant smile and a firm handshake in between drags of his cigarette. And then he starts giving me direction for each scene I will be doing over the course of my time on set. He started with the scene we were shooting and just kept going. In my head, I was like, "Should I write this down? Is he going to repeat any of this on the other days we shoot?" As we waited for them to rig the late '90s limo with camera gear, the DP approached and asked if I had ever driven a limo before. I was like, "No, but I should be ok." The AD was very concerned because the limo was old, long, it bottomed out, and it was rigged with lights and a camera blocking my view. I looked at David as if to say, "I got this." He looked at me, smiled, looked at his AD, and said, "He's got it." I mean, how can you not love this guy? I did a quick test run and we were off.

In the scene, I was driving, and Kyle MacLachlan was in the back, and we were talking through the rearview mirror. But there wasn't enough room in the back for the camera, DP, Kyle, and David. So Kyle sat out and I read my lines with David Lynch. Did you read that right? Here I am, just a stand-up comedian who does some acting from time to time, and I'm driving this old limo reading lines with David Lynch for *Twin Peaks*, one of the most iconic shows in television history. The scene ends with me pulling up in front of Naomi Watts' house. I get out and walk around and open the limo door. I get around to the door and I hear David yell cut. I walk around to his side and he rolls the window down, gives me some direction and says, "It's all great. Let's go again," and he rolls the window up. I walk back to the driver's seat thinking, "I'm getting direction from David Lynch out of a window of a 1990s limo. Who am I?"

David Duchovny (Denise Bryson): I was so happy to be asked back to do it again. Then to come back and be directed by David, but also to do a scene with him. I was quite nervous to come in.

I remember we did it on a Saturday night because I was shooting Aquarius at the time. So I had like a crew cut and I was playing this macho '60s policemen and I had to go on some Saturday night and just put the dress back on. I worked with David and he was totally cool. I remember saying, "This is a little vain." I was looking at myself in the mirror before going out to set and I was like, "Hmm, Denise, the years have not been kind," but I still had good legs. I was thinking, "I gotta lead with my best parts." And so David and I blocked the scene and I was behind the desk sitting the whole scene. I don't think I told David I wanted to show off my legs, but I said, "Could I at one point, maybe, just walk over to the front of the desk and kind of lean on it and play the rest of the scene on like that?" And he said, "That would make my character uncomfortable." And I said, "I don't want to make you uncomfortable".

[On "Fix your hearts or die"] It's a fucking great line. And something about those clown comics. It was just a weird but wonderful phraseology, man. There was a fan that made me pins, like little broaches, that said fix your heart or die. It is a great line.

As a director myself as well, it was just very interesting to watch David work and as a fan and a watcher of his work, it's a real opportunity and pleasure and honor just to see a guy who's so totally in control of the tone of what he does and for that tone to be so unique. It's just one of the high moments for me as a performer to be able to work with him and work on that show.

John Pirruccello (Deputy Chad): The first time you see Chad, he's leaning against the desk and I think that's like one of the last things we shot actually. Chad wants to make sure that he's getting credit for this arrest that's happened and so he's like, I did that. It's a simple little line where I just had to say, "I arrested that guy. It was a DUI. He blew a 0.20, could barely find his nose in front of his face" or whatever the line is. I have some learning issues and I sometimes swap things around and then just like get stuck there. I couldn't say it. I kept saying 2.0. I did it like three times in a row and it's at a certain point, I just walked out into the middle of the room and I looked over at David and I was like, "What the fuck is happening?" I don't even know what's going on. He's laughing and he's like, "Just get back there, you'll get it." So at that point once you get your head, it's hard to get out of your head. Cause then all I'm thinking about is just the literal line and not anything else. So I go [back to] leaning against the desk and I look over and Bob Forster goes, "See the guy blowing into the tube" and I went, "Oh ... Right!" Then Jody, who plays the dispatcher, she looks over and she sort of puts her fingers up to her mouth and blows just so quietly. It was very intimate. I felt completely supported by those guys and it was Bob that [noticed], John needs to be grounded right now and he's not grounded and he did what he could to ground me and it worked—the next take—perfect.

Dana Ashbrook: I always envied the Twin Peaks Police Department. I always wanted to be a part of it. So it was nice for me to finally get to play cops and robbers. I enjoyed so much working with Bob Forster, Harry Goaz, Kimmy Robertson, and Michael Horse. These guys are my dear old friends. That was a lot of fun for me.

The crying thing is not out of character for Bobby. I cried a lot. Then when you see me cry in the new one, it's like on track. Bobby is a crier. He's in touch with his stuff.

Harley Peyton: The introduction of Wally Brando is one of my favorite things that I've ever seen on the show. That's pure Mark Frost. That whole speech that he had. It's so great. It was so much fun.

Michael Cera (Wally Brando): Working on *Twin Peaks* was an enormous pleasure. My time on set only amounted to one night, but it was a very happy time for me. Nancy Steiner was doing the costumes and she's a good friend of mine. I was so happy to see a familiar face when I first got there. I asked her if she knew who I was going to be doing my scenes with and she said, "I can't say anything." The secrecy around everything was very intense, everybody was made to sign NDAs. When I signed for my per diem, I saw that Amanda Seyfried had also signed the sheet, and felt like I had accidentally learned something I wasn't supposed to know.

Mark Frost greeted me in my trailer and hung out with me for a bit which made me feel very welcome. Robert Forster introduced himself and gave me a letter opener as a gift which I still have to this day. Kimmy Robertson and Harry Goaz were both so warm and kind and encouraging. David greeted me with a big smile which put me immediately at ease and then went to meditate during the dinner break.

Kimmy Robertson: Having dinner before we shot with Michael Cera, who was going to be playing my son, that was really fun because we were right there near where the mill was and we were right by the sheriff's station eating outside in a tent. That was special.

Michael Cera: The whole scene feels to me like it took very little time to shoot. We rehearsed, David asked me to honor the pauses as much as possible, and then we shot. David told me that it was "money in the bank" when I held my fist up in a certain way. We did one or two takes, maybe three, and then it was done.

Ian Buchanan (Dick Tremayne) on Wally Brando: I thought he looked more like Dick's child with his sense of style.

Michael Cera: While they were turning around to shoot Robert Forster's side, there was a crew snack brought around of meatballs in some kind of broth. Mark Frost was eating them with a fork and there was some dripping happening, and David razzed him by saying "Hey!" and crouching down to show him the drops on the floor. Then he said, "Where were you raised? Eating soup with a fork!"

Dean Hurley (Music Supervisor): Au Revoir Simone is a band that David has been in love with for, geez, probably a decade, if not a little bit more. He was doing a Border's book reading like 10 years ago. And the curator of the in-store events paired his reading up with the girls playing music in between songs. That was his first introduction to them. It was kind of this random pairing of suggestive curatorial kind of alignment. I remember after that event, he was telling me about them and saying, "You got to listen to them."

David just fell in love with three women, three keyboards, the quality of their voice, their songwriting. It's unique and there's something about it that I don't think if somebody was trying to line up acts for David Lynch [for a] curated kind of event, maybe they wouldn't come to mind, but the fact that he fell head over heels in love with them, it's become part of his sound. (*KEXP, Morgan Chosnyk*)

Brings Back Some Memories

Bryon: We were very blown away by Kyle MacLachlan's playing Mr. C, Dougie Jones, and Dale Cooper. Although we were ready for the real Special Agent Dale Cooper to finally come back.

Ben: I was itching to see Dale Cooper again and, little did I know, I'd be itching for a long time. I figured it would only be a couple of episodes before Dale Cooper wakes up and goes searching for Laura Palmer in Twin Peaks. But I am a fan of Cooper as Dougie and I really enjoyed the breakfast scene with his son helping him out. Dougie spitting out coffee reminds me of when he spit out his coffee while demonstrating the rock-throwing technique in Season 1 Episode 2. "Damn Good Coffee and Hot!"

Favorites Quotes and Scenes

Bryon: My favorite scene and quote are put together for this part. FBI Deputy Director Gordon Cole has a meeting with Denise Bryson. Last time we saw Denise she was Drug Enforcement Administration Special Agent, but 25 years later she is now the Federal Bureau of Investigation Chief of Staff.

When Dennis made the transition to Denise, Gordon Cole told his colleagues, those clown comics, to "Fix their hearts or die." I love this saying. I feel over time this line has grown in popularity. It has joined the "Damn Fine Coffee" and the "Hell-o-o-o!" of the *Twin Peaks* lexicon. Gordon is saying that he accepts Denise for who she is and we need to move with the times.

Ben: That is my favorite quote as well. I think it's very appropriate for the times we're living in. We live in a very judgemental world and I think that's a good way to put it. To me, the message is, "Fix how you are towards others that might be different from you or don't be around me." That is how I interpret it anyway.

Bryon: I totally agree. Have some empathy towards your fellow man or woman. Be open-minded about others.

Ben: I always loved how opened-minded Dale Cooper was in the original series.

My favorite scene is Gordon Cole, Albert, and Tammy visiting Mr. C in prison. Mr. C as Cooper is a little off and not the Cooper that Cole and Albert once knew. He's talking slowly, repeating things and comes off as almost robotic. Outside the prison, Albert says, "This seems like a Blue Rose case," and Gordon replies, "It doesn't get any bluer," linking this case to the *Fire Walk with Me* mystery and opening the story wide open.

Community Commentary

Brittany Bowman: The very first time I saw any scenes or images from *Twin Peaks* was maybe 12 or 13 years ago while I was in college. I had recently discovered David Lynch after watching *Eraserhead*. I was weirded and grossed out by it, and then I became a bit obsessed with understanding it and finding out as much as I could about its creator and his other work. The internet, particularly YouTube, proved to be a great resource for discovering more of Lynch's oeuvre, especially his early short films. I clicked on a YouTube video of *Twin Peaks*, not knowing that the video was a clip from a TV series instead of a self-contained short. I saw some footage from the Season 2 finale; it happened to be the scene in the Red Room where "Señor Droolcup" slowly approaches Agent Cooper with a cup of coffee on a tray while repeating "coffee" over and over in a peculiar, otherworldly manner. The red curtains, the zig zag floor pattern, the décor, the little man in the red suit, the looks of confusion on Agent Cooper's face and his silence, the strange sound effects, the queer way that the characters spoke, the odd pacing … everything I was experiencing made me uncomfortable and deeply intrigued me. I understood nothing and yet I loved everything. I have been in love with this show, the cast, and all the mental, emotional, and existential challenges that the original show (and every iteration of it) entails ever since.

Chapter 38

**Season 3: Part 5
"Case Files"
Aired: June 4, 2017
Written by Mark Frost & David Lynch
Directed by: David Lynch**

In Memory of MARV ROSAND

The Log-line

Cooper, as Insurance Agent Jones, is given case files to investigate.

Behind the Curtain

Amy Shiels (Candie): When I met with [Johanna Ray for the audition], she said, "You know Amy, I have had this star beside your name for the longest time and I saw you in a screen test you did. And I really wanted to meet with you because there's some people I work with that I think you would work very well with. And I love your work and when you come to LA, I would really like you to call me and let me help you out."

Johanna Ray: If I put a star by their name it's because I believe they're going to be a star.

Kristine McKenna (Co-author of *Room to Dream*): The statue in the plaza outside Lucky Seven Insurance, that's based on a photograph of [David Lynch's] father. People thought it was Bowie, but it was his father.

David Lynch (Director): My father, when he was 19, worked at a fire tower. He had to hike once a week for five hours to get water and food, and then hike back, and then climb way up in this tower to scout out smoke and fire and call out to the firefighters if he saw anything. I'm not sure if he took the first selfie, but with a string he managed to take a picture of himself holding a pistol out with a stance, and that was the impetus for the statue. It doesn't even look like him really, but it's the pose. (From Festival of Disruption 2017 as told by Ivie, Devon. *"The Hidden Significance Behind Dougie's Favorite Statue in* Twin Peaks: The Return," *Vulture.com*)

Kyle MacLachlan: David was so encouraging, particularly with some of the shtick and the coffee stuff. It's meant to be funny, but absolutely with no wink and no commentary and nothing. It's funny because it's sort of sadly funny. You can't help but laugh. And so there was a lot of that going on on the set. Each day was a neat challenge. Each day we found the way through. It was kind of a slow, steady pace and [we] did a lot of laughing on the way through.

Elena Satine (Rhonda): Working with David Lynch was an absolute dream of mine. To witness and share in his artistry and to be a part of the *Twin Peaks* legacy will always be one of the greatest highlights of my career.

Amy Shiels (Candie): My one-on-one talk with David, which is the only talk we have before you go to film, all he really said to me was that [Candie's] dumb as a brick, but cute as a button. And that was it. And I said, "Do you want her to be Irish or American?" He said, "Why would she be Irish?" "Because I'm Irish." He said "What?!" I put on an act the entire time I was talking with him. I know people hear the Irish first and then say, "Ooh, she's not American. Her accent is slipping." Because a lot of people mix up your voice with your accent. He said, "No, she's American." So we laughed at that and then I went to off and decided, "I'm not going to have her just be these couple of lines on the page. If she's not going to speak with her words, she's going to speak with their body." It is true 70% of what we say is through our body language and that's something that you can really express. If you do have a small part, it helps if you just grab that and make that your own.

[On Candie's movement with her arm and hand in the Silver Mustang Casino:] I studied mime professionally for three years. There are very few times we can get to employ these tricks that you've learned over the years and you kind of wonder why you would ever use these things. So it was so nice as an artist to just put something in that now has been asked

Photo courtesy of Debbie Zoller.

so much about. It was a really proud moment for me actually. I'm grateful to David for keeping it in there. Some of the crew members ask me about it, too and ask me where it came from, what I was doing. Then one of them brought me over to David to discuss it with him. Marcel Marceau actually taught me that when I was younger. The artist himself. I believe he trained David Bowie too, and David Bowie is such an influence in the show as well.

We're all coming to the table with our own ideas of what happened before. I had a massive backstory that I worked on and I brought that into the physicality. Then once they had the costume and the hair and makeup, it really made sense to me. That would make her move in a different way than I would move and talk in a different way than I would talk. I found her voice and everything kind of came together then.

Dean Hurley: ["I Love How You Love Me"] was one of the songs that was actually written into the script. So that was like a very early choice and it's always cool to see those throughout the process of working in film when something is committed to the page so early on and as you're reading it, you can hear and experience the scene. A lot of times you think, "Oh, great song, great scene," but when they're really linked on that DNA level of the script page, it's when sometimes the truly remarkable combinations happen and that one was there. That is obviously a very Lynchian moment. All the cylinders start firing and everything clicks into place in that moment that you couldn't really just needle drop anything in there. It has to come from the creator.

It's a Phil Spector production. I'm a huge Phil Spector fan. David's a big Phil Spector fan and I think that sound that he had concocted, it's not even part of his wall sound sort of a spectrum. It's more of like in the vein of the Teddy Bears. The smooth silky productions that he did and the kind of teenage symphonies that he was doing. Seeing Becky go into her world, that music is a big part of it. I'm sure [David Lynch] was trying to manufacture those songs so that people could close their eyes and go away. (*KEXP, Morgan Chosnyk*)

James Morrison (Warden Dwight Murphy): It was a dream come true and so you just completely submit. You just go, "Man, here I am. I don't know if I'm still alive? Is this heaven?" The storytelling that Mark Frost and David Lynch are known for is so unique that you just have to completely submit and trust that wherever it's going to take you in the final product is going to serve that vision. Because you know it's a very specific vision and as a fan, you can't second guess it. You can't go maybe this would be better. You have to go with whatever they give you.

Dean Hurley: "Snake Eyes" by Trouble was specifically written and crafted for the show. It was kind of at a point where I had a lot of the things in front of me of what was probably gonna make it in the show. It's this kind of delicate balance between not everything was going to be ethereal and pretty in the Roadhouse, but needing some rougher edge things too. So Riley Lynch and I kinda sat down and tried to bring in kind of a harder edge to something. And then we had Alex [Zhang Hungtai] come by cause when you're making instrumental music, what is the voice in this particular instrumental music? Using that kinda crazy sax spotlighted color to just bring into a focal point that kind of straddles the line between acting as score and acting as digesting centerpiece of the scene. That was definitely Riley. I think also just really wanting to do something for the show. I think his dad was like, "Well it better be cool. It's not going in if it's not cool." (*KEXP, Morgan Chosnyk*)

Chrysta Bell (FBI Agent Tammy Preston): I don't think Tammy was written for me. I think that Tammy was really super bright; her descriptor was hyper-intelligent and professional. I think David knew me as a person and he had this visualization of Tammy and he brought the two together and it worked for him.

Juan Carlos Cantu (Officer Reynaldo): The thing that made working on *Twin Peaks* different from most productions was the way David Lynch and executive producer Sabrina Sutherland made everyone in the cast and crew feel like they were an integral part of the show. From background actors and day players to the stars of the show, from the grips and PA's to the 1st AD and DP, everyone was treated with the utmost respect and valued for their contributions. It was a real pleasure to work in such a great environment.

Dean Hurley: [On Johnny Jewel of the Chromatics:] He just started sending us things, too, to just consider and it was very nonchalant with no sort of illusions about what would happen to it. He was just getting excited about being involved. And I kept feeding David these pieces that he was making, these instrumental pieces, and David just fell in love with it, found places for it, started working it in, imagining places where it could continue. It was like nothing was really talked about. It was just this very kind of poetic, easy relationship there. I think that's really cool when someone just does that and just gives and doesn't sort of toxify any of the process with "Well, what about this? Are you going to use it or are you not going to use it?" It just allows something to really just kind of handshake and become forged together. (*KEXP, Morgan Chosnyk*)

Sabrina Sutherland: The "In memory of" is to honor those who passed away prior to our show but were integral to the show and we used their clips or people who were on the show who passed away before the show aired.

Showtime gave us special dispensation because usually they don't have "in memory of." And so one of the first things that we did in terms of negotiation was to say, "We need to say in the credits in memory of." (*Q&A at* Twin Peaks *Festival 2017*)

Marvin Rosand, for example, who played Toad. He was such an incredible guy, lovely to work with. He was the cook at the Double R Diner. I remember talking to him and he was thrilled to have been called back. He was in *Fire Walk with Me*. I think it was only a week later he passed away after working with us. We were still up in Washington when he passed away. As you know, we have NDAs and nobody's supposed to say anything to anybody. And he had kept all of this secret from his family. [They] didn't know that he was working on it. He was going to surprise them and they found out after he passed away. [He was] just such a wonderful man.

Brings Back Some Memories

Ben: In the Roadhouse, there were all these side characters talking to other characters and we were not sure who was important to the overall story.

Bryon: It was like we were eavesdropping in on these random people's lives at the Roadhouse and it made this world seem more alive. It was the modern-day *Invitation to Love* soap opera.

Ben: I like how Dougie works for an insurance company and the employees are called agents. Are they special agents? They have case files just like FBI agents and they have to investigate claims. Cooper/Dougie calling Anthony Sinclair a liar reminds me of when Agent Cooper was able to tell when he questioned people if they were lying. In Season 1 Episode 3, Truman and Cooper talk to Leo Johnson. Cooper asks Leo if he knew Laura Palmer and Leo says, "No," and Cooper tells him with no hesitation, he is lying. Cooper as Dougie still has the essence of who he is even if he is not completely aware of his surroundings.

Favorites Quotes and Scenes

Bryon: My favorite scene is seeing Mr. C in jail with his face looking into a small mirror and BOB's face overlaying his and Mr. C saying, "You are still with me. That's good." This was a very clever way of including BOB again even though the actor Frank Silva had passed away in 1995. A great scene that has been burned into my brain forever. It's very creepy.

Ben: My favorite scene is at the Double R with Norma and Shelly, concerned about Shelly's daughter Becky. They know Becky is in similar trouble to what they were once in with being with the wrong guy. They've lived through it and they wonder how can they help Becky not follow that same path.

Bryon: Shelly is still hanging out with the wrong people, as we will learn later on she is with Red. It was kind of sad to see Shelly not learn from her mistakes.

Ben and **Bryon:** Our favorite quote comes from Dr. Lawrence Jacoby AKA Dr. Amp who says, "Shovel your way out of the shit!"

Bryon: He selling products: flashlights, drinks, and now a golden shovel (two coats) that you can [use to] shovel your way out of the shit.

Ben: His message is basically the only way things are going to get better is if you do it yourself. No one is going to rescue you from your life so you gotta shovel your own shit.

Community Commentary

Russ Marshalek (A Place Both Wonderful and Strange band): *Twin Peaks* was in my periphery until I binged the entire (then 2-season) series with my then-girlfriend the winter the Gold Box was released. I was captivated, disgusted, compelled, repelled: all reactions that Lynch seemingly trades in. Who were these characters and what was this show? I wasn't sure I wanted to interface with *Twin Peaks* any deeper than a surface level, but the mood conveyed so perfectly by the opening notes of "Falling" stuck with me and was unshakable. The rest is history.

Listen to those opening notes, watch the lengthy intro (it's iconic!), feel the pull of the lapping of the waves Laura's body was found in. It's become everything to me.

Chapter 39

Season 3: Part 6
"Don't Die"
Aired: June 11, 2017
Written by Mark Frost & David Lynch
Directed by David Lynch

The Log-line

A child is struck by hit-and-run driver Richard.

Behind the Curtain

Lisa Coronado (Hit and Run Mom): People were getting called in for something at a local casting agency and nobody really knew what it was. I had known the casting director from a couple of other projects before and so I came in and she sat down and she's just like, "Can I ask you some questions?" I'm like, "Okay." We just started chatting and then she started asking me about being a mom and raising kids. It was really casual and I felt pretty comfortable with her to open up. And then she's like, "Thanks. That's it."

Kyle MacLachlan on finding out Laura Dern was playing Diane: I was so excited. It was one of those "aha" moments. Like of course, she'd be perfect to play Diane. Laura is an extraordinary actress and so intuitive as well and has worked with David obviously over the years. She brought in so much of that character and created her. It was really fantastic to see. She's so interesting. I love working with her. She's just one of those really, very special people. We both have kind of a similar sense of humor where it gets a little bit wry at times. She's definitely in that same style. We have a lot of fun. We're not above making jokes about David at David's expense. He comes right back at us. There was definitely some edgy humor between all of us.

Lisa Coronado (Hit and run mother): The first day on set, [David Lynch] came right over to me and introduced himself and I felt like I'd known him my whole life. He kind of has that impact on people. He makes you feel at ease and important, and he's just lovely. I don't know a lot of people like him so it's hard to describe him and I feel like everybody feels this way about him, which is so universally wonderful that this person that's created such interesting, phenomenal work is really just a down to earth, warm, open guy.

He made sure I was safe and that was really what I remember. He was always checking in and making sure how I was doing, how Hunter [the little boy that got hit] was doing and being really aware of the surroundings around us and the people. I just felt like I had space to really go there. It was a difficult, emotional journey we went on together. After we were done, he couldn't have been more sweet, supportive. And the little boy was great. He was such a trooper, and we got along right away.

I think it took me about five days to finally watch it 'cause it was tough. And so I watched it, and I was taken aback at how beautifully David Lynch edited it, and Harry Dean Stanton's performance, which I knew was going to be great because I was there ... He was so precious. I felt like I wasn't watching myself, which was nice. It was just this beautiful, tragic scene.

Jay Jee (patrol officer): Truly, one of the highlights of my career as an actor!

Josh Fadem (Phil Bisby): So many moments from *Twin Peaks* that I allowed my brain to soak up so I would not forget them. My character's name was "Phil Bisby" in the script. Someone on production mentioned to me that I was "Phil Blix," which I didn't question. When I went to set for a first rehearsal and met David I said "Hi I'm Josh," and he said, "Oh, are you Phil?" Then he gave me a couple of quick notes about the type of guy "Phil Blix" is and BOOM we were rehearsing. It was immediate and fun. Each day I'd see him and he'd say something along the lines of "Phil, great to have ya on board!" or "Phil Blix!" One day I asked him, "Is it Phil Blix or Phil Bisby? Because some people said Bisby," and he said "Phil Blix!" That was good enough for me. You can see that moment in the Making-Of Blu-ray doc. But there was a scene where I had to say into a phone speaker, "Phil Bisby here!" and as we were rehearsing he was told that legal couldn't approve "Blix." David got really bummed out for a second and then appeared to reason all the ways in his head Bisby could be good. Apparently, if there's like one or two Phil Blixes out in the world a production can't use that name, but if there's more it's okay. "I guess there's some Phil Blix out there just doin' it up," I said. "Yeah, he's out there cuttin' up a rug," David responded. Then he said, "But Bisby will put him to shame." Each time I've been in a situation where I've seen David, he always asks Phil how things are going at Lucky 7 and we talk about how Phil's career is going and if he has gotten promoted.

One day we were lining up a shot and they were trying to figure out which side of me the camera should face, for editing purposes. Someone said, "I think if it's on that side it's right." Meaning it would cut together properly, to which David shouted, "I don't care about RIGHT!" I loved it. Each day and moment there felt special to witness and be a part of.

I liked being near set whenever I could. I know during a long break I sat in a random chair near set and fell asleep. Kyle MacLachlan took a picture of me passed out and showed it to me later. I assume it exists somewhere.

Naomi Watts (Janey-E Jones): Most people know I'm forever indebted to David Lynch. Creating the part of Betty/Diane in *Mulholland Drive* was a career-altering and life-changing experience for me. One I'll never forget. I did, however, hop into a clumsy, heavy bunny suit with no eye holes, no possibility of temperature control, actually, no air circulation to speak of, and thought that would have paid off my debt to him [on David Lynch's Rabbits].

Then a decade or so later, the phone rang and there was my buddy Dave asking me about *Twin Peaks*. He said I'd need to come over to the west coast, leave my children, and work for free. I told him I wasn't living in a two-bedroom shared apartment on Sycamore Ave anymore. I'm now in New York City and I've got kids in private school. And a hefty mortgage!

He said, in his lovely and calm voice, "Now listen up, Buttercup. I just want you to have a read of some scenes, see if you like it. And if you do, we'll take some coffees, have some fun and make something beautiful."

I immediately knew I was on board based on his high level of charm factor. Then I read the pages and POW! I packed my suitcases and the rest is history. And on celluloid for keeps.

Like everything with David, the experiences are always memorable, unique, and so, so special. And no one gets me going on screen more than him. I feel I'm always at my best with him because we have full trust. And there's nothing greater than being led by someone you trust implicitly. Needless to say, I'm fully indebted again.

Tammie Baird (Lorraine): I had the most amazing time working on *Twin Peaks: The Return*. From the moment that David invited me to set, my heart was smiling so big. It was very hard to contain my joy due to the fact that my character Lorraine was not a happy person.

I loved sitting in Lorraine's office with David, talking about the scene. I was sitting at my desk and he sitting across from me. I had a quick moment where my internal monologue started to become star-struck. I was so thrilled to be sitting across from David Lynch having this one on one time. I quickly came back to the conversation, being the professional that I am, and hung onto his every word. I will always cherish that day. Even as I am talking about it, I am smiling ear to ear.

Jodi Thelen (Maggie Brown): David kept saying to me, "Don't move your hands so much." I wasn't aware of them moving. Must have been nervous energy being released. David is very spontaneous and a true auteur.

Dean Hurley: Brian Loucks at CAA has a relationship with Sharon [Van Etten] and I was familiar with her music, but Brian re-brought her up and she's kind of incredible. One of the interesting connections is the way that I got David kinda hyped on her. I showed him KEXP, her in-studio performance, where she played Tarifa. So that was how he experienced her for the first time.

When they're doing a small, intimate performance like that, it's stripping down the song and showing the songwriting in its most illustrious form. That song, originally, on her album, had horn arrangement in the chorus and in KEXP performance, it didn't. I eventually played the album cut and David was like, "No, no. I want it to sound like in the video, the way that she did it on KEXP." (*KEXP, Morgan Chosnyk*)

Favorites Quotes and Scenes

Ben: My favorite scene is one of the most tragic scenes in Season 3, with the hit and run of a child. In the same intersection from *Fire Walk with Me* where Phillip Gerard confronts Leland Palmer, we now witness the child get run over there by an angry Richard Horne. Lisa Coronado's portrayal of the hit and run mother is powerful and heartbreaking. Harry Dean Stanton's Carl Rodd, who witnesses what looks like a golden spirit ascend from the dead boy, is comforting to the mother without words.

Bryon: My favorite scene was finally meeting Diane. Diane Evans is found by Albert in a local bar called "Max Von's Bar" which seems to be a popular place among the young people. We follow Albert as he makes his way to the back of the bar where we see the back of a skinny woman with what looks to be a white hair wig on, wearing an Asian looking dress, with one hand holding up a cigarette. She slowly turns around and we find out that Laura Dern is playing Diane in one of the most mysterious roles in *Twin Peaks* history. We can finally put a face to the tape recorder.

Ben: I had a feeling that Laura Dern would be playing Diane the moment they announced her in Season 3. She's the perfect choice with the history she had with Kyle MacLachlan in *Blue Velvet*. They have amazing chemistry.

Bryon: My favorite quote comes from FBI Agent Albert Rosenfield [walking in the rain to Max Von's Bar]: "Fuck Gene Kelly, you motherfucker!" Agent Rosenfield is older and a little more serious during Season 3. I feel this might be because we are missing Harley Peyton's writing, but Mark Frost and David

Lynch still did a good job capturing his sharp wit and snappy comebacks for Season 3. This one line had me rolling in my seat. The next day, I recall everyone quoting that line on social media and it's just a great line.

Ben: My favorite quote comes from Janey-E when she meets with Tommy and Jimmy to pay back the money Dougie owes them, "What kind of world are we living in where people can behave like this? Treat other people this way without any compassion or feelings for their suffering? We are living in a dark, dark age and you are part of the problem. Now, I suggest you take a good, long look at yourselves because I never want to see either of you again."

Amazing performance by Naomi Watts. She gives it all she has and she really delivers with these lines and speaks truth to what is wrong with our society today.

Community Commentary

Aidan Hailes & **Lindsay Stamhuis** (*Bickering Peaks: A Twin Peaks Podcast*): We were too young to have experienced *Twin Peaks* in the flesh the first time around, but we were always aware of it bubbling behind everything else produced by our culture ever since, and were fascinated by the influence it had. And even though it took us a bit longer to fully embrace this world, we're glad we did because it enabled us to participate in what was probably one of the coolest experiences of our lives: podcasting during *Twin Peaks: The Return* in the summer of 2017 alongside some of the brightest minds in the fandom. That experience of engaging in real-time with viewers on social media, theorizing about what everything meant, trying to "break the code, solve the crime" all over again, and podcasting weekly about each episode after it aired trying to make it make sense ... we often sat back and thought, "How lucky are we?!" *Twin Peaks*, unlike virtually any other show out there, is built for this kind of audience participation and it felt like, for a time, various spheres of the cultural zeitgeist (podcasting, social media engagement, enforced weekly viewing in the age of streaming digital binge-watching, etc.) overlapped and produced something wholly unique that we don't think could ever intentionally be replicated again; it was a one in a million situation. David Lynch and Mark Frost gave us that. *Twin Peaks* gave us that. It's an incredible thing to think about.

Chapter 40

Season 3: Part 7
"There's a Body All Right"
Aired: June 18, 2017
Written by Mark Frost & David Lynch
Directed by David Lynch

In Memory of WARREN FROST

The Log-line

Deputy Hawk and Sheriff Truman look over Laura Palmer's missing diary pages.

Behind the Curtain

Michael Horse (Deputy Chief Tommy "Hawk" Hill): Robert Forster was a gas to work with. He was supposed to be the original sheriff, but he was working. I love those old-timers. "Come on man, let me buy you a dinner and tell me your whole life [story]." He would tell me how he got into the business and everything. Again, a sweet, sweet man. In the first couple of days, he goes, "Michael, I don't get this." I go, "You don't have to get it." After he realized that, he had so much fun.

Robert Forster (Frank Truman): You do not contradict guys like David Lynch, but I was tempted. After a short scene on *Mulholland Drive*, David came over and asked me to do the dialogue slower. I, of course, obliged. After the second take, he came over and again said I should try it slower. I gave it a thought and slowed my pace a bit more. Two or three more takes go by, and each time he wants me to slow it down. I listen to myself in my head. I'm thinking to myself, "I don't believe what I'm saying. I sound like a 78rpm record at the wrong speed." Months, maybe a year later, after the film had become a big hit and won the Palme d'Or, I realized I'd been in a dream sequence. You do not contradict guys like David Lynch!

Mark Frost on recording his father Warren Frost: There was just about a month before we actually started production, and we actually shot it on Skype with David in LA and my dad in upstate New York. I was there, and my brother Scott was there, and my son Travis. So we actually had all three generations together. Travis was the production assistant and Scott was helpful with the lighting. It was kind of fun.

Scott Frost: It was a fun afternoon. That was the last work Dad ever did, but he was basically retired anyway. Shortly after that, being able to do it again was just not gonna happen. He loved doing it because [he could be] a real hambone even though he was a sort of shy Vermont kid at another level. I guess that's why he was an actor. [It] gave him an out from that.

Mark Frost: I felt really good about that scene and spent a lot of time getting it right.

Clare M. Corsick (Hair Department Head): Pinnacle of my career. When you become part of David Lynch's team of artists, you realize that your creativity, your visions, will be asked to expand and go to new levels outside of any norm. David's heart and soul ask you to create outside of the norm and create on the spot, as his characters come to life the day that they show up on set.

Kyle MacLachlan: Diane could have been anything; could have been a person; could have been the name of the tape recorder, but I never made it specific for myself, which is actually kind of nice because it really [left it] open to interpretation by the audience.

Debbie Zoller: The Diane character was the one that I had the most sleepless nights over. Every fan, every person that knows anything about *Twin Peaks* has an image in their head already created of what Diane looks like. And that was the one that I was most concerned about because I didn't want to go the wrong direction. I was kind of the last person to fill in that look because David and

Laura Dern were speaking behind closed doors and on the phone the whole time. They figured out the wardrobe and then they figured out her hair, the cut, then they had to figure out the hair color.

Clare M. Corsick: In particular, Laura Dern has two different hairstyles. She had talked to me about a blonde wig and I felt, as David did, that her character needed her hair to speak bigger color. David gives you that freedom and trust in yourself to play all the way! He pulls it out of you and keeps you a part of the process through and through. So with Laura's wigs, we came up with two very different colors, and boy were they big and fun!

Debbie Zoller: Then the last thing that got filled in was me. So I was just as kind of shocked as anybody would be. When I got the word that her clothes are this inspiration, her haircut is this inspiration. Oh my goodness, where do I go?"

That was when I realized that her makeup had to be what's called monochromatic, which means that it has not necessarily a lack of color, but one color fades into the next, which fades into the next so that your eye doesn't clue in to a color. So I wanted you to see her face and her expression, but I didn't want the blush color to stand out, or her eyeshadow color to stand out. And the lip color was really my main concern. So when David said to me, "I want pink," and I'm [thinking], "Pink?" I don't associate pink with David, so that was really interesting. And I [said], "Well, what kind of pink?" And he [said], "I want it light pink." "Okay."

So it must've taken me two or three days. With Laura's help and with David's help, we kind of came up with this color. And then at the last second,

I realized with the monochromatic makeup that I had designed, I needed the pink to be an ombre pink so that it kind of followed the guidelines of being monochromatic, and so one color bleeds into the next, bleeds into the next, and that's when we came up with the monochromatic with the ombre pink.

Sabrina Sutherland: I think that's such an incredible collaboration. Her character looked stunning.

We reached out to Laura Dern to find out more about her transformation into Diane. Her response:

Laura Dern (Diane Evans): Fuck you, *Twin Peaks Unwrapped.*

Chrysta Bell: Laura Dern is so gifted that you're just in a moment with the woman who is Diane.

Kyle MacLachlan as Mr. C with David Lynch and Laura Dern: We know each other very well. Having to relate to them as the character of Mr. C where there's absolutely no humanity in there at all, that was really difficult for me because these are my good friends. When I had to look at them as just objects, it was very disconcerting, actually, to me.

Christophe Zajac-Denek (Ike The Spike): Working with David Lynch on *Twin Peaks* is one of the greatest highlights of my career. I am a huge fan of his work and it took all of my composure to not lose my mind when I found out I booked the role of Ike "The Spike"! David is direct, thorough, open, and funny. It was such a pleasure to work with a team that respects and understands the creative process at his level. I'm also so lucky to be absorbed into this family of such incredibly talented and kind people who work with David. The experience changed my life and I'm so grateful to be a part of *Twin Peaks*.

Favorites Quotes and Scenes

Ben and **Bryon**: Our favorite scene is Diane meeting Mr. C for the first time in years at Yankton Federal Prison, Sioux City with Gordon Cole, Tammy, and Albert. Diane demands ten minutes alone with Cooper. Ten minutes tops, or it's over when she says it's over. The anticipation of watching Diane hit that button to make the little wall go up behind the glass and see this dark and creepy version of Dale Cooper handcuffed to the chair with this almost demonic voice coming through the speaker, the look on Diane's face after seeing him for the first time says it all: horror.

Bryon: The exchange between the two about remembering that last time they saw each other put a lump in my throat and made me sick to my stomach, as the insinuation that what happened that night was not good. Diane asks, "Who are you?" and says, "Look at me." She sees something that others don't and whatever that might be, she can't take it much longer before closing that dividing wall again.

Ben: That whole "Look at me," and, "Who are you?" exchange is actually said in *Fire Walk with Me* by Laura Palmer when BOB visits her in bed in the middle of the night. Both of these women were sexually abused by the people they were speaking to.

Ben and **Bryon:** Our favorite quote comes from Diane Evans: What did you say your name was again? FBI Agent Tammy Preston: Tammy. Diane Evans: Fuck you, Tammy.

Ben: It's funny how we see Tammy, who is very by-the-books, trying to help out and then Diane, annoyed by her, can only say "Fuck you, Tammy." I question whether this is truly who Diane really is or someone she has become because of the circumstances of what happened with Cooper all those years ago and now she has evolved into this bitter, hateful, and angry person.

Bryon: I think so. It's comical at first, but we will later find out the dark truth of this verbal wall she has put up. This could be because she doesn't want to get close to anyone after what happened to her, and has built an emotional wall from getting too close to anyone again.

Community Commentary

Cameron Crain (25YearsLaterSite.com): I'm a weird one. I saw *FWWM* first. Then I had this roommate, Marc, in college who worked at Blockbuster so he could bring movies home for free. One night, it was *FWWM*. He and his buddies were really into it, apparently. They'd never seen the show either, although I think we all knew it was a show. It was only after getting on the internet, such as it was in the late '90s, that I figured that out. And then I had to see to the series, which we could only get through out of print VHS tapes at that point, but they were on eBay at least. So my friend bought a set and we watched them together. I think each session was about six hours, as we didn't want to stop.

I proceeded to make pretty much everyone I knew watch it: other friends, my girlfriend at the time, etc., and I'd read them at certain pivotal moments. It wasn't long until I'd lost track of how many times I'd seen the thing. But I always had them watch *FWWM* after the series, whereas I saw it first.

I never had that wonder about who killed Laura Palmer, but it didn't matter for me. It was always the weird that drew me in more than anything else.

Chapter 41

Season 3: Part 8
"Gotta Light?"
Aired: June 25, 2017
Written by Mark Frost & David Lynch
Directed by David Lynch

The Log-line

Mr. C is shot, and an atomic bomb goes off in the New Mexico desert in 1945.

Behind the Curtain

Harley Peyton: Part 8, I think, is one of those really rare moments when every cylinder is firing, and the two of them [David Lynch and Mark Frost] are kind of in perfect sync.

Dean Hurley: David was like, "I want Trent [Reznor] to be in the show." It was so cool because Trent has a history with David and essentially curated a lot of the music for *Lost Highway.* It was kind of like an open invitation. I don't think David really even thought of it in terms of Nine Inch Nails or some of the other myriad of [sic] projects that he has. He just wanted him involved. So when [Trent] sent over "She's Gone Away" it wasn't even labeled Nine Inch Nails, but eventually, it was, "Oh I think the thing is going to be Nine Inch Nails," and it was like, "Oh great, this is awesome!" (*KEXP, Morgan Chosnyk*)

Duwayne Dunham: The thing with Nine Inch Nails occurred to me that that had to happen in the middle [instead of the typical end of the part]. And it's what lets Cooper kind of wake up from that experience [of] having been shot.

Harley Peyton: I think that the whole notion of the atomic bomb tests and the way that links to other things, that to me is classic Mark, because I know he thinks a lot about that stuff. And actually you get a sense of that stuff in the *Twin Peaks* book that he wrote. So many people watch [that part] and talked about David's bravura directing. It was amazing, but for me that conceptually it was like, "That's Mark. I know it."

Duwayne Dunham: When David came back [from completing filming], we had a talk and I said, "Look, I've got so much to do just to cut these scenes together, and there are sequences here that only you know what you want to do with anyways. Why don't you tackle those?" So we made a big list and said, "Okay, David, these are yours." The atomic explosion [was one of them]. I had something in there, and a title card just as a very, very, very crude space holder. He ran that thing for me and I really caught myself and instead of saying what I would normally say something like, "Wow, it's maybe a little bit too long, don't you think?" I formulated the same idea in different words and said something like, "Wow, if those images hold up an audience's attention for that long, that's really going to be something."

Dean Hurley on composer Krzysztof Penderecki's Threnody to the Victims of Hiroshima: David loves Penderecki. I think a lot of film directors love Penderecki, and he's been utilized the best with people like Kubrick. They used the same piece, Threnody, in *Children of Men*. There's something about his writing or his aleatoric techniques of just these bizarre orchestral sounds that you're not used to hearing as orchestral sounds. I think that piece is a really special piece and the way it's used in this show, it's the testing of the terrible weapon that would eventually do terrible things and then the music that was essentially inspired by all those terrible things ends up scoring the test. So it's a really interesting collapsing of time that I think is a theme in the show, as well. It's kind of cool how that works, but even from a visceral standpoint, it's the sounds, the tones, the aggression, the energy, and violence in that piece is just insane. I think David is always looking for something that will jump, something just beyond; it's like everything is emphatic. If something is violent, he's going to want it to be extremely violent. If it's emotional, he wants it to be extremely emotional. And I think that piece is a great example of what you reach for when you're trying to go to eleven. (*KEXP, Morgan Chosnyk*)

Michael Horse (Deputy Chief Tommy "Hawk" Hill): I think [David is] just trying to figure out, "Where does that kind of evil come from? Why would you unleash something like the atomic bomb or why would you hurt a woman?"

Erica Eynon (Experiment): Working with David Lynch was one of the most thrilling and memorable experiences I've had as an actor. I had the privilege of watching his imaginative genius at play. He invents and creates what he envisions without apology. This artistry is truly inspirational and gives young artists the courage to create.

Dean Hurley: A shorter version of [Slow 30's Room] was actually born around that time [of Foundation Cartier *Air is On Fire* exhibition from 2007]. It's really interesting. It was made because David had done these postcard drawings of '30s rooms and they had kind of ornate patterns on the floor and Foundation Cartier had literally reconstructed one of those drawings in three-dimension in real-life like, life-size, so you could walk around one of these drawings of a room that David had done. I remember at that time, David said, "We need some slow thirties music." So slow thirties music was born. I've been here so long, maybe things that surprise a lot of people have ceased to surprise me. A moment like that is so cool because when I saw the dailies for this scene, it looked very similar to that drawn room that had been in that exhibition. When all the pieces come together, he's creating out of the same world, off the same singular palette that only he has. Wow, that room is a movie now. It's in the realm of cinema where before it started as just a drawing, then it became a drawing realized into something that someone could move around in and then it became part of it as cinematic alter narrative. (*KEXP, Morgan Chosnyk*)

Carel Struycken (The Giant/The Fireman): We are aware of only a tiny fraction of all that floods our senses; much of it is absorbed and stashed away. What I love about David Lynch is how he manages to give such splendid form to what emerges from the deep recesses of his mind while refusing to allow us to make sense of it all. There it dances on the edge of the known, and the unknowable like a beautiful Zen riddle.

Tikaeni Faircrest (Girl from 1956): Being cast to play the iconic role of young Sarah Palmer and getting to work with David and the *Twin Peaks* family was the best gift I could ever have dreamt of; I feel like Dorothy in the *Wizard of Oz*.

Debbie Zoller: First, David gave me a description of [the Woodsmen]. They're dirty. They're grimy. They are otherworldly. They live amongst us. They're homeless. And so I would just kind of chew on that information for a little bit.

Then we started shooting in Washington. We would go to these beautiful locations every day in the woods. And so every day I would pick a little tree bark or something or like this purple mushroom that was growing wild and I collected all these different colors from the woods that we were shooting in. Then I would take those colors and adapt them to make up colors. And then that's how the process started for the Woodsmen.

The Woodsmen were probably an hour each [to get made up]. There were a lot of details that went into those characters because it was color and texture and reflection.

Stewart Strauss (Woodsman): David Lynch was pleased with what he saw. He got to Robert [Broski] who was the last person in line and he just said to him, "Can you say 'Gotta light?'"

Robert Broski (Woodsman) on "This is the Water": I did not know about this til about 15 minutes before filming. I never saw a script, I received one page with my lines on it, then it disappeared afterward. All very secretive.

Stewart Strauss: I think the woodsmen, in general, were just the unexpected surprise. But what we were and why we were, was never, ever discussed.

Robert Broski : So what struck me during the shoot and after when discussing the direction was, when directing, Mr. Lynch knows what he wants, and allows us the freedom to give it to him! That is the best way I can describe how he would relate what he was looking for, but leave it open for our interpretation of how to bring it to life. WOW! It made you want to dig deep and give your best.

Duwayne Dunham: How to balance it so that each [part] had a beginning and had a proper ending that it felt like it ended. We always kept that in mind. It just so happened that [part] was the atomic explosion, and Cooper getting shot, and the woodsmen going in the radio station, and the girl and the frog moth, just some really strange and fun and interesting things. I personally loved that [part].

Dean Hurley: "My Prayer" by The Platters is another selection that was written into the script. It's cool how it ends up tying together this idea of radio broadcast and electricity. How these airwaves and the electrical lines kind of tie in all these things through time, through space in the show. We pop around to these various locations where everyone is experiencing that song. It's kind of a neat tie-in to the power of radio and the power of a song coming on that just resonates in a way frequency and emotionally. (*KEXP, Morgan Chosnyk*)

Debbie Zoller: We'd always talked about having screening parties. I was working on another job and couldn't get it together quick enough, but I remember calling Sabrina and going, "Okay, what parts should we screen and have the party?" And she said, "Part 8." And I said, "That's too soon and I can't do Part 8 'cause I was involved in this crazy job." [I replied] "Okay, I'll do Part 9." So we sent out the invitations and I decorated the whole house and got food and had everything together. But of course, the week prior when I watched Part 8, my mouth was on the ground and I was like, "Oh my God, we should have screened Part 8." I remember the following week Sabrina is like, "I told you." God damn it, but that part blew my mind. This is television history! I could not have been more proud of that.

Kristine McKenna (Co-author of *Room to Dream*): Part 8 is a technical masterpiece.

Favorite Quotes and Scenes

Bryon: Well, I could say the popular part of Part 8 for my favorite scene. The atomic bomb going off and unleashing all hell into the world, the music, and the imagery. All that is amazing, but after thinking about this for a couple of years now, I always go back to seeing Nine Inch Nails performing in the Roadhouse. Why would I pick this performance over one of the most daring things I have ever seen on television in years? I can't really say, or rather put in words. I've seen Nine Inch Nails countless times, live, and have been a fan since the early '90s, so why would this be such a thrill for me in 2017? I guess the fact David Lynch and Mark Frost are giving all kinds of artists air time on a cable channel is so refreshing. No ads, no time constraints, no bullshit, just pure heroin, echoing the sentiments of David Nevins, President of Showtime.

We just witnessed Mr. C get shot and a bunch of Woodsmen come out of nowhere and perform some kind of magic on him, and then we get this raw, dirty and powerful performance by Nine Inch Nails right in the middle of this part. Somehow they make this work because what comes next is anybody's guess. They performed "She's Gone Away" from *Not the Actual Events* album. Lynch wanted dirty, dark, and raw for this part and we got it. This was the opposite of a palate cleanser but a precursor of things to come.

Ben: My favorite scene has to be the Trinity bomb going off. I remember watching it the night of and saying to myself, "Is this going to be the whole episode?" It's crazy to think for ten whole minutes we just got lights and noises from the atomic bomb and yet I was glued to my seat in awe. It was kinda beautiful at times, like watching the fireworks on the fourth of July. Did we witness the birth of some kind of evil into the world?

My favorite quote comes from The Woodsmen who says to a driver, "Gotta light?" Normally this would be a friendly request to ask to light a cigarette, but in this context with the humming and electricity sounds, it comes off as more of a sinister offer. Is he asking for fire? Does fire represent the soul? Do you got a soul?

Bryon: My quote also comes from the Woodsman, "This is the water and this is the well. Drink full and descend. The horse is the white of the eyes and dark within." This dark poetry that repeats out of the Woodsman's mouth that sounds like it's coming out of an old static radio station still gives me the creeps. Nobody knew what Part 8 was going to bring us and it hit us like a freight train. These words are now being analyzed by every *Twin Peaks* fan and repeated like it's the new, "The owls are not what they seem." Just reading these words, you automatically hear the Woodsman's leathery voice slowly reading them in your own head. This is what Lynch and Frost do best.

Community Commentary

Patrick Cotnoir (Producer, *The Chris Gethard Show*, *Upright Citizen's Brigade Theater's ASSSSCAT 3000*, *The George Lucas Talk Show*): I came to *Twin Peaks* late. I finally finished the show after season 3 had already been announced and was mid-production. I had tried to watch it earlier and I was never in the right head space to get through it ... but I knew it was something that I'd enjoy so I kept giving it a shot. I don't know what changed in me once I decided that I actually really loved the show, but it was apparently a massive, seismic shift (equivalent to the one on July 16, 1945). It truly was the moment that season 3 ended that sealed the deal for me. Like many, while I was watching, I didn't really understand most of it or know the reason I kept coming back to it every week. It really became appointment television even though, in the moment, I wasn't sure I was enjoying it. It was a wild sensation that I don't know I've ever experienced before or since ... but once the season ended, I couldn't stop thinking about the show. I imagine something from that show creeps into my head every day, whether it was the creature crawling in young Sarah Palmer's mouth, tea kettle David Bowie, Ted Raimi stuck inside a huge chess piece, donuts spread out on a table, the man sweeping the floor, or ZZ Top. So many insane images, so many wild ideas. I understand why it doesn't click for some people, but I'm so happy that I finally came to my senses and gave in to the wild world of *Twin Peaks*.

Although, I do have to say that I think the biggest change in my life since I started watching *Twin Peaks* is that I've realized that I love creamed corn.

Chapter 42

Season 3: Part 9
"This Is the Chair"
Aired: July 9, 2017
Written by Mark Frost & David Lynch
Directed by David Lynch

The Log-line
Betty Briggs reveals to Bobby that his father left him something.

Behind the Curtain
Charlotte Stewart (Betty Briggs): David called me up and said, "Hey Charlotte, you want to go to work?" I said, "You bet!" He said, "Well, I got a little bit of Betty in this next project that we're doing and I want you to come up to North Bend and do your act." So that's what I did. It was one day.

I was very nervous, to tell you the truth, because I'm 78 years old now. I don't remember things like I used to, and I was so afraid I was going to blow it. I really was. I was terrified, and David was so sweet and so patient and so kind. He just had us go over the dialogue together, the guys and me, until I was comfortable, but he knew that I was on shaky ground and he didn't let on to anybody else.

Dana Ashbrook: I love Charlotte. She was awesome from the very start. She will always be my TV mom. She's the best. It was great just to have her to do that scene and see her working with David, and having them hammer out that scene. Beautiful.

Charlotte Stewart: I have a wonderful picture of [David Lynch] with his arm around me standing in back of that chair, the part where I open up the secret compartment and pull out the tube, and you see him. He's got his headphones around his neck and he's got his arm around my shoulder just talking to me, just making me feel comfortable and letting me do it a little at a time. It's a scary thing for an actor when you have little trouble with your memory, but he was very understanding and very kind.

I didn't know anything about the new series, number three. So I was watching it for the first time like everybody else, and I wasn't in it until Part 9. He didn't even tell me

Photo courtesy of Charlotte Stewart.

what [part] I'd be in. We're watching it and it was kind of weird and a little different than the original, and I kind of accept David's judgment and his talent. So I was shocked when Betty appeared, as I think a lot of people were because everything was so strange for the first eight (parts) and it was still a little bit strange in number nine. Then there's Betty, good old, wholesome Betty. Her son is now a deputy sheriff and life is good. Oh my god, there is sanity in the world. I was really grateful [to] Mark and David for bringing that up again, that Betty reiterated to her son how much his father loved him and believed in him. So that was very special. The spirit of Don Davis was in the room and that's definitely what was good.

Chrysta Bell (FBI Agent Tammy Preston): David wanted to meet on the Saturday before the Monday of filming. He was being thoughtful and mindful and aware that this was my first television acting experience, and that he definitely had given me a big opportunity with a certain amount of pressure involved. I think he just wanted to check-in. We were talking a little bit about Tammy and there were a few moments in the script I had questions about. He said, "You know on Monday you have your interrogation scene." I was like, "Hold up. Monday?! My first scene is the interrogation scene?!" He was like, "Don't worry, it's going to be great." This moment of my first day of being Tammy was going to be the most intense day of the whole script for my character. Personally, as far as the focus on her and the nature of the scene, I just embraced it and then it was comically beautiful.

Poor Matthew Lillard. Oh my God, the look on his face when I told him it's my first day and my first scene. He was like, "What do you mean?" "Well, I mean, I'm a musician. I've never actually acted before, but I'm really excited." Bless his heart because he had this insane delivery to give and  this performance that took so much. Even between the takes he was rocking back and forth, and he was rubbing his head, and he had to be in that state of anxiety and overwhelm for the duration of the filming. It's very taxing.

I gave everything that I had and so by the end of it, Matthew said, "I appreciate you." Apparently, a lot of actors in the business, if the camera's not on them, they're not there. They'll kind of just turn off. But for Matthew every performance I gave, I was fully in. Whether the camera was on me or not because honestly, I thought that was expected of me. But afterward, he gave me a little bit of props, saying "You were really in it even when the camera wasn't on you and from an actor's perspective, I appreciate that." And so that acknowledgment went a long way with me because I didn't want him to be so bummed out that he had to perform with a novice actor in this really challenging moment.

David believed I could do it. And then it becomes your own personal faith and then has nothing to do with David as much as it has to do with wanting to personally rise to any occasion and give it everything that you've got. And I think Tammy was doing that at the same time. So it was like both I and Tammy were expanding ourselves to do this thing that we knew we could do somehow, but we were maybe in ways untested. It was a beautiful opportunity to basically rise to an occasion that I might not have chosen for myself because I might've been too scared, but that someone believed I [could] do it. So I stepped into it with all that I had.

Matthew Lillard (William Hastings): There are times in your life when you know you're a part of something bigger. Working with David is one of those times. It's humbling. He inspires you not to suck.

Kimmy Robertson: My favorite scene is the sandwich scene. "I'm on my lunch. I'm on my lunch." That was a good sandwich, too. I think they made three of them. I wish I had that sandwich right now.

Ashley Judd (Beverly Paige): A pleasure and a treat to work with the humorous and sly David Lynch. Whenever I asked about certain plot points, he said, "Oh, I can't tell you that!" He was affable and made me feel so welcomed.

Jane Adams (Constance Talbot): Working with David Lynch is like finding yourself on Los Virgienes Road in a finely tuned shiny black sports car with the sunroof open, the Rolling Stones singing "Can't You Hear Me Knocking" on surround sound stereo, the bluest sky gliding past tinted glass before your eyes, and you wonder, while your fingers tap the wheel keeping time, "Do those giant clouds that I see more resemble cauliflower or nuclear explosions?" You think, "This is beautiful. I'd like to go this way more often."

Chrysta Bell: Everything is written to the letter. I had a conversation at one point with David, or I'd read something somewhere where people would improvise and he was not into that. He worked on that script, and he's thought about that script, and it was written exactly as he intended. So unless you're in the moment that he tells you to change something. The one exception was this smoking scene [with Tammy, Diane and Gordon Cole], and that was completely improvised. So it was either to the letter or 100 percent improvised which is such a thrill, and horrifying.

Kyle MacLachlan: I think this is true of David's work; it's not like we're shooting a draft. It's really refined to David's perspective, his point of view. So we shot everything pretty much [in the script]. Now while filming, there might've been certain things we've tried very slight variations [of] but nothing that was significant enough to alter the story markedly. It was all right there.

Brings Back Some Memories

Bryon: At this point, I still felt like Dale Cooper was in some sort of state of subconsciousness. Mr. C built these barriers to keep him from coming back.

You noticed the red heels on the lady in the waiting room were like the heels Audrey had worn in Season 1 of the original run. This seems to be another clue to Dougie's awakening.

We are all noticing these subtle callbacks and with the internet, we can collectively notice more. But we ask ourselves, "Are we reaching?" I would argue that we don't know until we have seen the whole show to really understand if it was reaching or not. But it was fun to try and find these subtle callbacks as each week went on.

Ben: In Part 9, I started wondering if Cooper-as-Dougie was following a similar structure to the Wizard of Oz in that Dougie was on a journey of self-discovery in finding a brain, a heart, and courage. Dougie working on case files represented his brain, caring and crying for his son represents his heart, and protecting Janey-E from Ike "The Spike" represents his courage. Him watching a woman's red heels walk by could have reminded him of Audrey Horne, or maybe he was thinking about Dorothy's ruby red slippers and how she said, "There's no place like home." The idea of "Where do you make your home?" was an important theme in Season 3 to me.

Favorites Quotes and Scenes

Ben: My favorite scene is the Gordon Cole, Tammy, and Diane hanging outside the police station on a smoke break. A classic one shot, no cuts; a long, hilarious two-minute take that has Tammy awkwardly standing around as Cole bums a cigarette off Diane.

Bryon: Part 9 had a lot going on, but one of the most memorable scenes for me is seeing Deputy Chief Hawk, Sheriff Frank Truman, and Deputy Bobby Briggs entering the Briggs home to visit Betty about the day Major Briggs died. This scene just builds, with the swelling of the music and the way

Charlotte Stewart delivers her lines, that I almost forget to breathe while I'm on the edge of my seat to see what she will tell or show them. She tries to break the tension with "Would you fellas like some coffee?" that all hosts would say to their guests, but just like me watching, they all decline because we want her to continue about Major Briggs. As she pops open a secret compartment on an old Victorian chair and pulls out a small silver tube, she speaks directly to Bobby.

Ben: This is my favorite quote from Betty Briggs, "Bobby, when your father told me this, you were a very long way from where you are today. Somehow, he knew that it would all turn out well. He saw this life for you. Your father never lost faith in you."

Bryon: I could hear the voice of Major Briggs saying all these things to Bobby as she spoke to him. This also reminds me of the scene with Major Briggs and Bobby at the Double R. Briggs tells Bobby about his vision of light and how one day Bobby would knock on his door. Major Briggs would see Bobby living a life of deep harmony and joy. That vision light would be Bobby's future. We now see that future for Bobby and he will get to help his father in return. As Betty finishes her story and gives them the silver tube, the music comes to a head when she breaks the tension with "Well fellas, let's have that coffee," and everyone remembers to breathe, including me. This scene evokes memories of the past while giving us some new mysteries in the Briggs household.

My favorite quote comes from FBI Agent Albert Rosenfield, "I know, I know. Fuck you, Albert." This is just funny because we now have two smart asses, Albert and Diane, and Albert shows that he is still on top of his game of quick wit and he's not going to be outwitted by someone else.

Community Commentary

Blake Morrow (Photographer/Art Director): When *Twin Peaks* aired in the early 1990s, I was in high school, living in a small rural town. Suddenly, my surroundings seemed much more mysterious and promising. The series helped me see my surroundings in a new creative light, and was one of the influences that guided me to my career in the visual arts.

Fast-forward to over 25 years later. I created my "Return to *Twin Peaks*" photo project for many reasons. While it was a reflection of my anticipation of the new season of *Twin Peaks* that would be premiering in 2017, it was also a creative space I needed to take refuge in. Many changes in my life occurred around the time I began to work on my photo series, with the most significant being my father's diagnosis of Alzheimer's disease. I knew I personally needed a creative way to process these changes, and my photo series became that for me. I went to Washington State and photographed actual filming locations from the TV series, and then digitally integrated the environments with models [that] I shot in my Toronto studio. The process of styling the models to reflect beloved characters from the show, and revisiting the mythology of that world, helped to make me stronger in this one. It means so much to me to hear fans tell me how much the photo series has entertained and comforted them, as it reflects what it felt for me to create it. (*See an example of Blake's art below.*)

Chapter 43

Season 3: Part 10
"Laura Is the One"
Aired: July 16, 2017
Written by Mark Frost & David Lynch
Directed by David Lynch

The Log-line

Candie swats at a fly and hits Rodney Mitchum.

Behind the Curtain

Mark Frost: This is a very simple story. [Robert Knepper] had been slightly injured on the set. An accidental light fell over and hit him on the cheekbone.

Jim Belushi (Bradly Mitchum): It was an industrial accident. A light diffuser was on a c-clamp on a post, and I don't know if the clamp was tightened up. It kind of just dropped and a corner of it caught his cheek.

Mark Frost: They'd already shot some scenes with him. So David devised this way of figuring out why there would be a band-aid or a scar or the trace of him getting that injury. I thought that he came up with a hilarious way of doing it.

Amy Shiels (Candie): David Lynch just came to me and said, "Amy can you make tears? Do you know how to cry?" and I said "Yeah, I do." David said, "So me and Mark are going to write something for you tonight."

Jim Belushi: Robert went to get stitches [after the accident] and we had Tom

Sizemore come in. It was the next scene we had to shoot. David and I did the off-camera for Sizemore. It was cool. I was acting with David.

Amy Shiels: The fly scene is of course up there [as one of my favorite scenes] and loved working with Robert. I think we work so well together.

I was devastated. Completely devastated because he's been so kind to her and how could she possibly hurt him that way. It was unintentional, but still, she could feel his pain.

Kyle MacLachlan on if Cooper was still Cooper when he took over the life of Dougie: He was definitely Cooper. Cooper was inside, but he just was not able to connect with him. It's just like the plug and the fuse wasn't connecting for whatever reason. It was really challenging.

It's so funny how this works because I went to training school at the University of Washington, three years of acting study. One of the exercises that I remember that we did in class [was] called object discovery. The whole point of the exercise is to come upon something and you have to imagine that you have never seen it before, whether it's a fork, a book, a car, whatever the sound, and you have to react to it as if you've never seen it before. So how would you approach that object? What do you do? How do you interact with it? Blah, blah, blah. So I went back to the archives, so to speak, and really, that was how it all worked.

John Pirruccello: The day that we shot [in Sheriff Station getting the mail], I think that might've been the first thing we shot. [David Lynch] came over to me and said "Okay, now let's talk about this character, and here's what you need to know about Chad. He's an asshole!"

Kimmy Robertson: An asshole telling me it's a beautiful day.

John Pirruccello: An asshole doesn't think they're an asshole, right? I go, "Well, I think he feels the world owes him something and he kinda has been wronged and feels like he deserves more than the respect then he's getting," and blah, blah. David's just looking at me like a dog pondering a signpost or something. Like, "What the fuck is he saying?" And then I get done talking and he goes, "No, you're an asshole!" So what was really quite brilliant about that, was that it was really just this one knob that he had to turn up and down. How much of an asshole [can Chad be]? So in [the getting the mail] scene, we would do a take and then he'd go, "You know, I think maybe just a little bit more of an asshole, John. You know, turn the asshole up a little bit. Now maybe let's come back just for a little bit from that." It was just genius in its simplicity. This guy knows just what he wants. He's paying razor-sharp attention to everything and just to completely trust him. I remember when I went out to get the mail from the mail truck and I was sort of kind of swaggery, I remember I was kind of bouncing around a little bit like I'm cocky and David's like, "No! No! No! You're committing a federal offense." The efficiency of that, it's like, okay, I know exactly what to do with that. I am committing a federal offense. I will behave as if I'm committing a federal offense. So there's real freedom in having the combination of very little information and complete trust in the person that's directing you.

Amy Shiels: I really quite enjoyed the scene where I leave to go and get Tom Sizemore and then when I come back with him because I feel like it was a very kind of cheeky moment for her where she was just being a little playful with the boys.

I know this summer it was melting in Los Angeles. I walked into many rooms last year saying how grateful I was for air conditioning and then I kind of laughed. I caught myself saying, "Oh my God, I'm literally saying lines from *Twin Peaks* in real life now!"

Rebekah Del Rio (Singer): "No Stars" is a song that David Lynch and John Neff and I wrote. (*Courtesy of Jill Watson*)

John Neff (Musician): "No Stars" originally started life as a Blue Bob song. It gave birth to this song. We had done a song in *Mulholland Drive* called "Pretty '50s," which was a light and airy kind of whimsical set of chords that evoked the '50s. Right after that, I got an idea for a heavy '50s song. It was really dark and so I wrote the chords to this thing and played it on the guitarkestra. David really liked it and we didn't know what we were going to do with it, but we decided to develop it. David was inspired to write some words for it and thought that it might be ideal for Rebekah.

Rebekah Del Rio: I had a phone call from my agent, and he said, "David has a song he's working on and he'd love for you to come and work on it with him." I had what they call the Nashville formula of writing a song, which is basically, verse, chorus, verse, chorus, bridge, chorus out. And in the chorus is the hook and then sometimes you'd have a B section or something like that. So I already knew what I was doing when it came to songwriting.

When I got there I saw that they had created this really cool track, John and David. I love the track. David gave me this little piece of paper that he had written a poem on and these different words for the song, but it wasn't like a verse or chorus or anything like that. It didn't have any structure at all. And I thought, "Oh, this is interesting. I could probably do something with this." David said, "Well, I'd like you to make this into a song and come

Ben, Rebekah Del Rio, & Bryon at Festival of Disruption in 2018.

up with the melody and write this song in Spanish." I said, "Yeah, I can do that. I'll take this home and I can bring [it] back in a few days. I'll bring you back different styles, different ideas, different melodies. And you could pick the one you like the best." And he said, "No, no, no. Not exactly what I had in mind, Rebky. I'd like you to do that now." I looked at my agent and I said, "Are you kidding me?" And then my agent, he said, "Well, you've never let me down before." So I was like, "Well, no pressure. Thanks."

So I kind of tried to go to the furthest part of that house so that I [could] be by myself. And I sat down with a cup of coffee and I just looked at this chicken scratch that [David Lynch] had written down. I thought, how do I make this a song?"

I happened to be listening to the Smiths and Morrissey. So I had this in my head. And that's when I was looking at the song and the different lyrics he had, I thought, "Oh, I can just repeat this." I was just trying to make it into an actual formula song, but then throw a little Morrissey twist to it, right? It works for Morrissey. It'll work for me.

I kinda got this idea to make it similar to [the song] "Llorando/Crying," but in "Crying," it's like word-for-word and it's completely in Spanish. I did have that interest to not exclude anyone so they could understand some of it. And I think even when I sing it, even the Spanish part, you don't really need to understand what I'm saying. You can actually feel that it's pretty sad. But it also has hope, 'cause in the lyrics, "My dream is to go to that place where it all began," it's like she's looking back, but it doesn't exist anymore.

I finished it and I don't even remember what David said. And [my agent] looked at me, looked at David, and said, "I told you she wouldn't disappoint you. That's my girl." I felt like I was on display. See, and there she did it. No, she did it because she worked on it. She had to feel it and she was under a lot of pressure and she fucking kicked ass. This isn't something that just happens and it's not just magic.

John Neff (Musician): Then [Rebekah] wanted this whole dreamy ending. So I had to change the ending chorus to just go back and forth and be no stars all the way out. We recorded it the next day. It was really amazing. Rebekah Del Rio's album called *Love Hurts, Love Heals* was released in November of 2011, and I mastered the album. It's a really nice record. We put "No Stars" on it. It sounds a little different than it does on [*Twin Peaks* Season 3 Part 10] 'cause the TV show is an unmastered version.

Rebekah Del Rio: Years later, David gets this *Twin Peaks: The Return* for Showtime. So I just called him up and I said, "David, don't you think 'No Stars' would be perfect for *Twin Peaks: The Return*?" And he said, "Yes, I do."

They told me, "You come camera ready," meaning we're not paying for your makeup, your hair, or your clothes, so figure it out. So I had gone to Macy's and I actually found that dress as they were literally closing the doors on me. I saw that dress in the corner of my eyes, I noticed some Chevron.

I wrote that song long before the third season and so many things happened between the time I wrote that song and the time that it was filmed for *Twin Peaks*, including this fact that my only son suffered from cancer and then passed away. That song had a different meaning for me singing it up there again. I felt like I was back at the tower in *Mulholland Drive* and all my hopes and dreams were still alive. My son was alive. I had a record deal. I had a brand new movie. I'd never been in movies. David Lynch for Christ's sake! And I, of course, was healthy and thin and beautiful and young. And then all these things happen. 2015, it's like, wow, I lost my son. I lost my husband. I lost my health. I wrote this song and it all comes down to one scene and I just feel like this must be the place where stars go to die. That song is so torturous, but yet so beautiful.

Favorites Quotes and Scenes

Bryon: Starting off Part 10 with Carl (Harry Dean Stanton) playing "Red River Valley" on his acoustic guitar at Fat Trout is such a touching scene, and even more after his death two months later after this aired in July of 2017. It felt like art and the real world colliding with each other when you hear him sing the lyrics:

> *Then come sit by my side if you love me*
> *Do not hasten to bid me adieu*
> *Just remember the Red River Valley*
> *And the cowboy that's loved you so true.*

It's about a cowboy saying goodbye, but now it takes on this whole other meaning. It feels like Harry Dean Stanton is saying goodbye. It's wonderful that David Lynch captured these little moments of life on film and shares it with the world. This will always be a standout scene of *Twin Peaks: The Return* for me.

Ben: My favorite scene is the Mitchum brothers telling Candie to go down to the casino floor and to bring up Sinclair. So she walks down to the casino floor and we can see her on the security monitors trying to get Sinclair back to the Mitchum brothers. We can't hear what she is saying but she seems to be describing things and the brothers are getting aggravated with how long this whole process is taking. It was very comical. So they finally make it back to the Mitchum brothers and they ask what took so long. Candie replied by saying how she was telling Sinclair how lucky we are with air conditioning. A very funny scene.

Bryon: I always thought Candie was the tulpa for someone else. It would have been interesting if she had ended up being Laura Palmer.

Ben and **Bryon:** Our favorite quote comes from the Log Lady, "Laura is the One."

Ben: Laura has always been at the center of the mystery of *Twin Peaks*. Even though she doesn't seem to be in Season 3 that much, she still has this presence that haunts the town.

Bryon: These conversations that Deputy Hawk and Margaret Lanterman (The Log Lady) have with each other during *The Return* are very special, but hearing Margaret say, "Hawk, Laura is the One," then fading away to the Roadhouse to hear Rebekah Del Rio sing "No Stars" just gives me chills. It was really well done and a heartbreaking moment.

Community Commentary

Sam Witt (/u/Iswitt on Reddit): I never understood people who became obsessed with fictional universes until I saw *Twin Peaks* in 2013. I'm grateful to everyone who, from 1990 to 2014 when the new series was announced, were so loyal and committed that the fire stayed lit and got us what was previously thought impossible: more *Twin Peaks*. I've joined old and new fans alike to do my part in keeping the fire burning for future Peaks fans to come. This may not be the biggest fandom, but in the words of Dale Cooper, this is one of the best.

Eeson & Becks, Time for Cakes and Ale: It's hard to pin down the reason why *Twin Peaks* gets under the skin of so many of us. Its defiance of the conventions of film and television invites us to fill up the empty spaces with a part of ourselves; instead of spectators, we become collaborators in Lynch and Frost's beautiful vision. Much like Hawk's living map, *Twin Peaks* is always current, open to a multitude of interpretations, and full of secrets.

Chapter 44

Season 3: Part 11
"There's Fire Where You Are Going"
Aired: July 23, 2017
Written by Mark Frost & David Lynch
Directed by David Lynch

The Log-line
Dougie delivers a check to the Mitchum brothers.

Behind the Curtain
Dana Ashbrook (Bobby Briggs): I loved working with Mädchen [Mick]. The Bobby and Shelly scenes were always so fun for me to do. Mädchen is a great friend and so it was just great to be back there. We wanted Bobby and Shelly to be together because we're stupid like that. It's just not the way life is.

Charity Parenzini (Carrie, the mom who took a gun away from her son): My son and I had the great pleasure of working on *Twin Peaks* with David Lynch and his stellar cast and crew. I can say, without a doubt, the tone Mr. Lynch sets is one of profound respect for everyone involved--from the PAs to the ADs to celebrities. That group of people is a tight-knit family. They are courteous, kind, happy, and set a high standard of professionalism. If only every set in the business of making films and television shows could be as delightful, this industry would benefit tremendously. It was a world I am so honored and proud to have been invited to work [in], even if just to scream at my husband in the middle of the street for one short blip of time.

James Grixoni (Deputy Jesse Holcomb): David Lynch is a master of his craft, a conductor of the spirit and subconscious. Working for him was the greatest experience I've had as an artist; putting on the Twin Peaks Sheriff's Department uniform and walking past security and onlookers as I did my first scene at the Double R Diner, I had a realization: I made it!

Michael Horse: I'm an artist. That's what I do. You know, that's why I have such deep respect [for David Lynch]. David and I have an understanding. We're both painters.

I used to work for some of the museums and I worked for the Museum of the American Indian in New York. Don't leave me in a museum because I'm going to go through everything you got. I went to their paper archives and I saw a plain form of art called ledger art. We used to paint on hides. That was our history books, our calendar. There was what was called a winter count, which would be a buffalo hide with all these little pictures of things. We're an oral society, but it would remind the oral storytellers of things that would happen [like a meteor shower or migration battles] and we can roll it up and take it with us.

On the reservation period, the late 1800s - early 1900s, the buffalo are disappearing, we started to get ahold of pieces of scrap paper, mostly pages out of the ledger books, records of things were brought to the reservation in force, old bibles, love letters. There were about four or five of us that actually brought this art form back and I paint on all the original documents. Most of it was done in crayon, colored pencil, but I paint in the Kiowa Comanche style, which is more like a pen and ink and watercolor.

David asked, "Would you do the map?" And I went, "Oh yeah." And then he goes, "How much you want?" I said to David, "I don't have any of your artwork, just give me a drawing." And then in the mail came one of his prints, very limited edition from his Paris shows, signed to me. It was a really good deal for me.

The Hawk gets it. There are stories of places where there's evil that comes from the ground and the stories of the sky people coming and bringing information. We understand that whole spectrum of the human condition.

Jim Belushi: My directing [on *According to Jim*] and David's directing are two different things altogether. We were doing high paced comedy sitcoms and things are all about quick rhythm jokes and higher energy. And when you have time constraints you really worry about things ending up on the editing floor and movies also. So I've learned over the years to pick up my dialogue a little quicker because if you leave too much room, the edit can get in there and just cut you right out.

The scene where I come down for breakfast after I have that dream, [David] wants me to walk in. So I walk in and in my mind, I'm going, "Oh they will cut this." They never use walk-ups and drive-ups. And then I sat down and took a beat and I started my dialogue. I was like, "I had a dream last night." And then David said, he called me by my character's name: Lynch: Bradley. Me: Yes. Sir. Lynch: This is your first meal of the day. Breakfast is a very important time for you. When you sit down and you look at the cereal, the choice you make of cereal is very important to you. I want you to put the cereal in the bowl and you put the milk in. First of all, you want to make sure it's milk and not skim milk. And when you pour the milk in, you don't want too much because you don't want to lose the crunch, but you want enough to moisten it. So you're very careful about the mixture of the milk. Then the coffee, which is the most important part, how much cream you want to put in it because you like it in a certain taste, a certain color? How much sweetener? After you've tasted your coffee, then you think about what happened and then you say your line.

Me: David, you want me to take that much time? Lynch: Absolutely. Me: Don't tell me to take time because I'll take a lot of time. Lynch: Take as much time as you need, Bradley.

So you watch that scene and I walk in. I sit down and look at the cereal. I read the box. I pour the milk and then I do my lines. And, by the way, I pause between my lines for answers and I thought to myself, "This is never going to make the film." Every single beat made it.

Sarah Jean Long (Miriam Sullivan): Working with David Lynch and the *Twin Peaks* crew is still one of the best experiences of my life. I feel so blessed to be a part of this unique family. If it wasn't for Johnna Ray finding me and David seeing me for me, I wouldn't be the confident actress I am today. Thank you for giving me the confidence I didn't know I had.

Dean Hurley: "Viva Las Vegas" by Shawn Colvin was a selective that David Lynch wanted. And actually he was cutting a scene and just put it in himself. So when I first heard and saw that usage, it was because he slugged it in the film. I have a haunting suspicion this song comes from a rhino compilation. It was called Till The Night Is Gone and it's a tribute to Doc Pomus and it has a variety of artists playing his songs. This came out in 1995 and also on this compilation album is a cover of "This Magic Moment" played by Lou Reed, which was featured in *Lost Highway*. So with the timing of that and everything, I just kind of wonder if he had heard this version of "Viva Las Vegas" and always wanted to use it and finally had a chance.

It's kind of a great usage because there's the whole Vegas side of *Twin Peaks* in the series, that whole storyline, and it's a very different, extremely different rendition. I think David has always had kind of an affinity for Americana music. He loves the Dixie Chicks, which is a big surprise to people. He likes Jewel. This song wasn't a surprise to me that he liked it and wanted to use it, but I think it may surprise other people. (*KEXP, Morgan Chosnyk*)

Jim Belushi: I just loved the way David talked to actors. It's no bullshit. He was just very clear about that character's motivation in that moment. He was very clear and it was easy to do what he says [As David Lynch], "This check. This man saved your life. This man is the greatest man that you've ever met. You are so happy when you see that check. When you see that cherry pie you are so relieved that you don't have to kill him." And there's the check and that's why I was hooting and hollering like a coyote that just made a kill.

Dean Hurley: Angelo and David have such a rich history that their partnership is unmatched. And so it was really awesome seeing them work throughout this process. They worked in a really interesting way, which was a kind of through Skype and another like ISDN sort of technology where Angelo's studio in New Jersey was linked to a David studio here in LA. Whatever Angelo played was broadcast at studio quality as if he was playing in the room that we were in. We had Skype up and they could both see each other and talk like they always had worked before. It was a very kind of sacred experience, a situation where David and Angelo wanted to be alone. So myself and Angelo, assistant Jim Bruening, we would just sort of set up everything and then leave the room. But then in coming back and sorting through the material, you could hear the conversations and the back and forth and the nudging and the takes. They have something really, really cool.

At a certain point, David called up Angelo and was just like, "Yeah, I need some Italian restaurant music. Give me like three songs. One of them should be kind of peppy. One of them should be slow and sad and heartbreaking." So without even seeing the scene or them even working through Skype or anything, Angelo just sent three songs and they just placed [them] in the timeline, one after the other, and they all fit. My mouth was hanging open because I'm just like, how is this even possible? That this was just so effortless and he hasn't even seen the scene, it just slides right in. And I think at the time David was like, "Well, it's because he's Italian." It just like worked out. I think it's a testament to their long-standing working relationship where the shorthand is kind of insane. It's literally if you blink, you miss the translation of the idea of back and forth. It was really cool to see that two people working in the dark and the idea working and just being so synchronous and uniform. (*KEXP, Morgan Chosnyk*)

Brings Back Some Memories

Bryon: I really felt that Candie was someone, like Laura Palmer. I was reading deep into what Candie was talking about, traffic and the heat. I felt she needed a purpose, but in the end, she was just Candie. We also felt that the Dougie storyline is coming to an end and that Part 12 was going to be his wakeup call.

Ben: Every week we thought he would wake up.

Favorites Quotes and Scenes

Ben: My favorite scene is Dougie delivering the check to the Mitchum brothers. I love that Bradley had a dream that Rodney's "Candie cut" was completely healed and it was. Again in the world of *Twin Peaks*, the characters' dreams hold answers to life.

Bryon: They also decided not to kill Dougie because of this one certain thing in Rodney's dream: cherry pie. Dougie delivers them a cherry pie in a box. He is a friend, not an enemy.

Ben: It's only because of a dream that Dougie's life is saved.

Bryon: My favorite scene is the Mitchum brothers sitting around this half booth with Dougie enjoying a celebration dinner at a fancy Italian restaurant. The piano man seems to be the main focus during this scene, playing what sounds like at times a slowed, stripped-down version of "Laura's Theme" from the original run.

Ben: There is music in the air.

Bryon: We see the casino woman again, this time all dressed up and she runs over to Dougie saying "Mr. Jackpots!!!" Hugging him and proceeding to tell her son all about him. That money he won for her has allowed her to have a new life. She kisses him on the right cheek just like Laura did in the Red Room. Dougie/Cooper seems to be getting close to having his awakening. The music, a kiss, cherry pie, and coffee, just the feel and look to this restaurant is very Red Room-like.

Ben and Bryon: Our favorite quote is from Dougie at the restaurant saying, "Damn good!" about the cherry pie.

Ben: It's a wonderful callback to Cooper's love of pie in the old days.

Bryon: Just hearing Dougie/Cooper say "Damn Good!" was pretty awesome. We were getting the old Dale Cooper back slowly, but surely.

Community Commentary

WWE Superstar Viktor: *Twin Peaks* is the greatest journey I've ever taken the pleasure of being lost within and not wanting to find my way out.

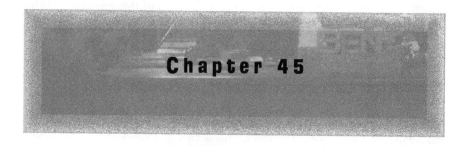

Chapter 45

Season 3: Part 12
"Let's Rock"
July 30, 2017
Written by Mark Frost & David Lynch
Directed by David Lynch

The Log-line

Tammy joins the Blue Rose Task Force and Audrey tells her husband that she wants to go to the Roadhouse.

Behind the Curtain

Chrysta Bell: Speaking for myself, part of what makes *Twin Peaks* so special is that there are these super vivid elements that are iconic. The blue roses are so arresting. The idea of it. [The] enigmatic nature of the blue rose ... and when I think of the blue rose, it's just this kind of untenable… it doesn't actually exist, but there's something about it that's palpable.

When I was reading the script and having to hold it all in because you can't share it [laughs], I was just kind of in awe that my character was going to have this strong position as part of the Blue Rose Task Force and just letting all this infuse into my being before the actual filming, before the show is on the air, before the aftermath or afterglow, both [laughs]. The idea of being on the Blue Rose Task Force with the [original] four, who were also a part of it. I really just couldn't believe it.

So my expression in my life is music. And so the Blue Rose just kind of worked its way into my own expression of music. Songs, they're ephemeral. If it's a song comes, you don't hold it too tightly because you don't want to scare it away, but you just have to remain really open. The "Blue Rose" was coming to me in this melody:

He calls me blue rose
My true love Like music in my mind
Floating through space and time
You send my love
Beyond the sun
He calls me blue rose
Blue rose
Nothing in this great big world like you and me
Nothing in this great big world like you and me

Ben, Chrysta Bell, & Bryon in 2017.

So when I played "Blue Rose" for David, he just smiled. He said, "I like it." And for David that was enough for me because he's never shy about giving his strong opinion one way or another.

David Patrick Kelly (Jerry Horne): The first season of *Twin Peaks* felt like being in The Beatles—amazing response among viewers and media to those first shows. *The Return* felt like a miraculous reunion with the added joy that David Lynch directed it all. I was running across a field shooting one of Jerry's scenes and I couldn't quite hear David shout "ACTION." I yelled to him, "David, could you say that louder? It's 26 years later and my hearing is not the same as it was!" David shouted back, "Join the club!"

Zoe McLane (Check-out Girl): Without the support of fans, a show cannot exist; however, the Peaks fandom is truly unmatched. They are kind. They are fun. Their attention to detail and ability to memorize multiple facts and word-for-word lines is impeccable. *Peaks* fans have welcomed us Season 3 newcomers with open arms. It's astonishing, considering this show and its characters have been beloved since April 8th, 1990.

Not only have I been a part of history, I've also been a part of something that has touched so many hearts around the world. I love witnessing the range of ages, faces, and walks of life who have followed us through this wacky world of *Twin Peaks*. I enjoy meeting and talking with every one of them at the *Twin Peaks* Festival.

Working with David Lynch was life-changing. His kindness seeps through every move he makes. His undeniable charm and wit warmed up the set. Working with a new group of people can be intimidating, but David makes everyone feel welcome and important. Grace Zabriskie was so kind and immediately introduced herself to me. David was so hilarious and quirky.

Twin Peaks has been so rewarding because of people I've been lucky enough to meet within the fan base, cast, crew, and, of course, David himself.

Kyle MacLachlan: One of the scenes that I love is when I'm in the backyard and my son, Sonny Jim, is giving me a mitt and I'm standing. He throws the baseball at me and I am like a child or a dog. I don't know what that is and what's coming to me until it hits me in the head. The challenge, of course, was not to react at all until after the impact. Obviously your tendency is to catch it or flinch or move, but this was not the case for Dougie.

Michael Horse: I'll tell you a really funny story. I'm supposed to go over to the house to see Grace. There are two houses and then they go, "Okay, action." I walk over and David goes, "You've gone to the wrong house." Hawk never got invited to anybody's house. I saw somebody come out of the house and I thought, "Oh, that's where they're filming." No, it's the house next door.

Grace is amazing. When Grace opened that door and yelled at me, all of my reactions, that's not acting. She's brilliant and she's really funny and really insightful.

Duwayne Dunham on Dr. Amp/Jacoby scene repeating in Part 12: The character [of Dr. Amp] was so good. Russ did such a good job with that character that we just wanted another Jacoby scene in there. As I remember, it's almost the same, but the reasoning was it doesn't matter. This is what the guy does. He just rants and so it doesn't matter when. Think about what we're talking about here because we're talking about hour 12 that didn't exist if David would've shot it, so there were only nine hours [of Season 3]. All of that story probably would have been condensed down and imagine if you can what that story looks like in half the amount of time.

Debbie Zoller on updating Audrey Horne: Audrey Horne is so iconic. I didn't want to change her too much. You had to immediately recognize her because her fans are insane. I would have been harassed if I had changed anything on her. So Sherilyn Fenn came to set very early on to talk to David and I saw her briefly and she had blonde hair. And I thought, "Oh My God! What's going to happen there?" And then I realized, "No, she was just confirming with David that she was going to go back to being a brunette." So she and I would talk and I'd worked with

Photo courtesy of Debbie Zoller.

Sherilyn before, so it was really nice to reconnect with her again. I sent her to go get her nails done and to get a facial. Just to make her feel pampered and to feel welcome. She was truly at the very end of our shoot of what, eight, nine months. So I wanted to make sure that she still felt connected to us, even though she wasn't coming until later.

Sherilyn Fenn: What David ended up writing for me was amazing. It was wonderful. I was so excited and challenged and nervous and thrilled. We had a great time doing it. It was a bumpy ride getting there. Once we got there, at the end we hugged and he's like, "It's great. Be happy."

Clark Middleton (Charlie): I'd been a fan of the original *Twin Peaks* and, of course, all of David's movies. I felt my acting sensibilities would fit in that world from the first moment I heard Angelo Badalamenti's iconic score. It's just one of those weird things that had no apparent logic to it, more of a feeling, a vibe. Like, "Oh, I belong there; that's where I'm supposed to be." Then 20 years later, I heard they were doing the reboot so I called my agent right away.

A few months after having sent a tape to David with me telling this crazy story about the time a friend of mine and myself bounced a car off a semi-truck in southern Virginia and the crazy, funny stuff that transpired when we wound up in the tall weeds in the ravine off the side of the road, I received an offer and the script with my scenes. I flipped through the pages and thought, "Oh my god! This dude Charlie has all of his stuff with Audrey. Man, how dang perfect is that!" Not only am I going to be working on *Twin Peaks* with David but also acting with Sherilyn whose work I loved in the first *Twin Peaks*.

I had a month to get under the hood of David and Mark Frost's incredible words, so by the time I arrived on the set I was ready to go, or so I thought. It became the most blissful acting experience because number one, David has this remarkable ability to say one tiny thing that'd spin your approach to the scene in the most remarkable and fun way. Although very professional and focused, the set had this low key vibe that felt like home-cookin'. It was beautiful hanging with David between setups, chatting very laid back while he smoked. He's so down to earth, unassuming and chill. Brilliant and funny but never off his breath. Then to watch him dream up how the scene should unfold in the moment; for my acting instincts, it was like cuttin' loose the hounds. It was the most perfect acting experience. And then to have been firing away in those scenes with the fiercely talented Sherilyn Fenn, man alive what on earth could be better for any actor? Beyond fun and tremendously inspiring. I'm so grateful for the experience. It sure did raise the bar for my acting appetite. I'd love to have more, more, more!

Dean Hurley: So when we had reached out to Johnny Jewel about a song of theirs, "Shadow," which everyone saw in the end of the second episode, he started sending me additional ideas and he would send some of the music he was working on at the time, an instrumental and a vocal version. "Saturday" we're using it as an instrumental and it's one of the first ideas that he sent over and kind of a second wave. It just leaped out at me because it was instrumental; it was so cinematic and left room for dialogue. It also just seemed to kind of poetically combine and be kind of this modern version of the kind of nostalgic *Twin Peaks* sound. So it just kinda wrapped up everything in a way that made it just feel comfortable and familiar, yet fresh.

I love that it's an instrumental and Ruth [Radelet] plays guitar on it and the three members on guitar are just kind of stoically standing there and swaying with the music. It's very eerie, ethereal and it just works really well, in a way. It's kind of a nice change in the Roadhouse to have kind of an instrumental cinematic backdrop to that space there. (*KEXP, Morgan Chosnyk*)

Brings Back Some Memories

Ben: I love that we see Gordon Cole hanging out with a French woman. Back in Season 2 Episode 25, he says, "That's the kind of girl that makes you wish you spoke a little French." And now 25 years later, he's hanging out with [a] French woman and I hope he's learned a little bit of French. Also, her working on leaving and him watching was so funny.

This episode was also special because we went to the *Twin Peaks* Festival in Washington (state) and were inside of the Roadhouse (the exterior was shot for the show) and we were surrounded by fans, friends, *Twin Peaks* cast and crew members as we all watched Part 12 together.

Bryon: Sabrina Sutherland had brought a computer with her that had the Part 12 on it for all of us to watch that Sunday night. I would say that Part 12 worked very well in front of a crowd. We all shared in the laughter of Dougie/Cooper getting hit in the head with a baseball, cheering after hearing Diane say "Let's rock." The impatience we all felt of watching the French Woman leave Gordon Cole's room so Albert could talk freely with him and we all cheered when the face of Audrey Horne finally, after all this time, graced that big-screen television.

Ben: I had accidentally found out that Audrey was going to be in this part a half hour before we watched it. I had forgotten we were on the west coast and people on the east coast were already talking about Audrey on Twitter. Also Sabrina mentioned that she had a message from David Lynch before we watched the show.

Bryon: Sabrina mentioned that David Lynch was watching it with us and I wanted to believe she put her phone on speaker and he watched at home listening along to the room's reaction.

Favorites Quotes and Scenes

Bryon: My favorite scene and quote are all rolled up into one. We get to see FBI Agent Albert Rosenfield and Gordon Cole bring in FBI Agent Tammy Preston to the Blue Rose Task Force. Diane walks into the room from behind a red curtain (kind of odd). They deputize her into the FBI and the scene ends with *Fire Walk with Me* music and sound and Diane says, "Let's rock."

Ben: "Let's rock" is my favorite quote and it takes us back to Cooper's Red Room dream and the words written on Chet Desmond's car in *Fire Walk with Me*.

Bryon: My prediction just based off the show title was that Cooper would wake up finally and his first words would be "Let's rock." But to be honest, what happens in the episode was even better than my prediction.

Ben: My favorite scene is with Audrey telling Charlie she wanted to go to the Roadhouse. It reminds me of the 1966 film *Who's Afraid of Virginia Woolf?* with Elizabeth Taylor and Richard Burton. They have an erratic marriage where something more is going on under the surface, but the audience is not let in on it. It's intense and mysterious and we watch these characters play mind games with each other and wondering why.

Bryon: I felt like were watching Audrey in therapy. That excitement was deflated after we saw Audrey and her possible husband Charlie play out and we were dumbfounded. We could not make heads or tails out of that scene. After we finished watching the part, all we could talk about was that Audrey scene. It seemed to be a mixed reaction from the crowd on the return of *Twin Peaks'* most beloved characters.

Ben: The scene really grew on me and I think the actors gave an amazing performance.

Community Commentary

Lindsey Bowden (Founder and Organizer of the *Twin Peaks* UK Fest): I was 14 years old when *Twin Peaks* first aired in the UK and was completely spellbound by it immediately. I loved the quirky characters, the small-town setting, the suspense of the murder story running through it, and it somewhat made me, as a slightly angst-ridden teenager, feel safe.

My favorite character was actually Windom Earle. Still is. I loved Kenneth Welsh's slightly maniacal performance, giving Earle an attractiveness and mystique of his own, despite him being crazed enough to kill. His performance is flawless.

Some of my favorite scenes in *Twin Peaks* are the llama coming face to face with Agent Cooper, the Tibetan rock-throwing in the woods, Major and Bobby Briggs' infamous father and son talk and, probably my favorite scene, Maddy's murder. That scene, and *Twin Peaks* as a whole really, was quite shocking for that era. Murder was never really that graphic on TV in the early '90s and indeed storylines were not pushed the way that Mark Frost and David Lynch pushed them. This led to breaking boundaries and direct influence on other writers. Their works inspired so many up and coming writers and you can see it clearly in shows like *Lost, Six Feet Under, Wayward Pines, True Detective* and *Stranger Things.*

I created the *Twin Peaks* UK Festival in 2010 and it's now ten years old. We celebrate this incredible piece of television with Peakies from all the world and stars from the show itself. We create worlds from *Twin Peaks* and allow the fans to lose themselves in this mysterious place. We also like to celebrate the fans by allowing them to contribute to our art gallery and Lynch Inspired Short Films. I love seeing how the fans are inspired by the show and how they bring their own creativity to the table. It's really a special event that brings people together. A world without *Twin Peaks* would be like Cooper without his coffee: not so damn fine!

Chapter 46

Season 3: Part 13
"What Story is That, Charlie?"
August 6, 2017
Written by Mark Frost & David Lynch
Directed by: David Lynch

The Log-line

Mr. C arm wrestles Ranzo.

Behind the Curtain

Jim Belushi: It was the party scene where we were doing the conga line into the [insurance] office. I'm a musician and an ensemble actor so my ears are hyper-aware of levels of sounds and drop in energy or sound. So I felt there was a kind of a hole and I kind of ad-libbed something. I can't remember what it was. It wasn't like a big sentence. It was like, "Oh yeah, love that." At the end of the take, cut, David was on his megaphone: Mr. Belushi? Yes, sir. Do I need to bring you into the principal's office? I said, "No, sir. He's just so funny and charming and he's just a doll. I love the way he did that.

Amy Shiels: It was a lot of fun shooting that day. Don Murray, he's a dear friend, so that was nice to have our scenes together and present him with all the prizes. How excited she was, making sure everything was so perfectly placed. She couldn't believe that she was giving a person keys to a brand new car. Can you imagine?!

Don Murray (Bushnell Mullins): Working with David Lynch and Mark Frost on *Twin Peaks* was an extraordinary experience for me. It was the first time I've worked with a creative team before I even met them. I've had the privilege of working with great directors such as Josh Logan, Otto Preminger, Fred Zinnemann, and Francis Ford Coppola. I am glad to say that David Lynch is in my top-tier of directors nonpareil; his enthusiasm and superb taste inspired me from day one on the show to the very end.

Grant Goodeve (Walter Lawford): Without a doubt, working with David Lynch (and everyone at Rancho Rosa Productions, especially Sabrina Sutherland) was the highpoint of my life as an actor. David's natural encouragement and appreciation of actors is without equal.

Everything about working with David Lynch was on the highest plane of creativity, artistic energy, and there was a vivid sense of unparalleled joy in the work itself. It was as rare a gift as one could hope to find in show business, not to mention, in life.

George Griffith (Ray Monroe): *Twin Peaks* and the worlds of David Lynch have been such a significant part of who I am and who I have become. *Twin Peaks* is more than a show or a film or a place to me. It represents a profound and continuing journey. It is a great, deep work of art filled with love and curiosity and mystery. I treasure it.

We live inside a dream. See you in the trees, fuckers.

Ben, George Griffith, & Bryon in 2018.

Derek Mears (Renzo): Working on *Twin Peaks* was phenomenal. When I finished shooting my last scene, I remember telling David [Lynch] the biggest compliment I could give him was that I applaud him for the family that he has created. The cast and crew's talent, kindness, and loyalty to him was a true testament to his heart and leadership. I thanked him for having me on the show and for the amazing life experience. He thanked me and then replied that I was "now a part of that family too." I choked up and exited before the emotional avalanche that his words created cascaded through my eyes. I will never forget that moment. David is an extraordinary talent and an even more extraordinary human being. I am extremely lucky and grateful to have been able to work with him.

Bryon, Ben and Joel Bocko arm wrestling Derek Mears at Rock and Shock Fest 2019.

Dean Hurley: David really wanted to reprise ["Just You"]. I think from the early idea of doing multiple acts in the Roadhouse, he was like, "I want James to sing 'Just You' in the Roadhouse." So we prepared that. James Marshall, the actor, was pretty excited to do it. It's kind of like, again the collapsing of time. Throughout the show where you have the characters older; their lives have changed; the world has evolved and we're back with that song. In the second season, it was such an interesting, bizarre usage and here he is, all these years later, performing it in the Roadhouse and kind of looking longingly toward his love interest. (*KEXP, Morgan Chosnyk*)

Favorites Quotes and Scenes

Ben: My favorite scene is the arm wrestling between Mr. C and Ranzo at The Farm. Mr. C dominates the situation and the funny thing is we want Mr. C to win the match.

Bryon: My favorite quote comes from Mr. C while arm wrestling Renzo, "Back to starting positions." Mr. C toying with this monstrous man Renzo at the farm was pretty intense. I honestly thought this could have been the end of Mr. C. Also, the phrase "back to starting positions" felt it could have a deeper meaning to the overall *Twin Peaks* story.

Ben: That scene really reminded me of the old 1987 arm wrestling movie *Over The Top* with Sylvester Stallone. It's kind of a crazy idea for *Twin Peaks* to have an arm-wrestling competition scene. It could have come off silly, but somehow all the elements came together and it worked.

Bryon: My favorite scene is James Hurley singing "Just You" at the Roadhouse. This was definitely a highlight for me. I know a lot of interesting things happened during this part, but for some reason, this performance was just as mysterious and dreamlike as anything else on the show. Seeing James Hurley playing his guitar with his two backup singers (I call them The Hurleyetts) singing "Just You" was magical. Who was the woman watching and crying? Was James on tour? Who were his backup singers? What was up with the Roadhouse? All questions we will never get answers to, but you know what? James is cool and now we know why.

Bryon, James Marshall, & Ben in 2017.

Ben: My favorite quote comes from Nadine Hurley who says to Dr. Jacoby, "And those drapes are completely silent. This is my tribute to you, Dr. Amp." Originally Nadine hoped her silent drapes would bring her wealth, things, a new life, love and happiness, but she learned from Dr. Amp/Jacoby that happiness comes from shoveling your self out of the shit. The scene was a sweet moment between Nadine and Jacoby. They clearly both care for each other.

Community Commentary

Jill Watson: *Twin Peaks* came to me, not the other way around. I grew up right down the street from Snoqualmie Falls, and it's always felt like home to me. My stepfather's job involved converting the old Snoqualmie Falls Lodge into what's currently the Salish Lodge/Great Northern Hotel. As a pre-teen, I spent a lot of time in the park beside the Salish and was lurking nearby during part of the pilot's filming. I was too young to watch the show during its original run, but I was also the only person in the house who knew how to program the VCR. I was enthralled. During high school, my best friend lived next door to the Palmer House in Everett. So, once again, synchronicity put me right there for filming. Years of watching the show at various points in my life, my relationship to the story continues to evolve.

Some of the dearest friendships in my life began with a shared love of Lynch and *Twin Peaks*. Some of the creative forces behind the show have become friends, and others have become artistic mentors. The benefits of Transcendental Meditation threw me into a creative life a few years ago and I haven't looked back. I still hike the falls almost daily, and I frequently lead tours through the filming locations in North Bend and Snoqualmie. *Twin Peaks* came to me, but I keep returning to *Twin Peaks*. I couldn't be more grateful for it.

Chapter 47

Season 3: Part 14
"We Are Like the Dreamer"
August 13, 2017
Written by Mark Frost & David Lynch
Directed by David Lynch

In Memory of DAVID BOWIE

The Log-line

The Twin Peaks Sheriff Department explores the woods near Jack Rabbit's Palace.

Behind the Curtain

Sabrina Sutherland: David loves his actors. David loves the show. He was insistent on having certain people in the show regardless. With Miguel Ferrer, we didn't know at the time that he was ill. He had a scheduling conflict where he wasn't able to work with us unless he [could] only work on the weekends and on certain days we were off. David said we have to have him and we changed our whole schedule to make sure that he could work with us. He knew we had to have him. The crew was going to kind of rebel cause we had just shot up here in Washington. We were working six-day weeks. We went down to LA and we planned, okay, we're now on five [days a week] and we can kind of take a breather cause it's very difficult to work six-day weeks. We had a production meeting and David made the speech. He says, "I really want Miguel. Miguel is part of our show. We have to have him and so we're going to have to work some Saturdays. I'm really sorry, but we want him; he's part of the family." And now looking back, it's so great that we didn't say, "Okay, we're going to recast him." And people were saying that, crude people or whoever, were saying, "Well let's recast." And it's like, "No, this is Albert." (*Q&A at Twin Peaks Festival 2017*)

Carel Struycken: I see [the Giant and the Fireman] as the same character. It is only Agent Cooper who calls me the Giant. So maybe my real function was the Fireman all along, putting out big fires. In this case, the world going up in flames. (*Courtesy of Tim Fuglei*)

Jay Aseng (Drunk): I went to go visit David Lynch on the set that day before I was going to show up to start shooting. I just ask him a little bit about what he was looking for. At that point, I had no direction. I had no script. I had nothing. I'd known that this was gonna be a drunk character in the Twin Peaks jail and that's all I knew [laughs]. He told me a little bit about what to expect and kind of what he was looking for, but even then he was kind of vague in his way. And that was really all I had to go off of. I never saw a script. I never saw anything like that. I had heard later from his assistant, Michael, and others that that character was in the script. I don't think he was necessarily written in a way where there were lines there because he's just basically kind of copying sort of what he hears in his sort of odd way. That was kind of how David talked to me about it, was just kind of to do that.

John Pirruccello: I have a lot of really fond memories of that time in the jail. Because that's where the two of them [Jay Aseng, the drunk, and Nae, Naido] sort of did that thing that they were doing. I had not been prepped at all that that was going to happen. Well, my reaction to it was really just amazement.

Jay Aseng: I love John [Pirruccello] so much. He was so kind of mystified and fascinated. It's almost like he couldn't believe what he was seeing happening around him. I didn't even know, honestly, that Naido was going to start doing that. That kind of just sort of came about. I'm guessing it was probably all part of David's master plan. When I was hearing around me, I was originally thinking I'm just gonna copy the actual words I hear people saying. But then she started making noises and I thought we should start doing something with that as well. I had no idea how that was going to come out because I tried to copy what she's doing, I can't come close to copying that, so it came out in this really demented way. But he seemed to dig it and it definitely seemed to drive both John's character and perhaps himself crazy to be in the middle of all that.

John Pirruccello: I had to do so many awful things. I had to speak terribly to people that I love and respect and I had to make light of things that were magical to me. So I just decided that anytime I was in wonder or amazement, I would just turn that into annoyance and anger. So I'm just sitting there just listening to the two of them go back and forth and it was just like a dream. In fact, I really have no recollection of when the lights were in there and when they weren't, when we were rehearsing, when we were shooting. It all feels like one thing. That whole sequence was very dreamlike, very magical.

Ben, John Pirruccello, & Bryon in 2017.

Jay Aseng: I think there is a school of thought that I'm not really there, or at least not in the conventional sense, like maybe I'm just the figment of Chad's imagination. Nobody else really seems to acknowledge me at all.

Dean Hurley: Lissie was definitely one of the acts that David wanted involved from the beginning. He's been a big fan of hers for years and discovered her by a series of videos she posted on YouTube covering Lady Gaga, Metallica, etc. This was 2010, I believe. It was definitely a learning lesson for me because seeing how he found out about her was one of the solidifying moments where

I saw what was important to him in terms of his experience of music and what thrills him. No one would necessarily listen to Lissie and say "this would be great in a David Lynch film," which is why only he could bring someone like her into his work. I don't want to speak for him, but I think it's obvious what he responds to in her. She is an incredibly emotive performer who completely embodies her music and gives everything. It's probably the same thing that guides his desire to cast certain actors for certain roles. He's looking for a super-strong emotive core which can illustrate and get across big feelings to a viewer for the roles that require that (and there's always a bunch of these types of roles in his work).

David doesn't attend a lot of concerts, but when she came through LA years back, he wanted to go. I can't emphasize how rare that is for him to want to go out to a show. An artist like Lissie thrives in the live performance arena. She's one of these people that almost can't be contained on a recording because she's the fullest realization of herself live. He raved about the show and particularly raved about the power and volume of the venue. When performance, emotion, and volume all come together in an optimal way, the artist's idea is translated with a certain power and that is what David works so hard at crafting and getting right in his own work. Volume is the only thing that he can't control in the realm of television, so I know I can speak for him on this front: watch *Twin Peaks* loud and on a good sound system! The experience will be richer as a result. (*KEXP, Morgan Chosnyk*)

Favorites Quotes and Scenes

Bryon: Part 14 is filled to the brim with exciting moments that really move the narrative forward but the one scene that sticks out to me is Sarah Palmer going to a local bar and being harassed by this trucker guy. I say trucker because of his shirt that says "Truck You" and he looks like a trucker. Before our very eyes, Sarah Palmer opens up her face like it was a refrigerator. We see what can only be described as a dark abyss. She asks, "Do you really want to fuck with this?" She closes her face and in a blink of an eye, she lunges out and rips part of this trucker's throat off. She seems to snap out of whatever spell she was in and starts to scream. Grace Zabriskie really shines. I believe this scene is one of the top moments people will be talking about for the next 25 years when it comes to *Twin Peaks: The Return.*

Ben: My favorite scene was when Bobby, Hawk, Andy, and Frank Truman go to Jack Rabbit's Palace. I just loved the atmosphere around it. I like the journey

SUNDAYS 8PM SHOWTIME

of these men going into the woods seeking and discovering supernatural things. Reminds me of season one with the men walking in the woods and running into the Log Lady's home and her providing answers. Also, it was great to see Andy have his moment with the Fireman and become a hero and protector.

Ben and **Bryon:** Our favorite quote is from Monica Bellucci who says, "We're like the dreamer who dreams and lives inside the dream, but who is the dreamer?"

Bryon: Gordon Cole tells Tammy and Albert that he had another Monica Bellucci dream.

Ben: *Twin Peaks* has always had dream elements in it, whether it's been through the music, visuals, or the words people have said. Cooper was in Cole's dream, but Cole couldn't see Cooper's face. Could Cooper be the dreamer?

Bryon: Are we the dreamer? I hope we are.

Ben: If Lynch/Frost is really talking to the audience, then we, the dreamers, keep the word of *Twin Peaks* alive with our conversations, theories, and love of the show.

Community Commentary

Em (Co-host of *Sparkwood and 21: A Twin Peaks Podcast*): I first encountered *Twin Peaks* when I was in middle school while living in Germany. My best friend at that time was a gateway for me regarding a lot of different things like movies and music among others. She told me about *Twin Peaks*, and I found it sometime later on the television. I remember I caught it right when James and Donna were burying the necklace, and subsequently, Donna's three-quarter profile became seared into my memory. I thought she was so beautiful, and I often thought about that image of her which is all I had of *Twin Peaks* for many years after that moment. My mother quickly caught me and stopped me from watching it. It came on during my mandatory study hour, and it was "too weird." It wasn't until the late '90s when I was living in San Francisco, I was able to watch more with a group of friends. Just the first season, anyway.

Steve (Co-host of *Sparkwood and 21: A Twin Peaks Podcast*): *Twin Peaks* is directly responsible for getting me to appreciate television as a legit medium, and Em is directly responsible for exposing me to it. One of my favorite memories is of us renting VHS tapes that had two episodes apiece, watching them, then driving right back to the store to get the next one. Twenty years and LOTS of TV later, *Twin Peaks* is still something that I think of, reference, or quote on an almost daily basis. The owls are still not what they seem.

Chapter 48

Season 3: Part 15
"There's Some Fear in Letting Go"
Aired: August 20, 2017
Written by Mark Frost & David Lynch
Directed by David Lynch

In Memory of MARGARET LANTERMAN

The Log-line

The Twin Peaks Sheriff's Department mourns the passing of Margaret Lanterman, the "Log Lady."

Behind the Curtain

Dean Hurley: Twelve years ago when I started this job, ZZ Top's "Sharp Dressed Man" was one of David's favorite songs. It's one of the touchstones in the talking points that we would always talk about when we were working on music. I think he always wanted to get at something that they were getting at in terms of this kind of hyper-stylized blues. It took me a while to see that song through his eyes, but once I did, it was like this chrome-plated, super-stylized version of the blues and from that album *Eliminator*. That was something new at the time and I think it caught his attention in his ear in a way that thrilled his soul.

One of his dream items was that it'd be great to have ZZ Top play the Roadhouse. Even though that didn't happen, it's sort of a great example that even though they don't appear in the Roadhouse, the essence and the energy of them appear in the Roadhouse in this [part]. I think because they weren't there is why David wanted to make this visual representation of how to listen to their music loud, even if it's being played off of a playlist or a record that the volume must be well into the red and this very visceral component. That song is a cool song and I feel like it's even cooler in a way in the scene because it somehow just leaps the thing to another level. The scene kind of also mirrors the quality that I've come to learn about what ZZ Top means to David. (*KEXP, Morgan Chosnyk*)

Wendy Robie (Nadine Hurley): What can I say about *Twin Peaks*? It was a cultural phenomenon that changed the face of television. Just think what was on offer on TV before *Twin Peaks* and after *Twin Peaks*. Then it came back decades later to take us all deeper into the trees, the wind, the falling water, and our own mysteries past, present, and outside time.

For me, the story began in Seattle in 1989 when David Lynch and Mark Frost cast me in a pilot called (for the moment) *Northwest Passage*. I remember wearing a shawl to the audition and quickly stashing it behind a chair as Mark and David told me about Nadine Hurley.

I adored playing Nadine in all her confusion, determination, rage, and pain. A half-blind dynamo with a spring in her step, Nadine was heartbreaking, hilarious, and weirdly innocent. Being a part of Mark and David's vision, playing Nadine, was the greatest adventure of my life. I will always be grateful.

Ben, Eben Moore, Wendy Robie, & Bryon in 2017.

Grant Goodeve (Walter Lawford), note to Peggy Lipton September 19, 2015:

I cannot express how wonderful the whole experience was working on *Twin Peaks*, especially working with you. Your beauty, talent, and wonderful spirit were a great blessing to me, as well as your encouragement and keen, deep insights into the wonder of working with David. I feel that I have been blessed beyond all imagining for the experience I had with you all on the set, and if I never act again, that's fine with me! This was an ultimate experience as an actor, and as a human being and my whole being is still ringing with gratitude and joy for what was clearly a gift out of God's clear blue sky.

Nathan Frizzell (the voice of Phillip Jeffries): I discovered *Twin Peaks* about two years before being cast in *The Return* and instantly became a fan. The idea of working with David Lynch, whom I'd admired since *Mulholland Drive*, and the task of voicing a character that David Bowie created was intimidating, to say the absolute least. But then I met David, who was extremely kind and supportive, and the work was easily one of the most surreal and rewarding experiences of my career. I won't soon forget the opportunity and am honored to be a part of the *Twin Peaks* world.

Harley Peyton: Mark [Frost] had his great cameo [as Cyril Pons] so I was happy to see that. Walking his dog through the woods. That was sweet.

Dean Hurley: I met Finn Andrews, I think it was back in 2015, and [The Veils] was one of the bands that I was just trying to put in front of David and sort of test the waters and see how he responded to that. Finn had reached out and we worked on a song together and recorded a song from the LP that "Axolotl" is from. And it was a song called "In the Nightfall" and we really hit it off. We had a great working relationship and as the show started to get going in the sort of peak secrecy of not revealing to people what was going on. There are certain relationships with bands that you want to have, a friendship there because it's an easy conversation and maybe there's an understanding of being considered for something but then ultimately it not working out. You know they're going to be okay with that and not talk to the media.

So when we had done "In the Nightfall," it has a *Twin Peaks* kind of reminiscent feeling about it. Mainly because of the main sense that Finn plays in that song. I had played that song for David just like with no expectation.

I just wanted to see how he responded to it. He didn't really say, "Oh, let's put this in the Roadhouse," but a couple of weeks later as Finn was kind of delivering and showing me different mixes from the album, he had "Axolotl" and I remember hearing that. I played it for David and of course, I didn't tell him anything about it, but he heard the song and he immediately was like, "This is amazing!" It sounds like Gene Vincent produced by a hip hop guy, which in a way is sort of what it was. The Veils have kind of a longstanding indie rock tradition and this new album kind of juxtaposes them with a variety of producers, but one of them being El-P.

And that was a really interesting kind of mashup combination there. And those are the types of things that I think spark David's mind and make him go, "This is interesting." Music here is colliding and seeing the collision between two vastly different things, it's sorta like seeing his playlist evolve. It's like all these items and elements that he responds to. It's a lot of collision and vastly different ingredients. It was one of the few songs that I played for him and he immediately was like, "This is going in the Roadhouse. I love this song. I love this guy. I don't even know who he is, but I love him." So that was thrilling to be able to relay that news to Finn. (*KEXP, Morgan Chosnyk*)

Charlyne Yi (Ruby): It was like crawling into a dream, and releasing all my pain in a series of belting cries.

Michael Horse (Deputy Chief Tommy "Hawk" Hill): How lucky do you get to say goodbye to the Log Lady? And she was my friend; we were friends, Catherine, Jack [Nance], and I.

People go, "Why didn't you cry?" I said, "I didn't want it to be sad. I wanted it to celebrate her bravery of doing that. Her dignity."

Charlotte Stewart on the passing of Catherine Coulson: Catherine and I became friends on *Twin Peaks* together. And then I've known her through the years. We stayed in touch. In fact, she did give me a call last summer to say she had lung cancer. She just wanted me to know. Then I saw her at the *Twin Peaks* Festival [2015], her last appearance there and she was quite ill, but she was so gracious and so available to all the fans.

Catherine Coulson: There are a lot of wonderful *Twin Peaks* fans, truly the nicest people in the world.

Charlotte Stewart: I just admired her. You know what? Catherine Coulson made me a better friend. Just knowing her made me a better friend and I miss her terribly.

Charlotte Stewart and Catherine Coulson at the Salish Resort in 2015

Photo courtesy of Jen Ryan.

Brings Back Some Memories

Bryon: This part gave me a roller-coaster of emotions. I was on cloud nine seeing Big Ed and Norma get back together, the edge of my seat watching Mr. C travel through classic places to reach a teapot that is Phillip Jeffries, finally finding out that Audrey is Richard's mother and Mr. C could be his dad, hearing what could have been Steven Burnett take his own life in the woods, the rocking sounds of ZZ Top at the Roadhouse while James and Freddie get in a fight and we see that green glove in action, Dougie/Cooper eating cake at home while more memories come flooding his way for his shocking return, and the death of one of the most beloved characters in *Twin Peaks* history, The Log Lady. David Lynch and Mark Frost are really delivering the goods in these final last parts.

Favorite Quotes and Scenes

Ben and **Bryon:** Our favorite scene is Big Ed and Norma getting together in the Double R.

Bryon: We finally get one of the biggest and sweetest moments which *Twin Peaks* fans have been waiting for all these years. Big Ed and Norma Jennings are together and are finally going to get married. This scene hits you on every level imaginable and will go down as my number one moment of *The Return*.

Ben: In the pilot, Big Ed and Norma are at the Roadhouse and Norma says, "I love you, Ed. I'm going to do what's best for both of us." And it took 25 years, but she does.

Ben and **Bryon:** Our favorite quote comes from Margaret the "Log Lady":

Margaret: Hawk, I'm dying.
Hawk: I'm sorry, Margaret.
Margaret: You know about death, that it's just a change, not an end. Hawk, it's time. There's some fear, some fear in letting go. Remember what I told you. I can't say more over the phone, but you know what I mean, from our talks when we were able to speak face to face. Watch for that one, the one I told you about, the one under the moon, on Blue Pine Mountain. Hawk, my log is turning gold. The wind is moaning. I'm dying. Goodnight, Hawk.
Hawk: Goodnight, Margaret ... [line clicks] ... Goodbye, Margaret.

Ben: It's hard to separate the Log Lady's words with Catherine Coulson the person, who was close to dying herself. It was very brave of Catherine to participate in *Twin Peaks* and to give us one last outstanding performance. She and her words were just so powerful and heartbreaking.

Bryon: This is the last phone call we would hear from Margaret. The sadness and fear we hear in her voice bring shivers down your spine.

Ben: I thought it was a nice touch to have Hawk, Sheriff Truman, Andy, and Lucy have a moment for her and then have her cabin in the woods lights slowly go out.

<u>Community Commentary</u>

J.C. Hotchkiss (Managing *Twin Peaks* Editor for 25YL Site and Bookhouse Babes Co-Founder): I was twelve years old when *Twin Peaks* came out. I was a theater kid, a performer. I loved all things dramatic and at twelve that is a lot! First time seeing Laura Palmer, she was beautiful, ethereal, and wrapped in plastic. Seeing Laura getting turned over by Doc Hayward and Sheriff Truman took my breath away. The second time that also took it away was the minute Special Agent Dale Cooper drove into town. The music, the cadence of his voice, and that profile was pure magic. Hearing him speak, "Diane, 11:30 AM, February 24th, entering the town of Twin Peaks" is something I will never, ever forget.

With the return of *Twin Peaks*, we have gained so much more. Besides the mystery coming back into all our lives, we got a glimpse of the genius that was in Frost and Lynch for the last 25 years. We were able to see incredible acting from Kyle MacLachlan, Grace Zabriskie, and Laura Dern. We became a *Twin Peaks* family once again. I gained gifted and damned friends all over the world who understand and still love *Twin Peaks* as much as I do. To all those who have come into my life, thank you, especially Ben and Bryon. I am honored to be on this damn fine journey with you. Here is to the speculating, theorizing, and reading, re-watching, and wondering, hopefully for the next 25 years and beyond.

Chapter 49

**Season 3: Part 16
"No Knock, No Doorbell"
Aired: August 27, 2017
Written by Mark Frost & David Lynch
Directed by David Lynch**

The Log-line

Agent Cooper wakes up and heads to Twin Peaks.

Behind the Curtain

Duwayne Dunham: David Lynch hadn't seen any changes while he was shooting. Even when he was back in LA and he'd come through on the weekend, I'd say, "Hey, do you want to take a look at anything or you want to look at this? I could use some help, some input." He'd say, "No, no, you'll figure it out." He finished shooting somewhere around the 23rd or 24th of April [2016]. And I think we were about maybe 16 hours at that time. Fully cut. I didn't even watch it with him. It took him a whole week just to watch the movie because he would do it in maybe three-hour chunks a day. It's hard to look at more than that and formulate your thoughts. So what we had May, June, July, August, we had four months [to complete the season of *Twin Peaks*]. The movie grew by two hours and we locked the whole thing.

Jonny Coyne (Polish accountant): Me to my manager: I understand it's David Lynch and I would love to work with him but why would I want to play an accountant? That's not exciting. Manager to me: Just do it. You'll have fun. It's David!

On set, chasing Tim Roth and Jennifer Jason Leigh's van on foot and emptying two clips into said van: David Lynch to me: Was that first burst about half? Me to David: Well, I counted sixteen. David Lynch laughed and it made me happy. Yeah. I'll play an accountant for him!

Tim Roth (Gary "Hutch" Hutchens): "Think Rag Doll Elvis." -Performance note on my death from David Lynch. Love that man.

David Lynch getting makeup on the set of Season 3 Photo courtesy of Tim Roth.

Kyle MacLachlan on Cooper being a little more present in the script: During the filming, there were moments where [Cooper] had some lucidity, primarily when he was communicating with the one-armed man when he had connected to that world. We shot those and ultimately, I think, David decided that wasn't part of the story that he wanted to expose. It just didn't make it into the series. But there were moments. There weren't a lot, but there were a couple where you did get a taste of that. For whatever his reasons, I think the despair that people felt and it grew over time, that Cooper might not actually ever return was much more powerful. And to be honest, the reveal at the end when he does finally wake up was a moment that people really responded to.

J.R. Starr (Roadhouse MC): *Twin Peaks* is one of the best shows I've worked on and the director, David Lynch, is the best. He respects the actors he casts to bring it to the production. His cast and crew: the best. Everyone works as a happy family. I had a great time working on *Twin Peaks*!

Duwayne Dunham on using index cards during the editing process: [The index cards] serve a number of purposes. I learned the system with Lucas. George would write with index cards and he'd have an idea of a scene or just an idea and pin it up on the board. You try to find a structure that way. So when we're editing, the first thing that I do is I go through the script. I like to do it myself because I get more familiar with the story. I do just an abbreviation of what the scene is, day or night, and the scene number and I put 'em up on a board in the order, the structural order of the script. And then when you get scenes cooked together and you kind of get enough material that forms one reel, then you put that designation up.

So in the end, during the editorial process, when you've got your cut together, you can just stand back and look at the board and visually you can see where you are. And I use a color-coded system that tells me I haven't touched the dailies on this scene or I've done my first pass or another color as my first pass waiting [for] David's notes on it. And then I have to do the notes. Then once it's all done, the pins go red. So I can look at the board and know our status very quickly. It was hard with *Twin Peaks* because it wasn't a board. It was the entire cutting room, up one wall down the other wall, completely 360 degrees. We have cards up. And I had a couple of moving platforms that had the last hour or two on it.

Editing index cards.
Photo courtesy of Duwayne Dunham.

You could stand in the middle of the room and then I color code even further and I'd say, "Okay, this color is bad Cooper. This color is Audrey. This color is Laura's mom. This is where Agent Cooper turned from Bad Cooper to this is Dougie and then this is the FBI guy we now see." The Roadhouse had a different color. So you could look and if you knew the color codes, you could see a balance and sometimes you'd stand there and say, "David, a really important story point happens right here in hour three. We don't come back to it until hour fifteen. Is that going to be a problem?" So you look at it and you go, "Well, no, I don't think so." So off you go. I just use it. It's a shortcut for me. I can see the entire movie on the wall. Then all of my assistants know that system and they update the board as we're cutting along and we always know where we are.

Dean Hurley: One of the unsung heroes bringing [Eddie Vedder] into the fold was Laura Dern, actually. He and Laura are really good friends. David had a relationship with him because he had done a benefit concert back in 2009 with Paul McCartney and Ringo Starr. David mixed that concert and loved Eddie, loved meeting him. But he and Laura Dern are our best friends and I think Laura was kind of planting that seed into David's mind about "you should ask Eddie to do something." And Eddie's one of the few musical performers that actually just wrote a brand new song for the show. I had a conversation with him on the phone and he was a super sweet guy. Super modest, but so warm and generous.

He was asking me about the show and I didn't know what to say. I mentioned a few maybe abstract themes from the show to him. After just mentioning those few items, he was just like, "Okay, well sounds like we're throwing darts at the wall." I thought that was a really good phrase.

Photo courtesy of Debbie Zoller.

He's just gonna try something, send it over. It's like throwing a dart blindfolded. He's an amazing dart player because the first dart he threw David to listen to, he said, "It's great. It's going in the Roadhouse. I love the song." It oddly, unknowingly kind of touched on some feeling and vibe of the show in terms of the lyrics and the overall abstract theme of it all. Very cool performance and just one of the most gracious people I've ever met. He gave me a Zippo, an Eddie Vedder Zippo as a gift on set. (*KEXP, Morgan Chosnyk*)

Debbie Zoller on that "Audrey in another place" scene: [Sherilyn Fenn is] wearing a lot less [makeup]. That's the kind of actress that she is though. She knew that it would play better if she was more revealed and more naked in that sense of the word for the character. So we took her way down and of course Peter with his lighting. I think it was such a beautiful, dramatic effect because you don't know from watching the scenes with her and Charlie, what is going on. I mean, I didn't even know what was going on when we were shooting it. "Did I miss something?" That was the one area that I [said], "Okay, where's this going?" I couldn't grasp it. And then when we did that scene at the very end with her so stripped down, that's when it all came together.

Dean Hurley on "Audrey's Dance": I think this was in David's mind that he wanted to reprise this kind of moment and it also kind of sums up this Audrey storyline in terms of there's something going on with her. "Audrey's Dance" from the original series was this very kind of hypnotic thing where she's almost overtaken and goes into a trance dancing to the song. So the same thing happens here and it almost ties into the story a bit where something's going on with her. It's anyone's guess what it is, but that music cue is somehow pivotal to the whole thing. I can't even speak to it because I don't know what's going on, but something's going on. I think that something is defined in David's head and why he wanted to do specifically this "Audrey's Dance" reprise and work that into her storyline. (*KEXP, Morgan Chosnyk*)

Favorite Quotes and Scenes

Ben: My favorite scene is Cooper finally waking up. It was a running joke with us that we would say, "Next week Cooper will come back" every week on the podcast. It finally happened and I think the entire *Twin Peaks* community was happy to get him back.

Bryon: The one scene that has stuck out for me is Audrey Horne's awakening.

When I first saw this play out in 2017, I was so confused about what was going on, but over time I feel I have more of a grasp on what I had witnessed. Audrey performs "Audrey's Dance," a fistfight erupts, Audrey snaps out of her hypnotic dance and runs over to Charlie in a panic saying, "Get me out of here!" Now, what we will see next will change everything that we thought was going on up to this point. This is why this scene is in my top moments of *The Return* and I'm sure it will be talked about for the next 25 years.

Audrey seems to wake up in a white room looking into a mirror with a white shirt on, no makeup, her hair is down and she's in a state of panic, not knowing what is going on. We hear the electric sound in the background as she is having this awakening moment as well. My theory as of now is she was raped by Mr. C while in a coma (confirmed by the Mark Frost book, *The Secret History of Twin Peaks*) and she, like Laura Palmer and to some degree like Dale Cooper, is trapped inside her own subconscious. Was Audrey escaping or trying to get back to reality? Where is she now and who is Charlie? I feel we will never really figure this one out, but that is the genius of David Lynch and Mark Frost creating expectations and then shattering them right before our eyes.

Ben: We had so many theories of what was happening to her. Was Charlie her shrink? It was a unique story-line that David Lynch wrote for Sherilyn Fenn and it leaves us wanting more.

Ben and **Bryon:** Our favorite quote comes from Dale Cooper who says, "I am the FBI."

Bryon: Once Dougie/Dale Cooper woke from the hospital bed, I think everyone watching that night probably cheered in unison. This was the moment we had all been waiting for, and it only took 16 hours. The cool thing about this awakening is Dale Cooper remembers everything that has happened to him, so he thanks Bushnell Mullins for his kindness and calls the Mitchum brothers for a favor, a plane ride to Spokane, Washington. But to top off this absolutely momentous occasion, Mullins asked "What about the FBI?" to Dale and just like an '80s action star Dale Cooper says back, "I am the FBI." This is very reminiscent of "I am Batman," or "I'll be back." For me, this goes down as one of the coolest moments in *The Return*.

Ben: It's these four words from Cooper, and the *Twin Peaks* theme music accompanying the words tells the audience Cooper is ready to get back to work and return to *Twin Peaks*.

Community Commentary

H. Perry Horton (Author of *IN DREAMS: A Unified Interpretation of Twin Peaks & Other Selected Works of David Lynch*): I found *Twin Peaks* in college, a few years after it aired. I watched the pilot with my roommate, who had the VHS set, and when it was over we just kept watching and watching and watching. 32 hours later we had mainlined it all and literally everything about me as a viewer, a writer, a film fan, a thinker, a spiritual being, and a human changed. Doors were open where there'd been no doors before. The world--life--got bigger. And all because of a TV show. *Twin Peaks* is the pinnacle of its medium, the singular greatest narrative accomplishment in American history, and an integral vertebra in the skeleton of my being.

Chapter 50

Season 3: Part 17
"The Past Dictates the Future"
Aired: September 3, 2017
Written by Mark Frost & David Lynch
Directed by David Lynch

In Memory of JACK NANCE

The Log-line

Agent Cooper confronts Mr. C and BOB at the Twin Peaks Sheriff's Department.

Behind the Curtain

Kyle MacLachlan: All of the locations in Seattle were filmed first. So that means the very end of the show was filmed in those first few weeks. And it was a sequence where I show up at the sheriff's station as Mr. C and I'm walking across and I see Andy for the first time. It was a bit challenging because it wasn't a contained space. It was daytime; it was in the light. And I wanted to make sure that there was still the power to him because he was going to be there to take out Sheriff Truman and waiting for Cooper and everything. So he was about to do some serious damage. So we picked it up right in the middle, but everybody felt pretty good about it.

Charles de Lauzirika (DVD and Blu-ray Producer and Filmmaker): On Kyle's first day, when you watch *A Very Lovely Dream: One Week in Twin Peaks*, the piece I made, you see that on the same day he played both Mr. C and Cooper and he had to do two completely different roles on the first day of shooting. Imagine me not having read the script or being told the story, I knew literally nothing about what the premise was of the new show. Other than obviously you see Mr. C, Bad Cooper, show up with the long hair and think, "Oh well, BOB is still inside of him in some form," and you start thinking, "Okay, well then it's many years later. BOB is still out there and then on the same day Cooper is there in his FBI suit, clean-cut, and looking like he did back in the day." And you start thinking, "Oh, so this must be the return to Cooper as well."

Now, I see a little piece of Bad Cooper and I'm seeing Good Cooper. You start to piece these things together. But even then, I wasn't sure because in my perspective I thought that the shots of Mr. C, Bad Cooper, were literally going to be the opening of the show at the sheriff's station. I thought that was gonna be how the show opened because you think, "Oh, it was all these years later he materializes in front of the sheriff's station." Andy says, "Agent Cooper, we were just talking about you." I thought, "Oh, that must be Episode 1 or Part 1 of the show." And then I thought seeing real Cooper or old school Cooper show up and run in and have to do something in the sheriff's station, I thought, "Oh, that must be the end of the series." I was wrong on both counts. They were totally different than what I imagined. So that was a lot of fun to watch the show as a fan, as everyone else is watching it unfold and realize that I was there and I still knew nothing.

John Pirruccello: My first day on the set, I got picked up at the airport and I had to go immediately to the set. Heading down to into the woods into those trees, into those magnificent trees. We pull up and it's the sheriff's station. I got out of my car just sort of shaking my head like, "This is amazing!" I walk into the sheriff's station and the first person that popped their head out was Kimmy Robertson. She said, "Oh, hello, hello welcome. Who are you playing?" And I said, "I'm playing Chad." She said, "Oh good. We were just talking about that. We were wondering who was going to play Chad. Come over here and meet everybody."

Kimmy Robertson on John Pirruccello: We all call him John Chad.

John Pirruccello: Bob Forester was sitting there. And so that was of course news to me that [he was playing Sheriff Truman], cause I didn't know anything. I look over the corner of my eye and there is Kyle and he's got black contacts in and his hair all scraggly. You just have to remember that I have no idea. Nobody did. Nobody had any idea about what was going on. I'm like, "That's Kyle MacLachlan, but that does not look like Cooper. What the hell is going on?"

Kimmy Robertson: My interpretation is that the real Cooper calls. You know, Lucy loves Agent Cooper. Always did. So she was able to just really listen to him and not think and not scream. He saves the day in many ways.

Harley Peyton: That penultimate episode really felt like that was where [Mark Frost] wanted to go. There's always a push and pull between the two of them [Mark Frost and David Lynch]. They've had a pretty unique creative relationship and there are going to be moments when one seems to step forward. I think Season 3 because David's directing was so much more like *Wild at Heart* then the original *Twin Peaks* and he was much more stylized and a lot more money to work with. So I think that was inevitable and it's not necessarily a bad thing at all. It's beautiful to look at. There were truly some amazing, amazing things in it.

Jake Wardle (Freddie Sykes): Working on *Twin Peaks: The Return* with David Lynch was absolutely incredible. I loved every moment of it. He has an ease about him and is also very specific and explains what he wants very well. He gives great feedback and encouragement. Between takes, he'll either ask you to go and talk to him or he'll come to you and explain everything in great detail. Being on set with him and all the other wonderful cast and crew was a joyous experience from start to finish. As a result, I have many happy memories from working on the show.

One that stands out, in particular, was during the filming of the BOB fight scene in Part 17. I had been instructed by David to gently punch the camera in order to get some POV shots of Freddie hitting BOB. They put a rubber ring around the lens and also added a lens protector. James [Marshall] had not been informed of this and when the camera started rolling and I gave it my first punch, he silently gasped, "Oh no, don't punch the camera!" As the scene went on, David then kept telling me to punch it "harder!" until finally the lens protector shattered into pieces and everyone gasped in shock, including me. This was then followed by laughter. There was a real sense of camaraderie on set that you don't always get with other productions.

Clare M. Corsick (Hair Department Head) on Laura Dern's red hair: David Lynch said red and I went with auburn. He saw the auburn and said maybe something redder. I showed him the cherry wig and he went nuts.

Brian Berdan (Associate Editor for S1 & S2, Additional Editor for S3): Shortly before I worked on the original show as an assistant editor, I visited the Pacific Northwest and fell in love with it, vowing to move there. Eventually, I did and ironically now live a stone's throw away from the Big Log on the beach where Laura Palmer's body was found. The chance to come back and work on the show after 25 years was like going to sleep and willing your subconscious to re-inhabit a wonderful dream you'd once had. And like a dream, you have no real control over where it goes or what it means, you just have to follow it.

Jennifer Lynch On the line "We Live Inside A Dream": I was raised in a home where dreams were things that caught us and gave us other ideas and allowed us to do things we otherwise could not do. So I never had the "Oh what a fucking bummer! It's a dream. What a cop-out!" You know what I mean?

Michale Horse: To native people, your dreams are as real as your waking life; that's your consciousness. There's a lot of things that I just got. People ask, "Can you explain this?" I go, "No, but you can't explain everything." Some people go, "Lynch is just trying to be strange." No, everything makes sense in David's world.

Kristine McKenna (Co-author of *Room to Dream*): He's just creating a bed for us to lay down on and dream. Really. He wants everybody to just go into that zone because that's his favorite place to be, I think.

Amy Shiels: Sometimes I would come in and I would do a scene that I had no clue what it was about. And I would worry like, "Did I just not prepare properly for this?" And then I realized, no, it wasn't a thing to prepare for. I wasn't given this scene. And then I think at one point, I came in and David said, "Now Candie says her line." And I'm like, "What line?" And he said, "Oh yeah, I forgot to tell her." So then he came over and whispered the line in my ear. "It's a good thing we made so many sandwiches."

Me, personally, I feel like home is where the heart is. To use that cliché, but it is--it's not a physical building. It's where your heart is and where you feel at home. Whether that for Candie was just wherever the Mitchum brothers are. Like you see how happy she is entering Twin Peaks. She's never even heard of Twin Peaks. She's so happy in her part. And she is so welcoming to everyone. She always wants to make sure everyone's looked after. They all get their finger sandwiches. They all get their drinks. They all get their snacks. She just wants to make sure her boys are okay. She's happy making everywhere a home, so she makes the hospital room a home for Dougie. She makes sure everyone's all ok and looked after.

Ben and Amy Shiels in 2017.

Dean Hurley: [On Julee Cruise singing "The World Spins"] That's the no brainer. Sort of the penultimate moment for the entire series is returning to the ingredient that she brought to the original series and her work with David and Angelo. She returns to the stage and it's that moment of nostalgia and wistfulness. I think it's well-timed at the end of the show. She's performing "The World Spins," which kind of sums up this entire run of 25 years later. And I think all the unspoken feelings that people have seeing a lot of these characters having grown older and yet they're still in this town of Twin Peaks. Haley's comet has come and gone. It's just actually reality. Just experiencing that eclipse and the stars turn and everything kind of moves on. So it's a real elegant comment on the end of the series.

One thing that I don't know if people are gonna pick up on so quickly, but I'll help them along, is her backing band in this performance, who are shadowy figures behind her, are actually comprised of the Chromatics. We kind of have this book ended like front end kind of thing, and this juxtaposition of the classic and the modern in her performance. And to me, it all kind of wraps up in this kind of poetic little package that takes this out of the entire series in making a comment on the music and the themes and the emotion of the entire show. (*KEXP, Morgan Chosnyk*)

Brings Back Some Memories

Bryon: Part 17 gave us some closure with BOB being defeated by Freddie Sykes's green glove. The original *Twin Peaks* gang and newcomers came together at the Twin Peaks Sheriff's Department one last time. But what threw us off was, "Did we just witness Dale Cooper go back to the past and save Laura Palmer from dying at the hands of her father that night?" This scene plays out in a way that could say he does or maybe he failed at doing so. This was a big sticking point the following day with the *Twin Peaks* Community. A heavy question for us, did Dale Cooper change history?

Ben: And if Laura Palmer was not murdered, where is she? I felt Part 17 was Mark Frost's *Twin Peaks* ending and the next and final part was the David Lynch ending. They both got to tell the stories they wanted to tell.

Favorite Quotes and Scenes

Bryon: Part 17 had a lot going on but the most interesting scene for me was finding out what or who is Judy. Gordon Cole tells Albert and Tammy the history of Joudy, which over time became Judy, this extremely negative force that Major Briggs discovered and wanted Cooper and Cole to help find. We finally get some answers about Judy after first hearing about her in *Fire Walk with Me*.

Ben and **Bryon:** Our favorite quote comes from Cooper who says, "See you at the curtain call."

Ben: I love the double meaning of the quote. Curtain call refers to the end of the show, the final bow, and there is actually a physical red curtain where Diane will meet Cooper.

Bryon: This reminds me of the quote by William Shakespeare, "All the world's a stage / And all the men and women merely players; / They have their exits and their entrances, / And one man in his time plays many parts, / His acts being seven ages." We can almost fit Dale Cooper's journey from *The Return* into that William Shakespeare quote. Dale Cooper playing different parts throughout this odyssey. Men and women coming in to help him along the way, playing their part. "See you at the curtain call" could have another meaning, too, that is a little more depressing. Once we all reach the end of our life journey, we will all meet again for one final curtain call.

Ben: I want to believe we all will meet again in the end. My favorite scene is when Laura Palmer meets Cooper in the woods. Cooper is there to take her home, wherever home is. As Cooper leads her through the woods, she vanishes and screams like she did in the Red Room in Part 2. Did this happen, or is Cooper still trapped in the Red Room dreaming about rescuing Laura Palmer? The mystery of show and not always getting clear answers is what I love about *Twin Peaks*.

Community Commentary

Merja Tahvanainen: My very first touch to *Twin Peaks* was when I saw a picture of dead Laura Palmer wrapped in plastic in the Finnish magazine and the title was "Who killed Laura Palmer?" It was the early '90s and I was twelve years old. At first, I thought it was real news. When *Twin Peaks* started it went straight into my heart and I was deeply in love with it. Since then, my life had a *Twin Peaks* vibe. Laura was my idol. I was in love with Sheriff Truman and BOB traumatized me. Even as an adult, I have seen nightmares about Maddy and Leland. I loved the whole *Twin Peaks* world and I still do, the music and everything. I also saw *Fire Walk with Me* as a teenager when it aired in Finland. I have made many *Twin Peaks*-inspired short films with my sister in recent years and the most amazing thing is my *Twin Peaks* friends all over the world. Without *Twin Peaks*, many things in my life would be different.

Tarja Kirvesniemi: I watched *Twin Peaks* for the first time in 1991. I was eleven. I'm so grateful to my mom she let me watch it. When the intro starts to play I'm, like, hypnotized, enchanted. That's the first thing I remember, the music. I fell in love with it and the people in the town of Twin Peaks, where nothing seems to be right but at the same time, everything is. That's what makes it interesting. The show is everything. It makes you laugh, cry, fear. It haunts you, like the murder of Maddy. But you want more.

For a long time, I thought I was a bit weird because I liked the show and my friends didn't. I'm lucky my sister loved the show too. I've made *Twin Peaks*-inspired short films with her, it's been so much fun. And now I have this big amazing *Twin Peaks* family from all over the world. And we are all weird. These people are the best! The show has given me so much. Thank you, Mr. Lynch and Mr. Frost!

Chapter 51

Season 3: Part 18
"What Is Your Name?"
Aired: September 3, 2017
Written by Mark Frost & David Lynch
Directed by David Lynch

The Log-line

Cooper searches for Laura Palmer and finds Carrie Page.

Behind the Curtain

Duwayne Dunham: It was just fun to go back into the world of *Twin Peaks*. Maybe personally I would have liked to have spent a little more time "in" *Twin Peaks*. But that's not what this story was. The story was more about Agent Cooper and the Black Lodge and all this other stuff.

Johanna Ray: It was wonderful on season three to see the actors who I hadn't seen since the very beginning. It was great. Well everybody who works on a set with David, it's pretty much one big love fest.

John Neff: When I saw the cast list announced, it came to my mind that what David was doing was making a magnum opus or his grand unified field of all of his work. It's definitely his magnum opus. It's an 18-hour movie. It's just stunning.

Mike Malone (On-Set Dresser): Having been honored with the pleasure of being on the set of every iteration of *Twin Peaks* (except the Pilot), this film geek cannot begin to express the huge impact it's had on my life. I've worked alongside heroes, forged bonds with some of the best people I know, and been lucky enough to simply be in the presence of Genius Level Creativity. *Twin Peaks* is a pop culture phenomenon, an ever-evolving journey, and most importantly, a loving family that will always enthrall my heart and soul.

Dorothy Mae (woman at Judy's restaurant): Behind *Twin Peaks* lies the heart of David Lynch where genius navigates gifted talent to take viewers into a visual cinematic world of wonderment where no man has gone before. I'm beyond blessed to be a small part of the journey.

John Pirruccello: [On working on *Twin Peaks*] It's like being in a family; you can't leave. I mean you can avoid your family, but you can't leave the family, like it or not. And I like it. I love it! I am part of the *Twin Peaks* family and it's rewarding.

Debbie Zoller: Carrie Page was kind of the character that has had a really hard life. You don't know what's going on with her. You don't know her past. You don't know anything. You just know that when Agent Cooper walks through the door in Texas that there's a dead guy on her couch and that pushes her to when he says let's go, she [says], "Absolutely. Let me get my bag," you know?

You don't really know a back story on her. So I had to tell that story with makeup. You had to look at her and say, this girl's had a hard life. She's lost a lot of sleep, sleepless nights. But she's a fighter. She's a survivor. All of those traits get translated into makeup so that when you see her, you instantly say to yourself, "Ah, I know who this character is

Photo courtesy of Debbie Zoller.

or I recognize that trait." I had to make sure that she was not affluent [so] I used makeup products that you buy at like Walgreens or Target or CVS that the everyday Texan waitress can afford to buy. So that's how I translated her makeup. I think it turned out great.

Jay Aaseng: It's such a gargantuan, sprawling world that [David] created and it's just kind of fun to just even be in a small part of that and inhabit a literal, tiny little corner in a cell of that word.

Mary Reber (Alice Tremond): I was thoroughly blessed and humbled to be asked and considered to do a small acting part in *Twin Peaks: The Return*. The cast and crew that I worked with and met were class acts to say the least! To meet David Lynch and Sabrina Sutherland and work directly with them was one of the most amazing experiences of my lifetime!

It was incredible for me to share my house, the Palmer residence, in this epic show as it is a landmark of *Twin Peaks*. It was a fantastic opportunity

to share it with the fans and a chance for me personally to meet so many wonderful people from all over the world and hear stories of how this show has touched their lives! Thank you and bravo, David Lynch!

Sheryl Lee: I just did a lot of introspective work about time and what does time mean? Being in that energy of David's circle of time does various strange things to one and sort of being part of that process and also witnessing what was going on in my life around that time that we were filming also. It's almost like that period, that year of my life that we shot *The Return*, I kind of put in a little box and put in the back of the closet because it's something that I really, really need to take out when I have more time and open and really process through it because it was so, so trippy. And it was emotional and it was nostalgic and it was melancholy. There were tears and it was beautiful and it was heartbreaking.

It deserves time to process. And I haven't carved out that time yet or maybe I'm too scared to carve out the time, but I promise I will. I will process through that. (*Courtesy of Fire Walk with Me event with special guests Ray Wise & Sheryl Lee at Studio 35 Cinema & Drafthouse, July 19 - 21, 2019*)

Duwayne Dunham: Even in the script, I was like, "David, I like it. I don't know what this ending is. I'm a little confused by it. Am I missing something?" I pretty much felt the same way when we cut it together and it was over. What exactly was that?

Mark Frost on *Twin Peaks: The Final Dossier*: My thinking evolved after we'd written the scripts and before we got into production. I knew I wanted to write up at least one *Twin Peaks* book, but then I realized I wanted to write two. I wanted to go back in time and weave a kind of in-depth mythological history for the region and the people and fill *Twin Peaks* into a larger American context. So that became the *Secret History*. And then I felt I wanted to bring you up to date on the people that were in danger of kind of being left behind or forgotten. The two books act as a companion piece and maybe sort of bookend for the series. I think it's a fun way to look at the *Twin Peaks* experience through a different medium.

I think it was the chance to kind of close the book on a lot of the characters that we've not had a chance to catch up with and put the rest of lingering questions about certain characters that I think had haunted viewers for a long time. I felt we'd left a lot of things unanswered and things that we didn't have time to address in *The Return* and this was a way I thought to bridge that gap.

Ken Scherer: I have great admiration for both [David Lynch and Mark Frost]. I was so happy for them that they came back together cause they created in the archive of film history, they created an incredible piece of work. And maybe there's more, I don't know, but to be able to bring it back and have another iteration of it from a creative standpoint is really satisfying. And I'm happy for the two of them.

Michael Horse: People say, "Will they do another one?" I think it's over, but you never know. I didn't think it would ever come back in the first place. One part of me didn't want it to. It's like James Dean, it died before it's time. That's part of its legend.

Kimmy Robertson: Not that I know anything about it, but it's just that it seems to me like it would be really easy to make a whole new show. Didn't it even look different? The last hour. When [Cooper] came out of the motel. It was a different motel. Different car. A different guy?

Sherilyn Fenn: David Lynch said that he loves doing [*Twin Peaks*] so much. He said if people like the show that he would do more. Now David can change his mind, as we know. But he said the hardest part is writing it. It's just really buckling down and getting it written. He said, "Sherilyn, you never know." That's the truth, right? They could love it. They can hate it. But he loves doing it so much.

Kristine McKenna: [On *Twin Peaks*] That's David's basic world. It's like *Blue Velvet*. It's that neighborhood. He'll always go back. He's told me he loves the Palmers; he loves the characters. In his mind, I think it's such a fluid armature that he can explore all kinds of things through it as he certainly did in season three. Yeah, that's just his home base, kind of, is *Twin Peaks*.

Mark Frost and David Lynch wrote the script, but then David just continued writing and it got longer and more elaborate and layered. I think he could continue burrowing into that world forever.

Dean Hurley: There are so many great moments. It's been really cool to not only have been there and see everybody work toward this but also [to] see it all laid out and see friends and the Internet watch every weekend and see these moments that I had a small hand bringing to fruition. Just happy that I've been working with David for so long and that I was able to be along for the ride on this. (*KEXP, Morgan Chosnyk*)

Sabrina Sutherland: My all-time favorite thing is there was one point where everything was kind of put together, and David had done his pass with the editing and then I got to sit with David and watch it for the first time for me to go through from the beginning to the end. I'd seen pieces, but David didn't want me to see it put together until a particular time. And then he said,

"Okay, now's the time." Then I sat with him and I watched each show. And that was probably my favorite part, just to see the stuff come alive. I had seen everything being shot. I had seen things as they were being edited, but I hadn't seen it as one big thing. That was the best part.

Kyle MacLachlan: I would say this to myself in the morning. I get up, four-thirty or five o'clock in the morning whenever I have to get up and get to work, I'd be like, "I am so excited to go to work." In my kitchen, before I would go to work, I'd make my coffee and I'd have something to eat. I drove myself, too, which I really liked to do. The whole thing was like, I'm going to go work with my good friend David. We're going to be working on something that I'm so proud of. And I'm so excited to be this character and I feel like it's going really, really well. And I love the people involved. Every day was a joy in the work process. Every day was special.

Behinds the scenes with Cast and Crew.
Courtesy of Mike Malone.

Brings Back Some Memories

Bryon: I remember watching those final two parts back to back three times the night of September 3, 2017. Each time, I was noticing different things. I think it was my third viewing that night that I noticed that Cooper gets out of a completely different hotel than the one he went into the night before and his car goes from an older model to a newer car overnight, as well. Was Dale Cooper trying to save Laura Palmer on a different plane of existence? Did Laura Palmer run away instead of dying that night? David Lynch and Mark Frost smashed all expectations and didn't give us the ending we wanted, but the ending we needed.

Ben: I really had mixed feelings about the ending. In 1991, the Season 2 ending was a punch in the gut with Cooper seeming to be possessed by BOB forever. Now Season 3 ends with Cooper and Carrie outside the Palmer house, unsure of what to do. It left me wanting more and wondering, what was Season 3 all about? I had hoped for a happy ending for Cooper, Laura Palmer, and all the Twin Peaks townspeople. I thought Laura Palmer would be the one to defeat BOB or face her mother (aka Judy) or even confront her father. Of course, Lynch and Frost have always played by their own rules, which I do appreciate. I'd like to think Cooper and Carrie, who I think is Laura Palmer, went on trying to figure out when and where they are and maybe discovered more about themselves along the way.

Favorite Quotes and Scenes

Bryon: My favorite quote comes from Dale Cooper: "What year is this?" Not only are these the last words uttered by Special Agent Dale Cooper, but they very well could be the last words we will ever hear from Special Agent Dale Cooper. These last four words ended *Twin Peaks* in such a way that the quote from Winston Churchhill comes to mind, "It is a riddle, wrapped in a mystery, inside an enigma." These last few words have stuck with me ever since Cooper said them that night, bouncing around the frontal lobe of my brain like a ping pong match after drinking down a Slurpee in one minute and getting brain freeze. In other words, those four words make my head hurt. What a way to end 18 hours of television, with "What year is this?" followed by a scream from Carrie Page (Laura Palmer), some crazy noises, and an electric pop, and then black, nothing. The void of blackness with the reflection of ourselves staring back dumbstruck as Carrie's scream echoes away from us.

Ben: Even though we are left with a lot of questions, my favorite scene comes from Cooper and Carrie/Laura's journey to the Palmer House, getting to the Palmer house and not getting the outcome expected. You assume that Sarah Palmer is in that house but once they get there it's another woman who answers the door. I take away from this is that you can't go home again because time passes, things change, we all change. I believe that Carrie Page is Laura Palmer and we hear that sound of Sarah Palmer calling out to Laura that was from the original pilot, "Laura, Laura." This sound might be a trigger that wakes her up, her memories as Laura Palmer flooding back.

Bryon: We had a series of awakenings in *The Return*. Audrey had one, Cooper, Naido, and we see Laura have hers here. But to really understand what is going on, we had to understand what Cooper went through.

Ben: Is Carrie trying to suppress the horrible life she lived as Laura Palmer? Is Cooper forcing her to remember?

My favorite quote comes from the new Dougie. When he embraces the Jones family he says, "Home." I love the idea of home and what it means to Cooper. By Cooper making a copy of himself, he is able to live two lives. It reminds me of that poem by Robert Frost "The Road Not Taken." The poem is about a traveler looking back on his life and knowing he could have done things differently if he had traveled down a different road. Two Coopers: one, Dougie 2.0, chooses the family life, while the original Cooper goes off being an FBI Special Agent in search of finding and rescuing Laura Palmer and fulfilling what he thinks is his mission in life. Our Special Agent Dale Cooper took the road "less traveled by, And that has made all the difference."

Community Commentary

Jeff Jensen (*Entertainment Weekly*, writer on *Watchmen* (2019)): In 1990, *Twin Peaks* inspired me to think about television differently and expect more of all television, in general. It also captured my imagination for the artistry of David Lynch, and I've been following him down every lost highway and into every inland empire ever since.

When he and Mark Frost announced *Twin Peaks: The Return* [as being] officially a thing that was going to happen, what excited me most was the prospect of getting 18 more hours of moving pictures crafted by one of the most important directors in the history of film. While I was deeply interested in getting resolution to the fate of Agent Dale Cooper, my favorite TV character ever, it was the Lynch of it all that thrilled me the most. *Twin Peaks: The Return* was deeply satisfying in all the ways I hoped it would be, and then some. I didn't expect a TV show that would do for me what *Twin Peaks* did the first time around, but it did. *The Return* inspired me to rethink what TV can be and challenged me to want more from it. I was also delighted to get an experience that pleasured my nostalgia for *Twin Peaks* and grateful that it was presented in a form that challenged and interrogated my nostalgia in general. To be able to engage it and analyze it and talk about it in the mediums and with the fellowship of 21st-century cultural conversation, with critics and fellow fans, made it all the more fulfilling.

Watching *The Return*, I was convinced we were watching a masterpiece from a masterful artist and with each passing year, I'm even more convinced that what we experienced in 2017 was something truly special. *Twin Peaks: The Return* is one of only a few shows that I've rewatched in full since it originally aired, and I suspect I will be returning to it over and over again for the rest of my life. It is that profound, that essential. Of course, I would love it if Lynch and Frost made more, but I also believe *The Return* was enough of the show for a lifetime of puzzling and discussion.

Chapter 52

Curtain call

Bryon: It's been 30 years since *Twin Peaks* first aired on television and each year new people are discovering what many of us have loved about the show.

Ben: This book represents our version of the history of *Twin Peaks*. People like Craig Miller, John Thorne, Brad Dukes, who came before us, inspired us to learn more about *Twin Peaks* and share it with the community. We hope someone reading this will be inspired to continue telling these stories and keep the mystery that is *Twin Peaks* alive.

Bryon: The *Twin Peaks* community is a beautiful thing and we are so lucky to be part of it and are humbled by your support and friendship over these past five years.

Ben: As we publish this book in honor of the 30th Anniversary of *Twin Peaks*, the *Twin Peaks Unwrapped* Podcast will celebrate until the end of 2020 by continuing to discuss *Twin Peaks* episodes with the community and having interviews with cast and crew. We hope that in sharing our love and appreciation for one of the most unique and groundbreaking shows ever to come to television, we've given you all a closer glimpse into the magical and mystical world that is *Twin Peaks*. Thanks for listening ... I mean for reading.

Ben and **Bryon:** See you at the Curtain Call.

SPECIAL THANKS

Ben: I have to start by thanking my amazing wife, Tracey, and my children Seth, Emily, and Mia. You've all been so supportive of the weekly podcast and now this book, even though I was gone many weekends writing it. I have the best family.

We are so lucky to get so many cast and crew of *Twin Peaks* contributing to the book. Thank you to the representatives who returned our emails and helped us get in touch with so many of the people. Thank you Kristine McKenna for all of your encouragement and guidance. Thank you to Richard Beymer for letting us include one of your fantastic photos.

Writing a book is a lot of work, but Bryon Kozaczka made it fun. Thank you Bryon for co-hosting the podcast with me for as long as you did. As Kyle MacLachlan once said to me about us having 200 shows, "I didn't know there was that much to say." There is so much to say about *Twin Peaks* and I am so glad we got to share it in this book. Thank you for taking on this project and believing in us. You've always been a good friend and after the podcast and the book, I consider you one of my closest friends.

In 2013, my 14 month old daughter Callie passed away from unknown circumstances. What was once a wonderful blessed life became a life of pain, agony, depression, and deep sadness. It wouldn't be until March 2015 at my 40th birthday party that my wife would say she hadn't seen me so happy in a long time. Family and friends were there to support me on my day and that same day Bryon and I made a pact to create a podcast. Weeks, months, and years passed discussing and laughing about *Twin Peaks*. It was Bryon and the community, even though the pain still resides, that brought great joy to my life daily. Thank you so much.

Thank you Kyle MacLachlan for bringing life to the charming, quirky, and brilliant Agent Cooper. And finally thank you to David Lynch and Mark Frost for the strange, beautiful, and dreamy world you conceptualized.

Bryon: I would like to thank my loving and supportive wife, Allison Lovell, for half-listening to my ramblings about *Twin Peaks* over the last five years and for fully listening to all the cool interviews we have had, not that you had much choice. I appreciate you putting up with my late nights and Sundays focusing on the podcast and this book instead of you. Love you!

I would also like to thank all my close friends and family, especially Mom, Dad, Tony, and Nick, for not truly understanding what *Twin Peaks* means to me but at least caring enough to pretend they do (they say they will listen to the show but they never will). And a very special thank you goes out to Marc Warnock and Sandra Zukowski for allowing us to record our show almost every week in their studio.

In addition, a big thanks goes out to all the friends I have made over these past five years in the *Twin Peaks* community. I never thought a show like *Twin Peaks* would bring so many people together, but it truly does ... on levels I could never explain. I'm thankful and humbled by your genuine encouragement and friendship.

Finally, I would like to thank Ben Durant for motivating me to start this podcast with him five years ago and for this crazy idea of writing a book together. It's been the chance of a lifetime and quite a ride! You are a true friend and an inspiration.

Ben and **Bryon:** A thank you from us goes out to Scott Ryan for giving us the awesome opportunity to publish a book and his support throughout our *Twin Peaks* journey. We don't care what David Bushman says about you, Scott— you're one hell of a guy.

A big thank you to everyone who has supported us over the years. A special shout out goes to everyone who pre-ordered this book. We couldn't have done it without you. Here is the list of the first 200 people that placed an order: Aaron Cohen Eileen Holmes Josh Minton Charles Wald Jason Lloyd Rob King Ben Rojas Ito Atsuya Robert Hart Tobias Heinrich Ben Saari Jim Budds Willem Rekers Michael Mitchell Erica DeFrain Christian Hartleben Jon Parker David Heath Sean Blevins James Donato Michael Keaton Brian Regan Dan Neff James Ciccarello Aaron Tuller David Bushman Reid Nelson Blaise Ambrose Rob Schmitt Bonnie Manuel

Ryan Armentano Michael Nau Kylee Karre Jake Meyer Daniel Marks Kathy Weber David Lopatin Janet Jarnagin Gerald Owens Paul Billington John Salinas Jennifer A Keaton Mike Restaino Christopher Counsil Jen Christensen Thor Amli Andreas Halskov Josiah Lambert Garrett Kostin Bob McDonald Alison Seligson Pattie Mulderig Amy Kirschenbaum Pamela Mastrosimone Espen Risvag Julian Porter Joe Berendt John Sanchez Ryan Potter Brian Carey Thomas Heijmans J.D. Lafrance Justin Morris Kate Ross William Maranto Anthony Trapani Brian Johnson Troy Grillo Johanna Pitkaranta Marco Schindler David Chapman Dave Somers Steven Miller Rachael Grygorcewicz Melissa Ziemba Alison Harville Scott Engel James Bashaw David Holmgren Melissa Banister Julie Cotnoir Kevin Evans Sean Craypo Andrew Ryan Sean Langmuir Uwe Muench Kyle Thomas Stephanie Coonce Adam Black Richard Barrack Mark Mulvey Jeremiah Beaver Eric Leibowitz Rachel Ravitsky Mark Collier Jason Gibbs Rob Parrish Joshua Preston Allison Lovell Pamela Tarajcak Scot Polk Michael Dixson Don Appleby Don Amussen Andy Bentley Joel Bocko Aaron Reed Jon Adams Joseph Minanno Amy Flanagan Jeanetta Kreg Rikki Robinson Henrik Nielsen David O'Brien Joseph Cowart Alex Brunelle Bill Abelson John McCaffrey Mandy Bricker Ronald Vega Brian Moakley Robyn Norris David Mischoulon Brett Vickerman Linda Dorland Tom Proven Jason Kirkham Elizabeth Brozek Alex Hovis Henry Self Jeff Lemire Josh Mcjunkin Guido Sanchez Kimberly Honnel Daniel Kehoe Sabbe Cattrysse Jacob McCord Catherine Charleton Quentin Guilloteau Kevin Dittman Kirk Colton Bernard Seilhamer Peter Glessman Matt Marrone Ashleigh Raczkowski Dale Zavadovics Robert Perino Susan Warren Michael Benz Carri Ables Wayne Van De Graaff Rebecca Rajendra Cyril Schreiber A.M. Starr Janice Wallis Jason Smith Vince Melone Jason Hindo Richard Schweitzer David Hailes Michael Leary Peter Canavese Gianluca Voglino Adam Hultman Ronald Goss Patrick Cotnoir Erik Thompson Darren Shapiro David Kirshenbaum Patrick Odenweller Timothy Hack Brittany Bowman Shannon Hotchkiss Thorsten Meyer Kevin Halstead Jason Watkins David Owens David Schuessler Gina Worth Jocelyn Lermusieaux Margaret Hayes Richard DuBois Glenn Shepart Jr. Lacee Rains Alan Kenny-Rudolph Robert Cargni Jeffrey Eganhouse John Leibee Richard Mann Michael Chang Zach Dietrich Emily Marinelli Ian Witt Lars Trygve Rømmerud James MacCuaig Aaron Beard Katherine Cavanaugh Time Hofman Morgan Bennet

We also want to thank everyone who has contributed to this book:

Charity Parenzini, Stewart Strauss, Billy Zane, Amy Shiels, Jay Jee, Charles de Lauzirika, Don Amendolia, Ken Scherer, Chrysta Bell, Erica Eynon, Robert Baur, Ian Buchanan, Moira Kelly, Kristine McKenna, Carlton Lee Russell, Bob Engels, Ethan Suplee, Jay Aaseng, Kimmy Robertson, Jodi Thelen, Sabrina Sutherland, Mary Jo Deschanel, Nicole LaLiberté, Catherine Coulson, Sarah Jean Long, Galyn Gorg, Willie Garson, Lisa Coronado, Juan Carlos Cantu, Michael Horse, Tikaeni Faircrest, Michael Cera, Charlyne Yi, Clark Middleton, Mary Reber, Tom Holland, Tim Hunter, Karl Makinen, J.R. Starr, Richard Saul Wurman, Bellina Logan, Don Murray, Lara Flynn Boyle, Ken Welsh, Michael Caputo, Heather Graham, Keith Poston, Julee Cruise, Christopher Gray, Steven James Tingus, Zoe McLane, Nae, Chris Mulkey, Brian Berdan, Robert Forster, Robyn Lively, David Patrick Kelly, Jay Larson, Jen Lynch, Lenny Von Dohlen, Ricky Aiello, Debbie Zoller, Jim Belushi, James Grixoni, Richard Beymer, Stephen Gyllenhaal, Mark Frost, Elena Satine, Sherilyn Fenn, Tony Krantz, Johanna Ray, Nathan Frizzell, Dorothy Mae, Geoffrey Gould, Wendy Robie, Gary Bullock, Mak Takano, James Morrison, Carel

Struycken, Charlotte Stewart, Ray Wise, Josh Fadem, Harley Peyton, Connie Woods, John Neff, Dep Kirkland, Jonny Coyne, Grant Goodeve, Joan Chen, Vincent Van Dyke, David Eubank, Jane Adams, Brenda Strong, Naomi Watts, Mike Malone, Carel Struycken, Piper Laurie, Chris Rodley, Tammie Baird, Christophe Zajac-Denek, Brett Gelman, Richard Hoover, Ashley Judd, Clare M. Corsick, Joe Adler, Jed Mills, Robert Broski, Laura Dern, Matthew Lillard, Isabella Rossellini, Jake Wardle, Erika Anderson, Duwayne Dunham, David Duchovny, Lesli Linka Glatter, Scott Frost, Caleb Deschanel, John Pirruccello, Tim Roth, Dana Ashbrook, Rebekah Del Rio, George Griffith, Sheryl Lee and Kyle MacLachlan. Our three incredible editors; Tracey Durant, Jill Watson and Rebecca Saunders. Josh Howard who designed the greatest *Twin Peaks* book cover. David Laribee and Alex West, of Nerd/Noir podcast, who allowed us to use excerpts of their amazing Jen Lynch interview. Morgan Chosnyk, from KEXP, who allowed us to use excerpts of her enlightening Dean Hurley interviews.

A big thank you goes out to the *Twin Peak* community at large; Damon Lindelof, Morgan Higby Night, Viktor, James Roday, David Bushman, Sam Witt, Rob King, Andrew Grevas (and everyone part of 25 Years Later site), Scott Ryan (and everyone at Blue Rose Magazine), John Bernardy, Mya McBriar, Kirk Salopek (and Silencio), Aidan Hailes, Lindsay Stamhuis, Rosie (and *Diane* Podcast), Clare Nina Norelli, J.B. Minton, J.C. Hotchkiss, Ben Rojas, Joel Bocko, Steven Miller, Twin Petes, Eeson & Becks, Courtenay Stallings, Mark Givens, Laura Stewart, Jeremiah, Brad Dukes, Aaron Cohen, Lindsey Bowden, Patrick Cotnoir, Tom Wubker, Sean Glass, Rikki Robinson, Russ Marshalek, Jeff Lemire, H. Perry Horton, Andrew Blossom, Cameron Crain, Andy Bentley, Bretagnarchy, Blake Morrow, Andreas Halskov, Connor Ratliff, Jill Watson, Rebecca Saunders, Jeff Jensen, Em & Steve (Sparkwood & 21), David Wirch, Merja Tahvanainen, Terja Kirvesniemi, Mark O'Brien, Chris Counsil, Glenn Docto, Brett Vickerman, Red Room Podcast, Andy Bentley, Adam Stewart, Eben Moore, Jubel Brosseau, Christian Hartleben, Jen Ryan, Francine Sogno, Schaffer The Darklord, The Pink Room: David Lynch Burlesque and John "The Godfather" Thorne. To everyone else we may have missed a big ol' Dale Cooper thumbs up in your direction.

Reference Page

Amy Shiels, TPU Ep 143, February 21, 2018
Bob Engels, TPU Ep 118, August 29, 2017
Catherine Coulson, TPU Ep 8, July 29, 2015
Carel Struycken, TPU Ep 203, September 16, 2019
Charles de Lauzirika, TPU Ep 138, January 16, 2018
Chrysta Bell, TPU Ep 151, April 16, 2018
Charlotte Stewart, TPU Ep 50, May 18 2016,
    TPU Ep 100, May 3, 2017, TPU Ep 200, Aug. 5, 2019
Chris Rodley, TPU Ep 157, June 1, 2018, TPU Ep 166,
    August 7, 2018
Debbie Zoller, TPU Ep 155, May 14, 2018
Dean Hurley, The Morning Show on KEXP, Morgan Chosnyk,
    www.kexp.org
Geoffrey Gould, TPU Ep 105, June 8, 2017
Gary Bullock, TPU Ep 102, May 15, 2017
Harley Peyton, TPU Ep 37, February 17, 2016, TPU Ep 69,
    Sept. 28, 2016, TPU Ep 103, May 25, 2017 TPU Ep 122,
    September 19, 2017, TPU Ep 185, January 14, 2019
Ian Buchanan, TPU Ep 180, December 10, 2018
James Morrison, TPU Ep 85, January 20, 2017
Jen Lynch, Nerd/Noir Podcast Ep 3 July 08, 2015,
    TPU Ep 170, September 3, 2018
John Neff, TPU Ep 98, April 21, 2017, TPU Ep 112, July 19, 2017
Julee Cruise, Red Room Podcast Ep 157
Keith Poston, TPU Ep 43, March 30, 2016
Kristine McKenna, TPU Ep 164, July 24, 2018, TPU Ep 190,
    March 11, 2019
Kimmy Robertson, TPU Ep 124, October 4, 2017
Lisa Coronado, TPU Ep 11, August 19, 2015
Mark Frost, TPU Ep 72, October 18, 2016, TPU Ep 128,
    November 6, 2017
Michael Horse, TPU Ep 34, January 27, 2016
Michael Caputo, TPU Ep 43, March 30, 2016

Ray Wise, TPU Ep 199, July 23, 2019
Richard Saul Wurman, TPU Ep 66, September 7, 2016
Richard Beymer, TPU Ep 141, February 5, 2018
Sabrina Sutherland, TPU Ep 121, Sept 14, 2017,
    TPU Ep 137, Jan 9, 2018, TPU Ep 203, Sept 16, 2019
Sheryl Lee, TPU Ep 199, July 23, 2019
Sherilyn Fenn, TPU Ep 87, July 31, 2017
Stewart Strauss, TPU Ep 184, January 7, 2019
Todd Holland, Red Room Podcast Ep 125

COMING IN 2022 FROM FMP

ORDER AT FAYETTEVILLEMAFIAPRESS.COM

MORE TWIN PEAKS PRODUCTS

Order the only print magazine about *Twin Peaks*: *The Blue Rose*.
13 Issues and counting. Order at **bluerosemag.com**

Laura's Ghost: Women Speak About Twin Peaks
by Courtenay Stallings with a Foreword
by Sheryl Lee. Women discuss how Laura
Palmer influenced their lives.

Order at **FayettevilleMafiaPress.com**
ISBN: 9781949024081

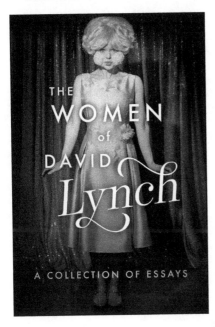
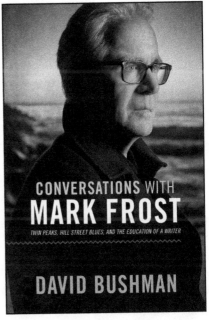

CPSIA information can be obtained
at www.ICGtesting.com
Printed in the USA
LVHW082302150921
697926LV00025B/855